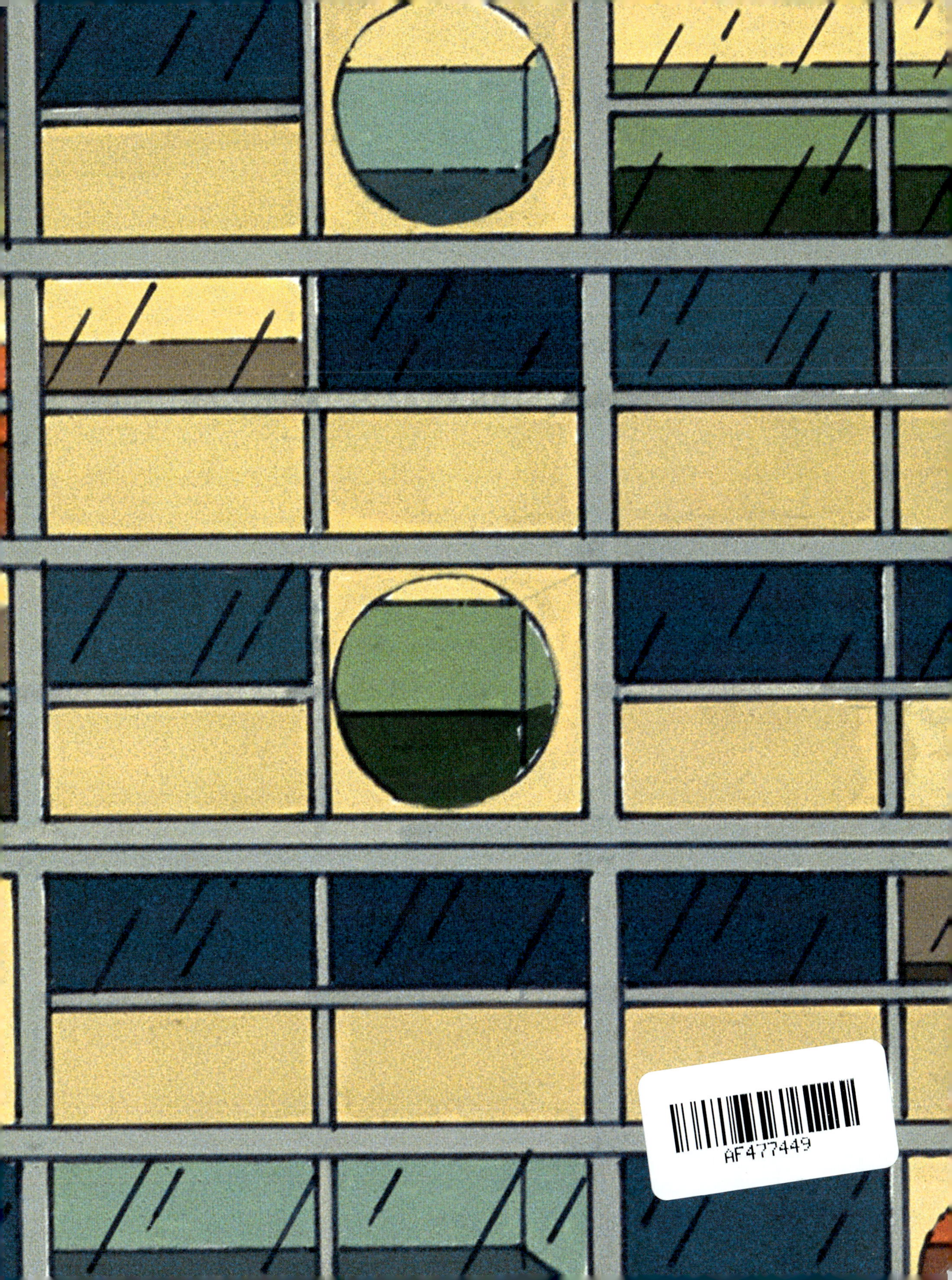
AF477449

Andrea Zittel

Gouachen und Illustrationen Gouaches and Illustrations

ausgewählt von / selected by
Andrea Zittel

herausgegeben von / edited by
Theodora Vischer

SCHAULAGER®

STEIDL

Diese Publikation ist anlässlich von

Andrea Zittel, Monika Sosnowska. 1:1

im Schaulager Basel (26. April bis 21. September 2008) erschienen.
Die Ausstellung wurde konzipiert und organisiert vom Schaulager Basel
in Zusammenarbeit mit Andrea Zittel.

The publication was produced on the occasion of the exhibition

Andrea Zittel, Monika Sosnowska. 1:1

at Schaulager Basel (April 26 to September 21, 2008).
The exhibition was conceived and organized by Schaulager Basel
in collaboration with Andrea Zittel.

Inhalt   Contents

Grusswort / A Word of Welcome   7
Maja Oeri

Einführung zu den Gouachen und Illustrationen von Andrea Zittel   8
An Introduction to Andrea Zittel's Gouaches and Illustrations
Theodora Vischer

Bildteil / Plates   15
mit Kommentaren von / with commentaries by
Andrea Zittel

Bildlegenden / Captions   170
zusammengestellt von / compiled by
Bettina Friedli

Ausstellung im Schaulager / Exhibition at Schaulager   179
zusammengestellt von / compiled by
Annamira Jochim

Biografie / Biography   203

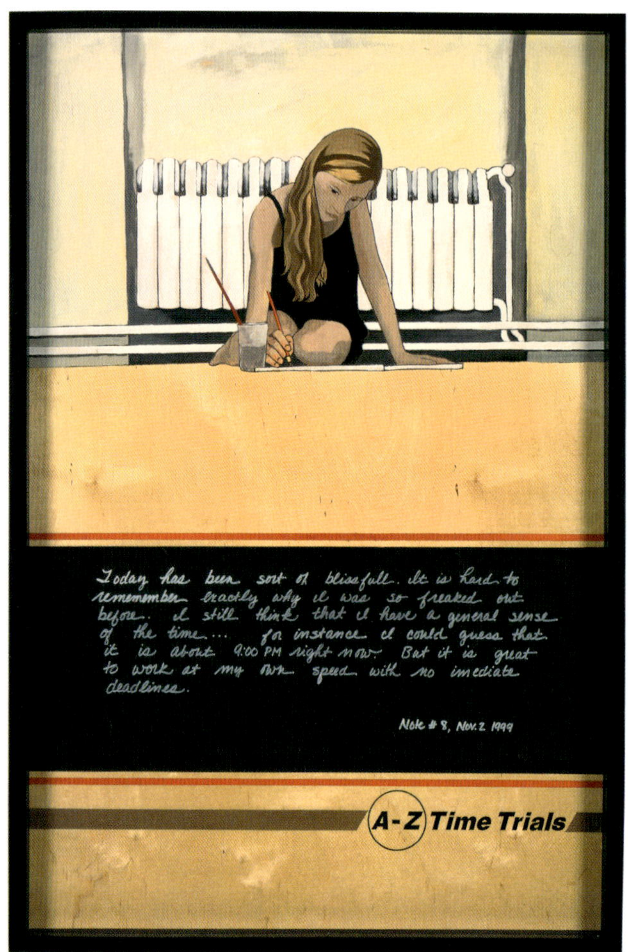

A—Z TimeTrials, Note #8 2000 (S./p. 170)

Maja Oeri

Präsidentin Laurenz-Stiftung   President Laurenz Foundation

„Andrea Zittel. Gouachen und Illustrationen" erscheint aus Anlass der Schaulager Ausstellung des Jahres 2008, die den beiden Künstlerinnen Andrea Zittel und Monika Sosnowska gewidmet ist. Seit 1996, als Theodora Vischer im Basler Museum für Gegenwartskunst eine Ausstellung Andrea Zittels zeigte, hat die Emanuel Hoffmann-Stiftung regelmässig Arbeiten der Künstlerin erworben. Sie besitzt heute wohl eine der grössten Werkgruppen Zittels in unterschiedlichsten Medien. Es war deshalb nahe liegend, die Künstlerin einzuladen, ihr vielschichtiges Werk in einer Ausstellung im Schaulager zu präsentieren.

Eine breit angelegte, narrative Abfolge von Werken entwickelt sich nun im Erdgeschoss des Hauses. In einer Art Entdeckungsreise kann der Besucher Zittels künstlerische Welt erkunden und stösst dabei immer wieder auf neue, verblüffende Facetten. Zusammengehalten wird dieses Universum durch die von der Künstlerin entworfene und konsequent gelebte Philosophie. Die vorliegende Publikation ist kein eigentlicher Ausstellungskatalog, sondern beleuchtet einen wesentlichen Aspekt des Gesamtwerkes, die von Zittel so genannten ‚Flat works'. Sie werden in der Ausstellung im Schaulager zum ersten Mal in ihrer ganzen Fülle gezeigt und dienen – mehr noch als bei anderen Künstlern – als Schlüssel zum Verständnis ihres Lebens und Schaffens.

Der Künstlerin und allen, die am Zustandekommen von Ausstellung und Buch beteiligt waren, gilt mein grosser Dank.

Andrea Zittel: Gouaches and Illustrations is being published on the occasion of Schaulager's exhibition for 2008, which is devoted to the artists Andrea Zittel and Monika Sosnowska.

Since 1996, when Theodora Vischer curated an Andrea Zittel exhibition at the Museum für Gegenwartskunst Basel, the Emanuel Hoffmann Foundation has acquired the artist's works regularly. Today it has probably one of the largest collections of Zittel's works in various media. It was therefore only natural that Schaulager should invite the artist to present her multilayered oeuvre in an exhibition.

A broadly conceived, narrative sequence of works evolves on the building's ground floor. Viewers can explore Zittel's artistic world on a kind of journey of discovery during which they will repeatedly encounter astonishing new facets. This universe is held together by a philosophy sketched out and rigorously lived by the artist.

The present publication is not really an exhibition catalog; rather, it sheds light on one essential aspect of Zittel's oeuvre: the works she calls "flat works." They are being shown in their full diversity for the first time in the Schaulager's exhibition, and they serve—even more so than is ordinarily the case with artists—as a key to understanding her life and work.

I wish to express my profound gratitude to the artist and to everyone involved in producing the exhibition and the book.

The present publication concentrates entirely on Andrea Zittel's gouaches and paintings on wooden panels. The works presented here were selected by Zittel herself. The subdivision of the book into seven sections resulted almost of its own from the more or less chronological sequence of the works. It is characteristic of Zittel's procedure that she combines her works into groups of related works and gives these groups titles. Accordingly, the gouaches and panel paintings also belong to various groups, whose titles are indicated in this book on the margin of the page in question. It is striking that, without exception, these group titles refer to Zittel's sculptures and objects. It seems therefore reasonable to see a close connection between the two, and in particular to understand the gouaches as nonautonomous preliminary works for the objects and sculptures. These works have indeed ordinarily been treated that way. Whenever they have been included in an exhibition at all, they remain in the background as accompaniment; in publications they are often treated principally as explanations of Zittel's three-dimensional works. When examining Andrea Zittel's oeuvre more closely in preparation for this exhibition, I realized what a presence the gouaches and paintings on wood have been since the beginnings of her creative work in the early 1990s, and that they tell their own, very special story. If we consider, moreover, that painting and drawing are the only artistic media apart from writing that Zittel can execute by herself, without the help of the third parties who are usually necessary to produce her objects and sculptures, then it seems more than justified to dedicate our full attention to these media for once.

All of Andrea Zittel's gouaches and paintings have titles, just like the other works; there are no works known as *Untitled*. The earliest gouaches were studies for objects and sculptures—for example, *Study for A–Z Carpet Furniture*, *Study for A–Z Ottoman Furniture*, or *Study for A–Z Personal Panels*. Later, in addition to sketches for projects, they are primarily illustrations of the use or presentation of sculptures and objects, such as *Me in A–Z Personal Panel with Poppy* or *Gray A–Z Personal Panel on My Bedroom Floor*. The technique and style of all these works is particularly striking. The paintings are very carefully executed. They are marked by clear and simple draftsmanship and painted in rich and glowing colors. The depictions are very legible; if there are people it is almost always the same young woman, who in the titles is identified as the artist; the situations shown are familiar but at the same time emphatically neutral and emotionless. There is also a certain 'innocence' to them. They are beautiful and attractive images whose eloquent, almost emblematic visual idiom recalls illustrations that are familiar less from the world of art than from the world of advertising and entertainment (illustrated books, for example). This proximity is affirmed by Andrea Zittel: "Even early on, starting to paint in a more commercial and illustrative manner felt completely liberating, as I was no longer struggling with the ideological weight of representation in fine art. Because we already understand images to

Theodora Vischer

Einführung
zu den Gouachen und Illustrationen von Andrea Zittel

An Introduction
to Andrea Zittel's Gouaches and Illustrations

Die vorliegende Publikation konzentriert sich ganz auf die Gouachen und Malereien auf Holztafeln von Andrea Zittel. Ausgewählt wurden die hier vorgestellten Arbeiten von Zittel selber. Die im Buch vorgenommene Aufteilung in sieben Abschnitte hat sich aus der mehr oder weniger chronologischen Aneinanderreihung der Arbeiten fast selbstverständlich ergeben. Es gehört zur Eigenart von Zittels Schaffen, dass sie ihre Werke insgesamt in Gruppen von verwandten Arbeiten zusammenfasst und diesen Gruppen Titel gibt. Dementsprechend gehören auch die Gouachen und Tafelbilder zu verschiedenen Gruppen, deren Titel hier jeweils am Rand der Buchseite aufgeführt sind. Es fällt auf, dass diese Gruppentitel ausnahmslos auf Skulpturen und Objekte Zittels verweisen. Es ist daher nahe liegend, zwischen beiden eine enge Verbindung abzuleiten, und insbesondere die Gouachen als unselbständige Vorarbeiten zu den Objekten und Skulpturen zu verstehen. So werden diese Arbeiten gewöhnlich auch gehandhabt. Falls überhaupt in eine Ausstellung einbezogen, stehen sie begleitend im Hintergrund; in Publikationen werden sie vorwiegend als Erläuterung zu den dreidimensionalen Werken von Zittel behandelt. Bei der vertieften Sichtung des Werkes von Andrea Zittel zur Vorbereitung dieser Ausstellung realisierte ich, wie präsent die Gouachen und Malereien auf Holz seit den Anfängen ihres Schaffens zu Beginn der 1990er Jahre sind, und dass sie eine ganz besondere, eigenständige Geschichte zu erzählen scheinen. Wenn man zudem bedenkt, dass das Malen und Zeichnen neben dem Schreiben das einzige künstlerische Medium ist, das Zittel allein, ohne den Beizug Dritter, der bei der Herstellung ihrer Objekte und Skulpturen meistens notwendig ist, ausführen kann, erscheint es mehr als gerechtfertigt, diesem Medium für einmal die ganze Aufmerksamkeit zu widmen.

Alle Gouachen und Bilder von Andrea Zittel, wie die übrigen Werke auch, tragen einen Titel, es gibt keine Werke „Ohne Titel". Am Anfang stehen Gouachen, welche Entwürfe für Objekte und Skulpturen darstellen – „Study for A–Z Carpet Furniture" zum Beispiel, „Study for A–Z Ottoman Furniture" oder „Study for A–Z Personal Panels". Später entstehen neben den Projektentwürfen auch und vor allem Darstellungen, welche die Anwendung oder Präsentation von Skulpturen und Objekten illustrieren, so etwa „Me in A–Z Personal Panel with Poppy" oder „Grey A–Z Personal Panel on my Bedroom Floor". Besonders auffallend ist die Technik und der Stil all dieser Arbeiten. Die Bilder sind sehr sorgfältig ausgeführt. Sie sind von einer klaren und einfachen Zeichnung geprägt und in satten und leuchtenden Farben ausgemalt. Die Darstellungen sind gut lesbar; treten Personen auf, ist es fast immer dieselbe Figur einer jungen Frau, die in den Titeln als jene der Künstlerin ausgewiesen ist; die gezeigten Situationen sind vertraut, gleichzeitig betont neutral und emotionslos gehalten. Darin ist ihnen auch eine gewisse ‚Unschuld' eigen. Es sind schöne und attraktive Bilder, die in ihrer ansprechenden, fast emblemhaften Bildsprache an Illustrationen erinnern, wie man sie weniger aus dem Bereich der

serve a function of persuasion in advertising they are already read as a potential 'fraud' or 'lie,' which somehow makes them feel more truthful since their role as propaganda is so transparent." The quotation is from one of the commentaries that Andrea Zittel wrote for this publication. Because writing is employed in her work as a supplemental artistic medium, such texts have a different status than the statements found in interviews or conversations. A good example of the particular nature of her writing is the publication *Andrea Zittel: Diary #1*, which was published in 2002 by Tema Celeste Editions in Milan. This diary, which covers the period from June 14 to September 6, 2001, describes, in the same emblematic and selective way she does the illustrations of her life and work on the West Coast, where she had settled several months earlier. In the present book, Zittel talks specifically about her painting for the first time. She titled the seven sections of the book "Planes and Panels," "Modeling," "Suburban Foothills," "Posters," "Measure and Marking," "The American West," and "I Know Everything and I Know Nothing." The titles already reveal what reading the commentaries makes clear: namely, the gouaches and illustrations are a kind of material for reflection, a subtext by means of which Zittel advances her artistic work. Such a function for drawings is by no means unusual among artists, especially sculptors. In Zittel's case, however, they are not rapidly dashed-off drawings, sketches, or notes of thoughts in which an idea is discussed or a project planned but usually worked-out images in which the ideas and project are presented as already realized and can be imagined as such. They are thus at once a place for self-reflection and for representation directed outward.

Leafing through the gouaches and illustrations, we are able to find numerous references to Zittel's life—albeit with many gaps and just a few cues. It begins with the sheets in the first section, "Planes and Panels," from the early 1990s, at a time when Zittel had settled in Brooklyn, New York, and had founded her artistic project A–Z, which would form the framework in which all her subsequent research and works would be sketched, produced, and tested. The biographical sketch ends with *Prototypes for Billboards* in the Californian desert near Joshua Tree, east of Los Angeles, where Zittel now lives and continues her work under the label A–Z West. This close connection between biography and artistic work is not only found in the illustrations and texts—*Diary #1* is marked by this as well—but is also characteristic for Zittel's artistic approach in general. In the uncertainty of their status between autonomous artwork and functional object, all her sculptures and objects move within the border zone between art and reality. It thus comes as no surprise, though it is still noteworthy, that they sometimes reveal formal affinities to movements inspired by social utopias and by concrete efforts to bring together life and art—for example, the social utopias of the second and early third decade of the last century in Europe or the frontier movement in the United States. One need only think of the homestead cabins developed on the frontiers or the clothing designs of Russian Constructivist women artists.

The question what the striking presence of the artist and her surroundings in the gouaches and illustrations does say about the significance of this medium in particular is not yet

Kunst als aus dem Bereich der Werbung und Unterhaltung (etwa von Bilderbüchern) kennt. Diese Nähe wird von Andrea Zittel bestätigt: „Schon von früh an empfand ich das Malen in einer eher kommerziellen und illustrativen Weise als grosse Befreiung, da ich mich nicht mehr mit dem ideologischen Gewicht der Repräsentation in der bildenden Kunst herumschlagen musste. Da wir ja wissen, dass Bilder in der Werbung Überzeugungszwecken dienen, werden sie von vornherein als potentieller ‚Betrug' oder als ‚Lüge' wahrgenommen, und das macht sie irgendwie wahrhaftiger, da ihre Rolle als Propaganda so durchsichtig ist."

Das Zitat entstammt einem der Kommentare, die Andrea Zittel für diese Publikation verfasst hat. Da in ihrem Werk das Schreiben durchaus als zusätzliches künstlerisches Medium zum Einsatz kommt, haben solche Texte einen anderen Stellenwert als Aussagen, wie sie in Interviews oder Gesprächen zu finden sind. Als gutes Beispiel für die Eigenart ihres Schreibens sei auf die Publikation „Andrea Zittel. Diary #1" verwiesen, die 2002 bei Tema Celeste Editions in Mailand erschienen ist. Das Tagebuch, das den Zeitraum vom 14. Juni bis zum 6. September 2001 umfasst, beschreibt in derselben emblemhaften und selektiven Weise wie die Illustrationen ihr Leben und ihre Arbeit an der Westküste, wo sie sich einige Monate zuvor niedergelassen hatte. Im jetzt vorliegenden Buch äussert sich Zittel zum ersten Mal konkret zu ihren Malarbeiten. Die sieben Abschnitte hat sie mit „Planes and Panels", „Modeling", „Suburban Foothills", „Posters", „Measure and Marking", „The American West" und „I know everything and I know nothing" überschrieben. Bereits mit diesen wird angezeigt, was bei der Lektüre der Kommentare deutlich wird, dass nämlich die Gouachen und Illustrationen eine Art Reflexionsmedium darstellen, ein Subtext, mittels dessen Zittel ihre künstlerische Arbeit vorantreibt. Eine solche Funktion für Zeichnungen ist im Werk eines Künstlers, insbesondere eines Bildhauers durchaus nicht ungewöhnlich. Nur handelt es sich in Zittels Fall nicht um schnell hingeworfene Zeichnungen, Skizzen oder Gedankennotate, in denen eine Idee erörtert oder ein Projekt entworfen wird, sondern zumeist um ausgearbeitete Bilder, in denen Idee und Projekt als schon realisierte präsentiert und vorstellbar werden. Sie sind damit Ort der Selbstreflexion und der nach aussen gewendeten Repräsentation in Einem.

Beim Durchblättern der Gouachen und Illustrationen lassen sich – wenn auch sehr lückenhaft und nur stichwortartig – zahlreiche Hinweise auf das Leben von Zittel ablesen. Es setzt mit den Blättern des ersten Abschnitts „Planes and Panels" Anfang der 1990er Jahre ein, in einer Zeit, in der Zittel sich in Brooklyn, New York niedergelassen hat und ihr künstlerisches Unternehmen A–Z begründete, ein Projekt, in dessen Rahmen sie seither alle ihre Recherchen durchführt und ihre Werke entwirft, produziert und testet. Die biografische Skizze endet mit den „Prototypes for Billboards" in der kalifornischen Wüste bei Joshua Tree östlich von Los Angeles, wo Zittel heute lebt und ihre Arbeit unter dem Label A–Z West weiterführt. Die enge Verbindung von Biografie und künstlerischer Arbeit findet sich nicht nur in den Illustrationen und Texten – auch „Diary #1" ist davon geprägt –, sie ist charakteristisch für die künstlerische Vorgehensweise von Zittel insgesamt. In der Unentschiedenheit ihres Status zwischen autonomem Kunstwerk und Gebrauchsobjekt bewegen sich alle ihre Skulpturen und Objekte in einem Grenzbereich

answered with a reference to the close connection of life and work. From the outset the model-like figure is an element of these works; it appears average and unspecific, lovable and anonymous. It is therefore ideal as the bearer of an advertising message, except that this message does not concern a commercial product. Instead, the figure presents the sculptures and objects that Andrea Zittel actually creates. The construction of this "persona," as Zittel once described it, is crucial and of great consequence. For it does not just appear in the gouaches and illustrations but is truly embodied and lived by Zittel herself. Only in combination with this figure do the sculptures and objects become the kind of hybrid forms that obtain their beauty and fascination precisely from their uncertain status between the art work and the functional object. As such, they also speak of the attitude associated with the development and use of such objects, of the concept of life that can ultimately be derived from that. The construction of the figure began with the founding of A–Z in Brooklyn in 1991. But it has found its representative form in the gouaches and illustrations.

zwischen Kunst und Realität. Kein Wunder daher, wenn auch bemerkenswert, dass zuweilen formale Affinitäten zu Bewegungen aufscheinen, die von sozialen Utopien und konkreten Versuchen, Leben und Kunst zusammenzuführen, getragen sind – so zum Beispiel die Sozialutopien der zehner und frühen zwanziger Jahre des letzten Jahrhunderts in Europa oder der *Frontier* Bewegung in Amerika. Hingewiesen sei hier lediglich auf den Bautypus der *homestead cabins*, wie er von den *Frontiers* entwickelt wurde oder die Kleiderentwürfe der russischen Konstruktivistinnen.

Was die auffällige Präsenz, welche die Figur der Künstlerin und ihr Umfeld in den Gouachen und Illustrationen innehat, über die Bedeutung dieses Mediums im Besonderen aussagt, ist mit dem Hinweis auf die enge Verquickung von Leben und Werk im gesamten Schaffen noch nicht beantwortet. Die modellhafte Figur ist fast von Anfang an Bestandteil der Darstellungen, in der Erscheinung durchschnittlich und unspezifisch, liebenswert und anonym. Ideal also als Trägerin einer Werbebotschaft, nur dass die Botschaft nicht einem kommerziellen Produkt gilt. Stattdessen führt die Figur die Skulpturen und Objekte vor, die Andrea Zittel auch tatsächlich realisiert. Die Konstruktion dieser *persona*, wie Zittel sie einmal bezeichnet hat, ist entscheidend und von grosser Tragweite. Denn sie tritt nicht nur in den Gouachen und Illustrationen auf, sondern wird von Zittel selber real verkörpert und gelebt. In Verbindung mit dieser Figur erst werden die Skulpturen und Objekte zu den hybriden Gebilden, die ihre Schönheit und Faszination gerade aus ihrem unentschiedenen Status zwischen Kunstwerk und Gebrauchsgegenstand gewinnen. Als solche sprechen sie auch von der Haltung, die sich mit der Entwicklung und Verwendung solcher Objekte verbindet, vom Lebensentwurf, der sich letztlich daraus ableiten lässt. Die Konstruktion der Figur hat mit der Gründung von A–Z in Brooklyn 1991 angefangen. Ihre repräsentative Form aber hat sie in den Gouachen und Illustrationen erhalten.

Bildteil Plates

mit Kommentaren von   with commentaries by
Andrea Zittel

I learned to paint from my grandmother. She was a desert landscape painter who lived on a ranch in California near the border to Mexico. We would work in her small, bright painting studio and practice landscapes of the fields, deserts, and the animals around her home. I grew up with a familiarity of painting that was born of an embracement of daily life—I suppose that we were hobby painters, but there was an ordinariness and an interconnectedness to the act of painting that was completely free of the fine art distinctions to which I would later be introduced. Years later on a whim I took an art course in college—and that led to more classes in painting, drawing, and then art history. It was as if art history spiraled into my life with all of its intricacies and complexities—a moment that was both intellectually exhilarating and infinitely confounding. From this point onward, though, the act of creativity would be forever bonded to a latent set of intellectual and cultural codes and values.

As a result of these ideologies, painting became something new to me—it became an expression of one's larger beliefs and society's moral and mental structures. At this time the idea of representation became immeasurably complex. For if I were to paint an image what did that mean? Should it be a form of endorsement or of critical distance? And if I were to paint an abstraction what would grant it any more significance than the pattern on my linoleum floor? By what right would I bring these things into the world? By nature I am both fascinated and haunted by these mental structures and intellectual codes as they play themselves out as intricate puzzles of existence both in my works and in my brain.

A few years after I started to study painting, the discovery of sculpture offered a salvation—a way to sidestep these issues and to create a direct manifestation or embodiment of ideas and actions—rather than struggling with the politics of how or even why to represent them. And of course making a work that serves a function like eating or sleeping solves that problem of giving core reason for an object to live. Although my primary practice is integrated with sculpture and with life itself, crafting an image of an idea is something that has a history within my life as well as my repertoire—these images are evidence of the importance of this parallel aspect of my practice.

Das Malen habe ich von meiner Grossmutter gelernt. Sie malte Wüstenlandschaften und lebte auf einer Ranch in Kalifornien in der Nähe der mexikanischen Grenze. Wir arbeiteten in ihrem kleinen hellen Atelier und malten die Felder, Wüsten und Tiere in der Umgebung ihres Hauses. Ich bin mit Malerei vertraut aufgewachsen, weil diese bei uns etwas ganz Alltägliches war; ich denke, wir waren Hobbymaler, aber der Akt des Malens war etwas ganz Gewöhnliches und Selbstverständliches für uns, ganz frei von den Kategorien der bildenden Kunst, mit denen ich später Bekanntschaft schliessen sollte.

Jahre später belegte ich im College aus einer Laune heraus eine Kunstklasse, was weitere Kurse wie Malen, Zeichnen und dann Kunstgeschichte nach sich zog. Es war so, als würde sich die Kunstgeschichte mit all ihren Schwierigkeiten und Komplexitäten in mein Leben hineinwinden, ein Moment, der intellektuell belebend und zugleich unendlich verwirrend war. Doch von diesem Punkt an sollte der kreative Akt für immer latent mit einer Reihe intellektueller und kultureller Codes und Werte verknüpft sein.

Als Ergebnis der damit verbundenen Ideologien wurde die Malerei etwas Neues für mich. Sie wurde Ausdruck der eigenen umfassenderen Überzeugungen und der moralischen und mentalen Strukturen der Gesellschaft. Damals wurde die Idee der Repräsentation zu etwas unendlich Komplexem. Denn wenn ich ein Bild malen sollte, was war dann überhaupt damit gemeint? Sollte es eine Form der Billigung oder eine der kritischen Distanz sein? Und falls ich ein abstraktes Bild malte, was würde dann gewährleisten, dass es auch nur eine Spur bedeutsamer wäre als das Muster auf meinem Linoleumboden? Mit welchem Recht setzte ich diese Dinge in die Welt? Von Natur aus faszinieren und verfolgen mich solche mentalen Strukturen und intellektuellen Codes, da sie sich sowohl in meinen Werken als auch in meinem Gehirn als komplexe Daseinsrätsel abspielen.

Einige Jahre nachdem ich das Studium der Malerei begonnen hatte, erwies sich die Entdekkung der Skulptur als Rettung für mich. Sie war eine Möglichkeit, diesen Fragen aus dem Weg zu gehen und eine direkte Manifestation oder Verkörperung der Ideen und Handlungen zu schaffen, statt mich mit der Frage herumzuschlagen, wie oder gar warum ich sie darstellen sollte. Und natürlich löst die Herstellung eines Werks, das eine Funktion wie Essen oder Schlafen erfüllt, das Problem, einen sonst wie stichhaltigen Grund für dessen Dasein zu finden. Obwohl mein primäres Tun in die Skulptur und das Leben selbst eingebunden ist, ist das Anfertigen von Bildern einer Idee etwas, das eine Geschichte in meinem Leben und in meinem Repertoire hat: Diese Bilder sind der Beweis für die Wichtigkeit dieses parallelen Aspekts meiner künstlerischen Praxis.

The early 1990s was a period when I began to rediscover painting. It started with a series of studies for a project—the *Carpet Furniture* series. I began working with gouache on the smooth backside of watercolor paper. Gouache is a medium that I had loved in the past—it is fairly opaque and velvety. Although mostly stable after it has dried, it can still be wetted and melded into successive layers of color. Gouache is also interesting because it was the medium of choice for graphic designers of past eras when making camera-ready illustrations. Having always had a love of graphic design, the crispness and neutrality of the gouache added to a certain illustrative deadpan picture quality that I was after.

The *Carpet Furniture* works themselves are carpets, which are imprinted with plan views of furniture, which can be used the same way that you would use the furniture. These are connected to a larger grouping of works such as the *A–Z Personal Panels* and *A–Z Covers* which all are composed from the format of a panel.

The idea of a "panel" is interesting because it is sort of a plane liberated in space. A "super plane" that can transcend the limitations of two-dimensional space without actually becoming three-dimensional. The *Carpet Furniture* already had a painterly reference as it hovers between being a representation of something and that actual thing itself (the furniture was meant to be used just like any other furniture), and using the gouaches to plan new variations of the furniture worked out in both a practical sense and on a conceptual level. Later these paintings also extended to plan views of *Ottoman Furniture* (trying to show various configurations through which they might serve differing functions) and the *Personal Panels*, which are rectangular pieces of fabric that can be worn as garments.

In den frühen 1990er Jahren begann ich die Malerei wiederzuentdecken. Es begann mit einer Reihe von Studien für ein Projekt: der „Carpet Furniture"-Serie. Ich fing an, mit Gouache auf der glatten Rückseite von Aquarellpapier zu arbeiten. Gouache ist ein Medium, das ich schon früher sehr gemocht hatte, denn sie ist ziemlich opak und samtig. Obwohl sie nach dem Trocknen recht fest wird, kann man sie wieder anfeuchten und zu verschiedenen Farbschichten vermischen. Gouache ist aber auch interessant, weil sie früher einmal das Lieblingsmedium grafischer Gestalter war, wenn es um kamerafertige Illustrationen ging. Ich hatte schon immer eine Schwäche für Grafikdesign und die Frische und Neutralität der Gouache trug noch zusätzlich zu einer gewissen illustrativ-ausdruckslosen Bildqualität bei, um die es mir ging.

Die „Carpet Furniture"-Arbeiten selbst sind Teppiche, die mit Grundrissen von Möbeln bedruckt sind und die man genauso benutzen kann, wie man auch Möbel benutzen würde. Sie sind mit grösseren Werkgruppen wie den „A–Z Personal Panels" und „A–Z Covers" verbunden, deren Komposition durchweg auf dem Format eines *panel* beruht.

Die Idee des *panel* ist interessant, denn es handelt sich gewissermassen um eine im Raum befreite Fläche. Um eine ‚Superfläche', die die Begrenzungen des zweidimensionalen Raums überwinden kann, ohne jedoch tatsächlich dreidimensional zu werden. Die Werkgruppe „Carpet Furniture" hatte bereits einen Bezug zum Malerischen, da sie zwischen der Darstellung von etwas und der Sache selbst schwankte – die Möbel sollten genauso wie irgendwelche anderen Möbelstücke benutzt werden –, und der Einsatz der Gouachen für die Planung neuer Möbelvarianten funktionierte sowohl in einem praktischen Sinne als auch auf einer konzeptionellen Ebene. Später wurden diese Gemälde auch auf Grundrisse von „Ottoman Furniture" – mit denen verschiedene Konfigurationen aufgezeigt werden sollten, durch die sie unterschiedliche Funktionen erfüllen können – und die „Personal Panels" ausgeweitet, bei denen es sich um rechteckige Stoffstücke handelt, die man als Kleidung tragen kann.

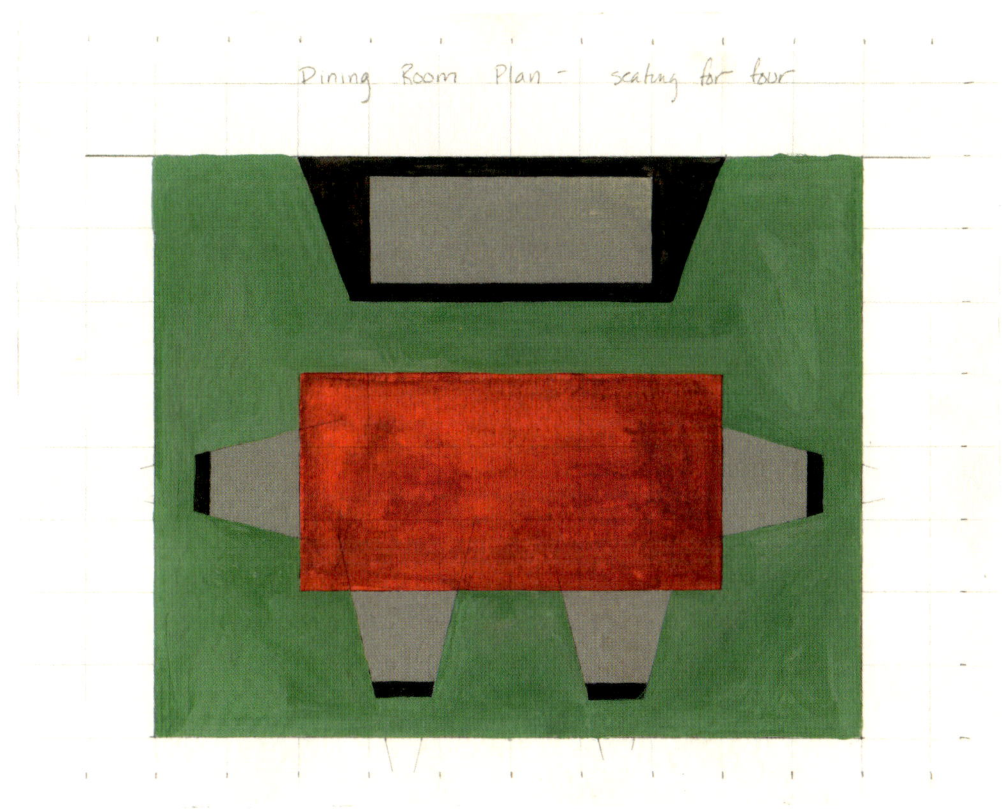
Dining Room Plan — seating for four

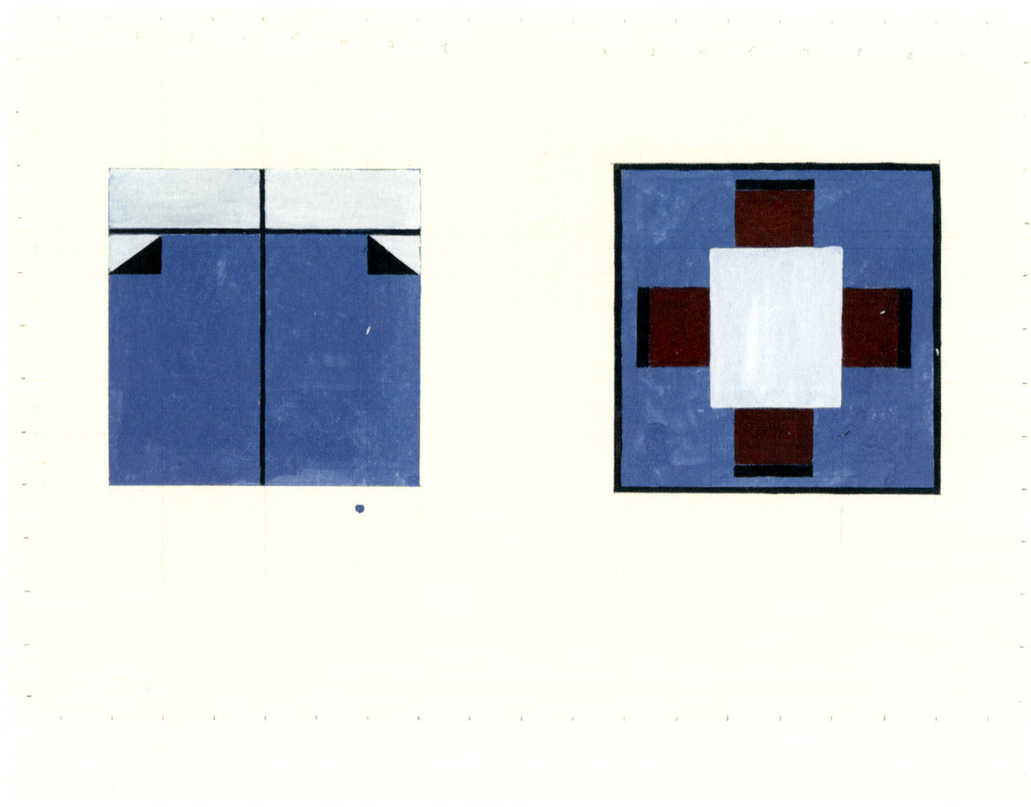

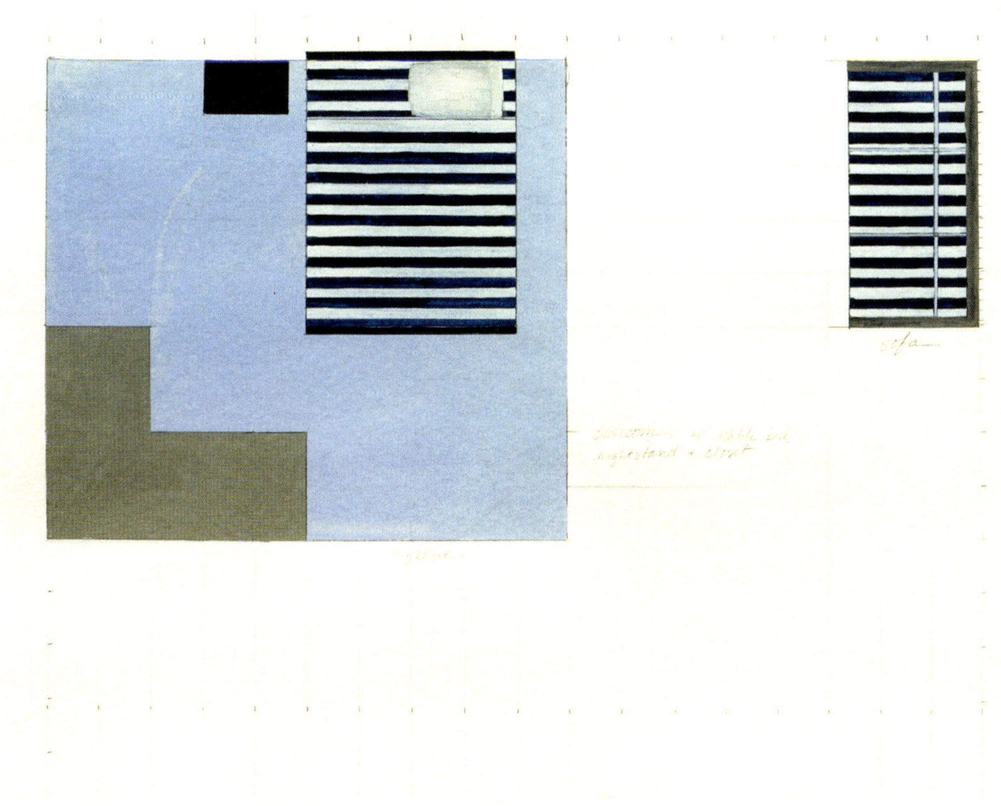

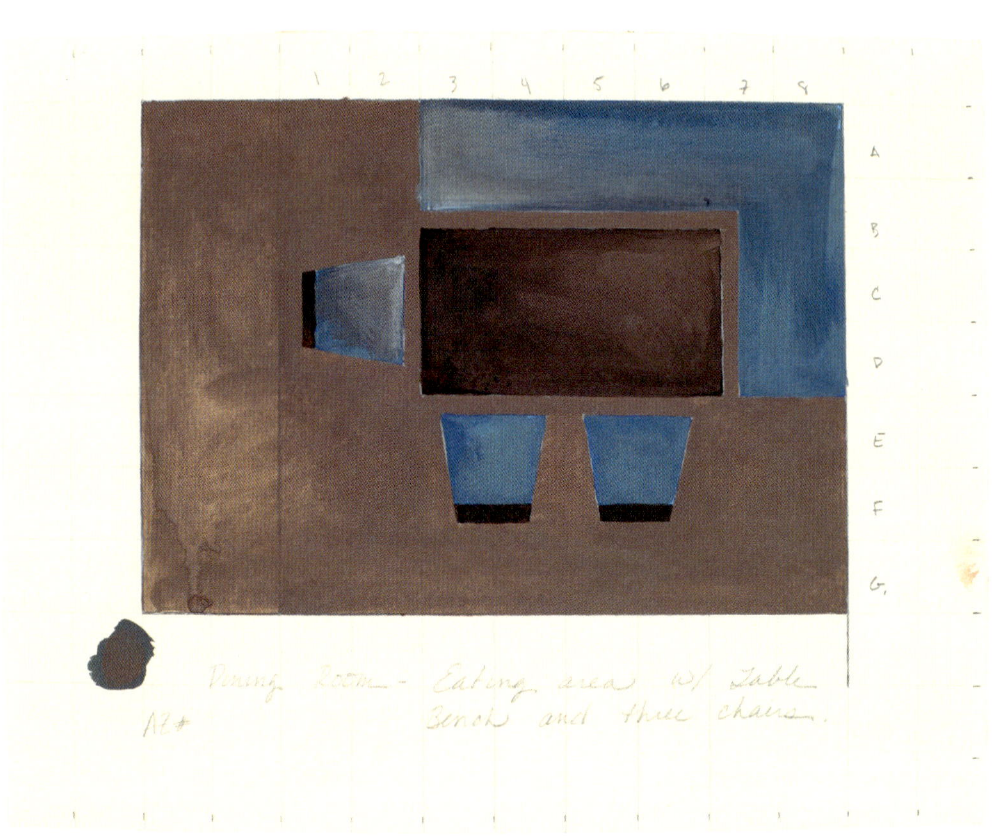

Dining Room — Eating area w/ Table
Bench and three chairs.

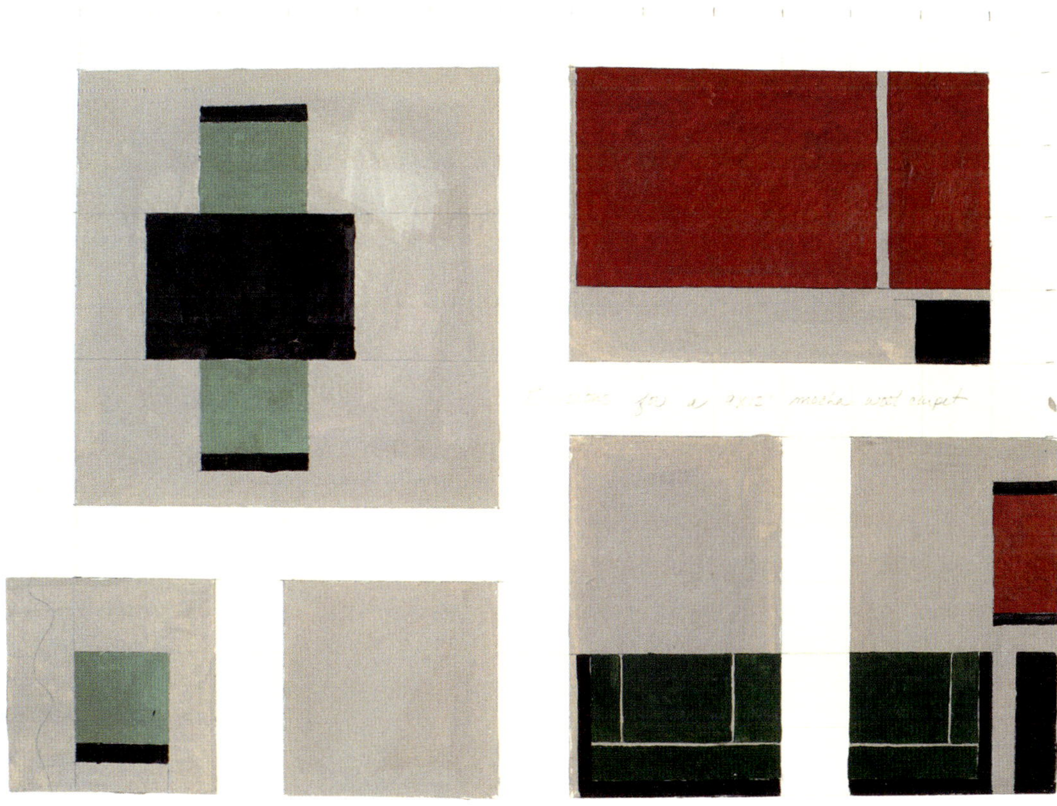

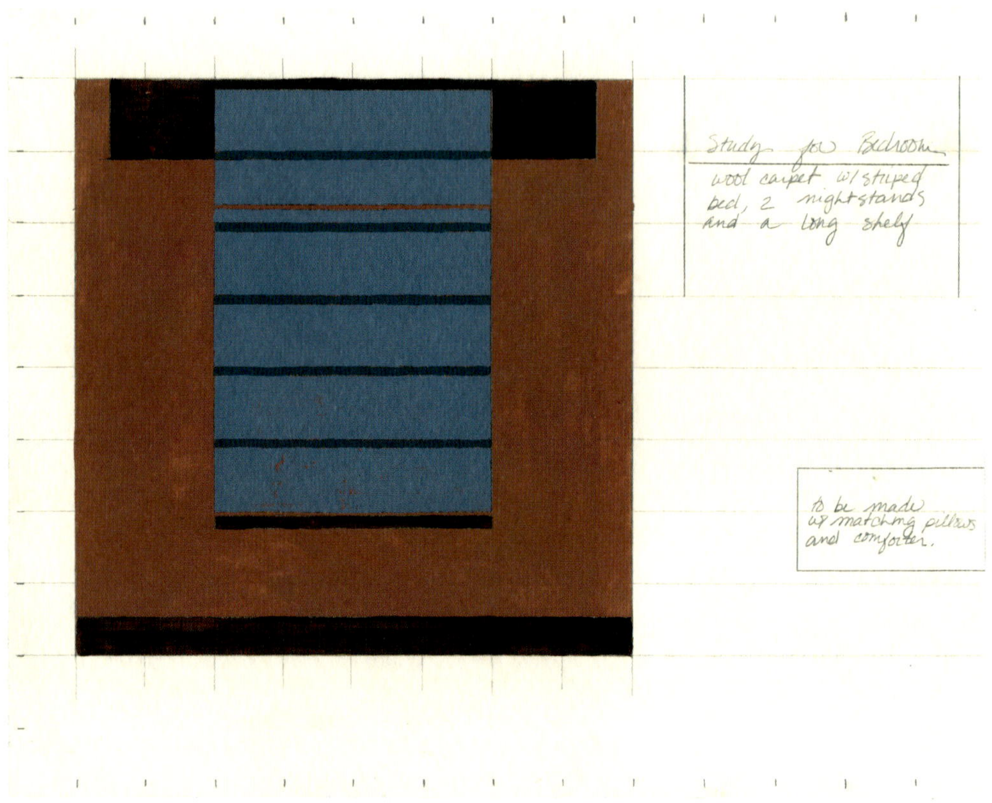

Study for Bedroom
wool carpet w/ striped
bed, 2 nightstands
and a long shelf

to be made
up matching pillows
and comforter.

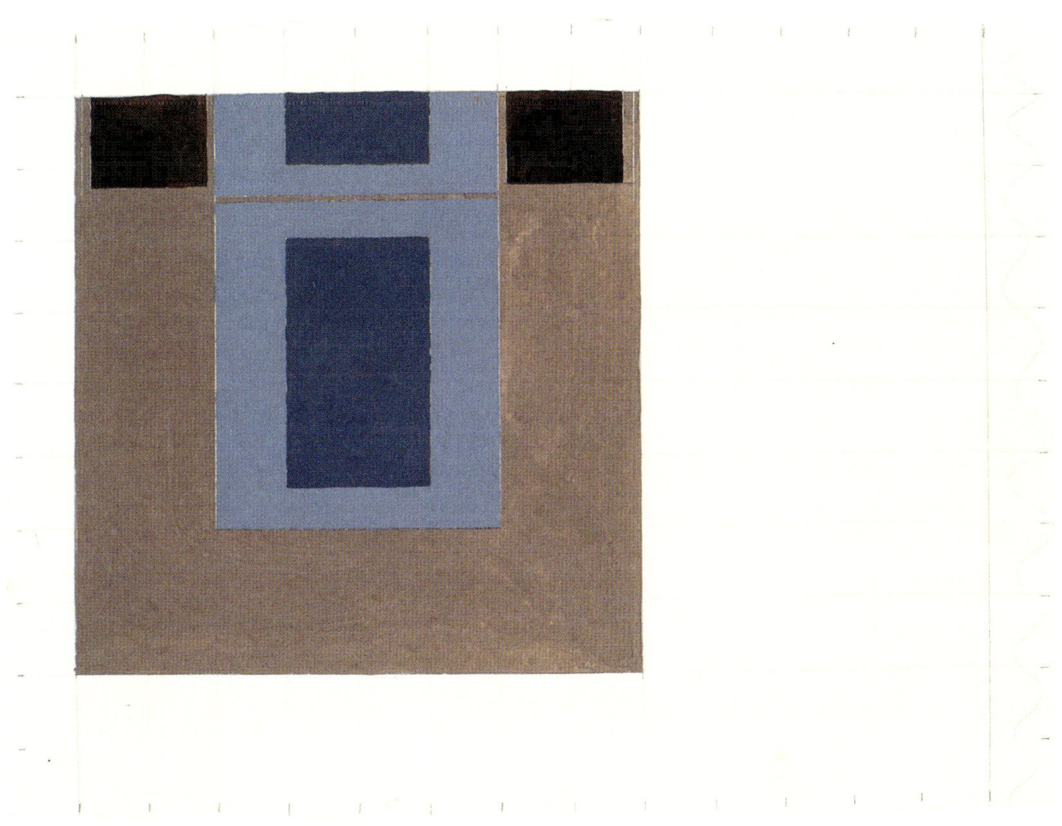

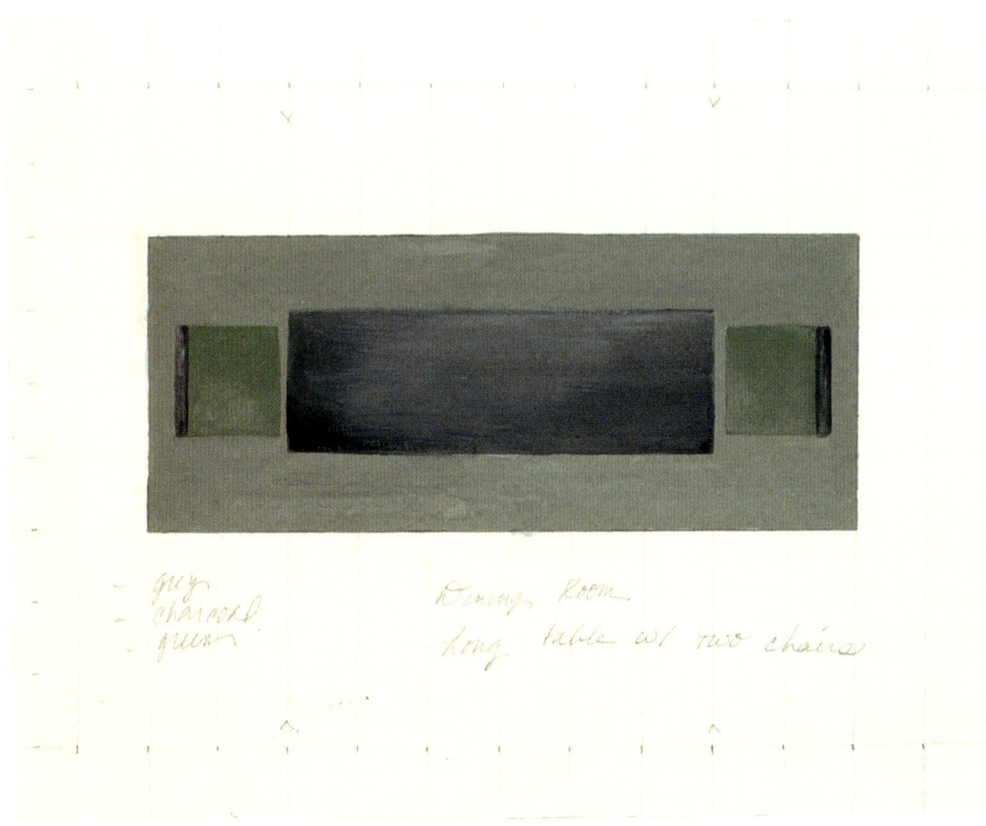

- grey
- charcoal
- green
Dining Room
Long table w/ two chairs

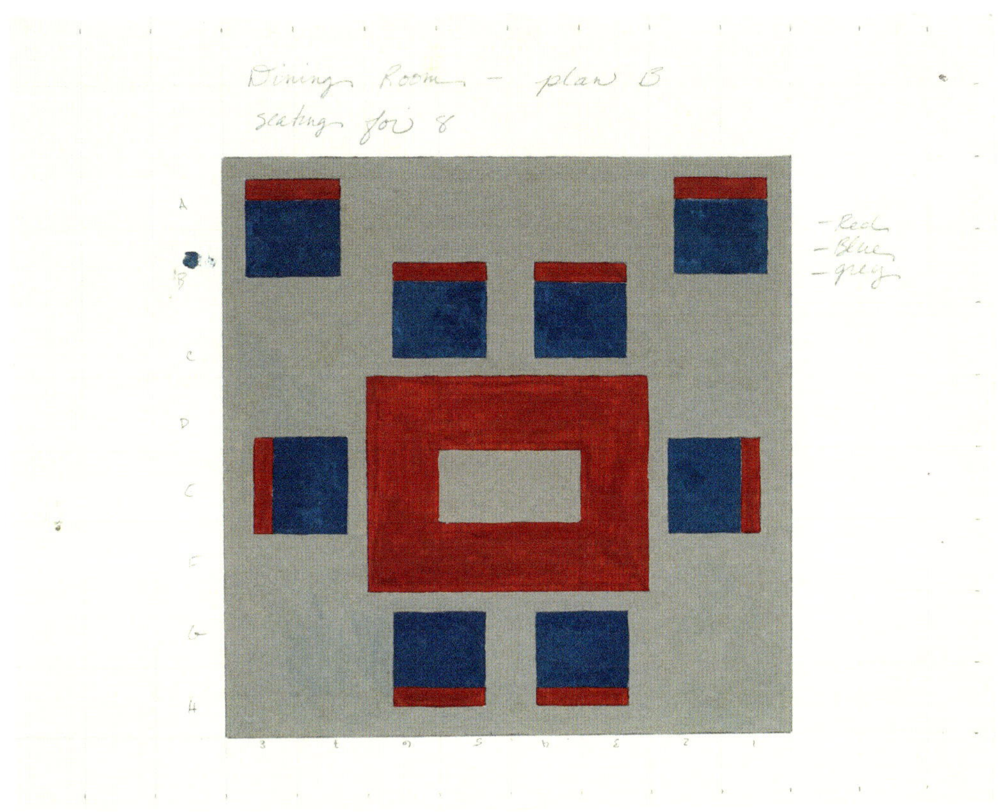
Dining Room - plan B
seating for 8
- Red
- Blue
- grey

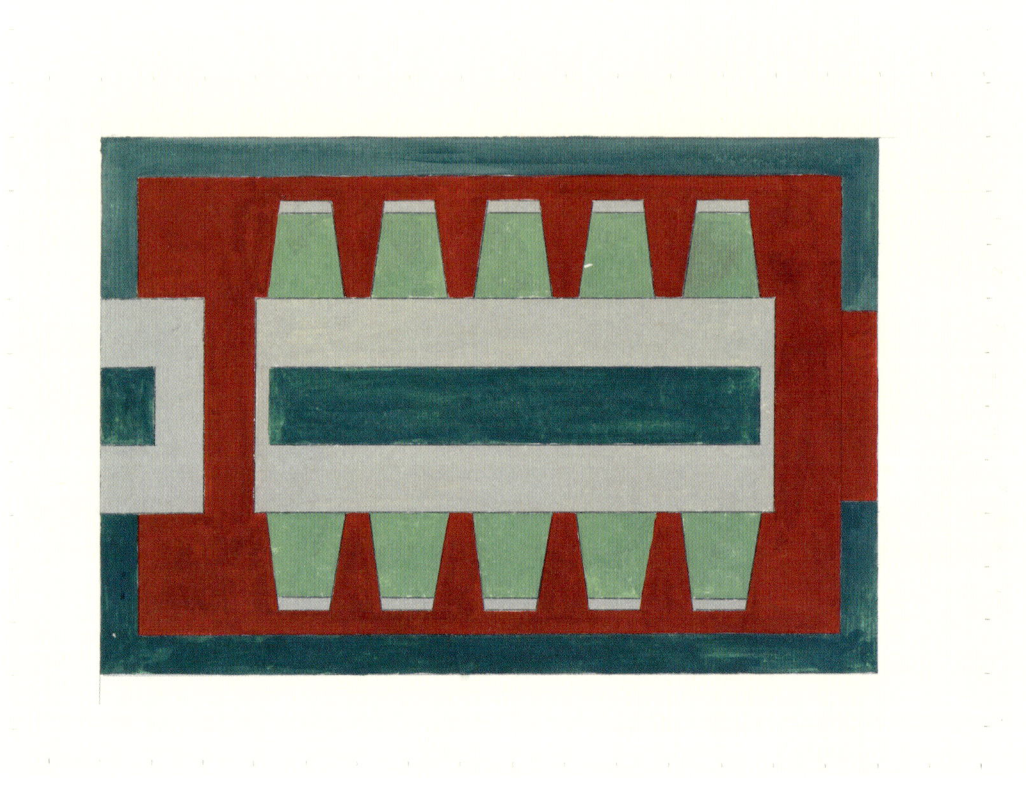

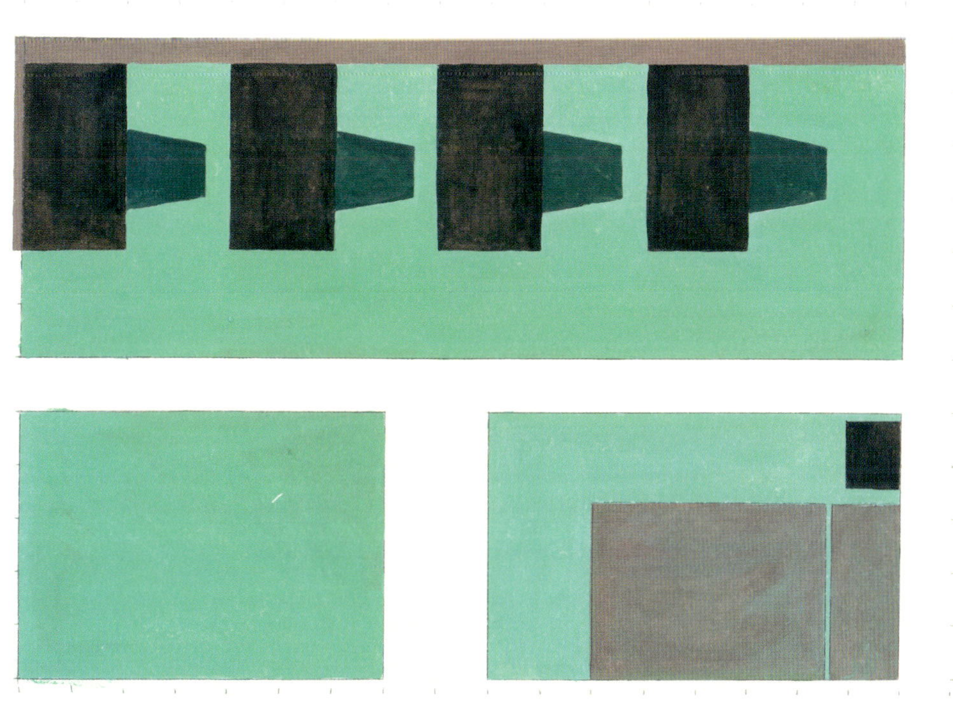

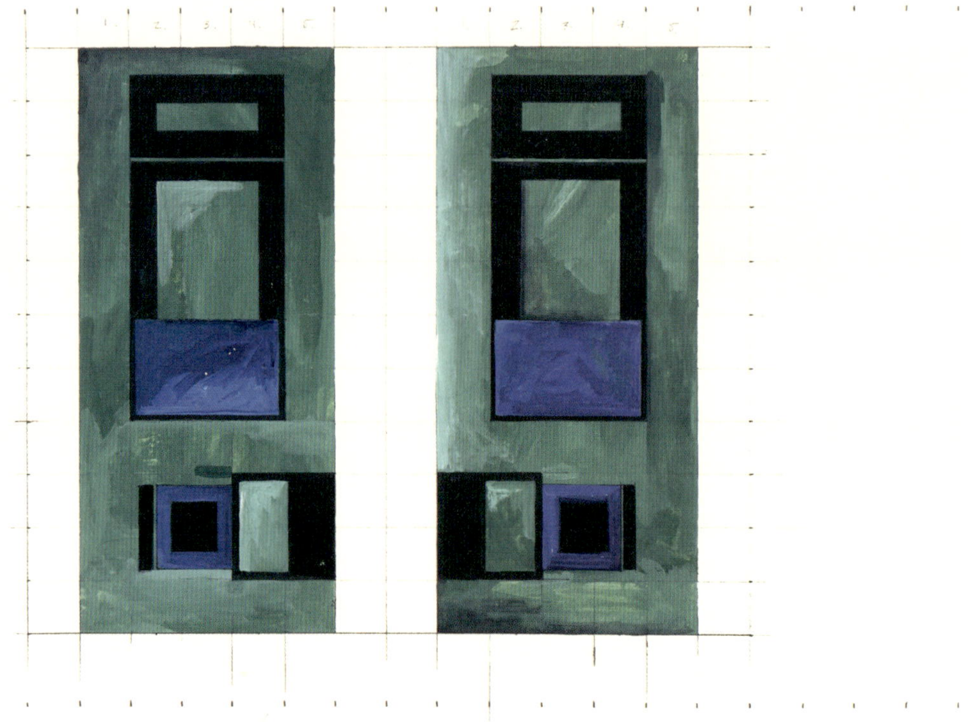

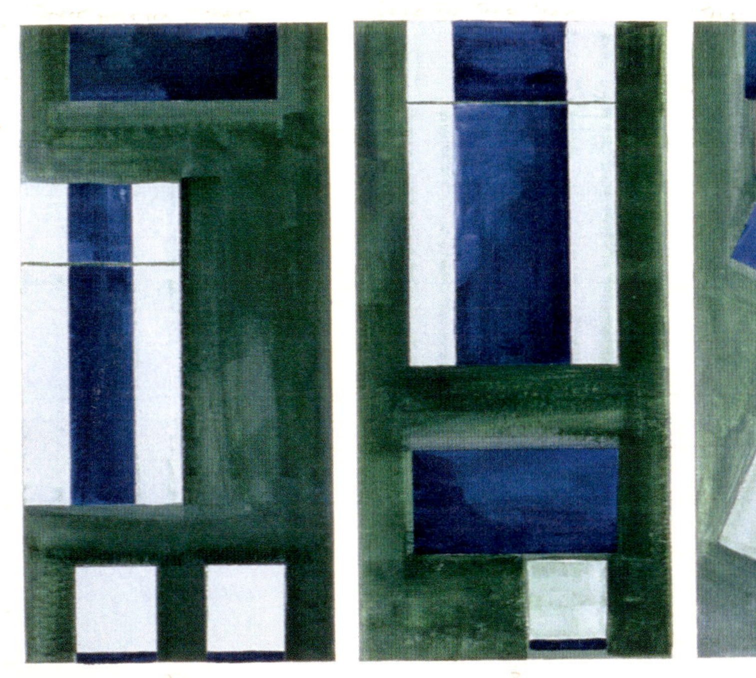
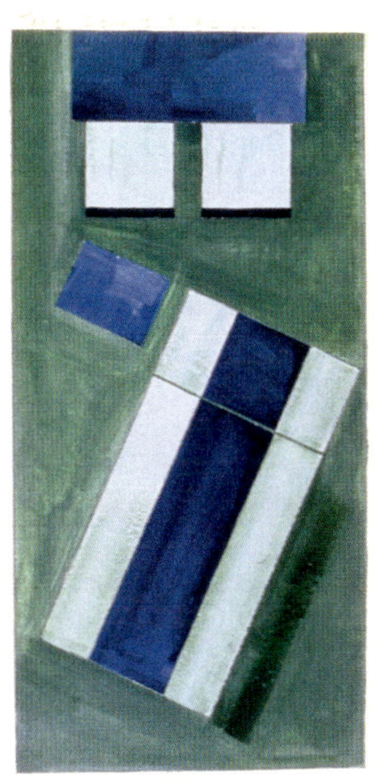

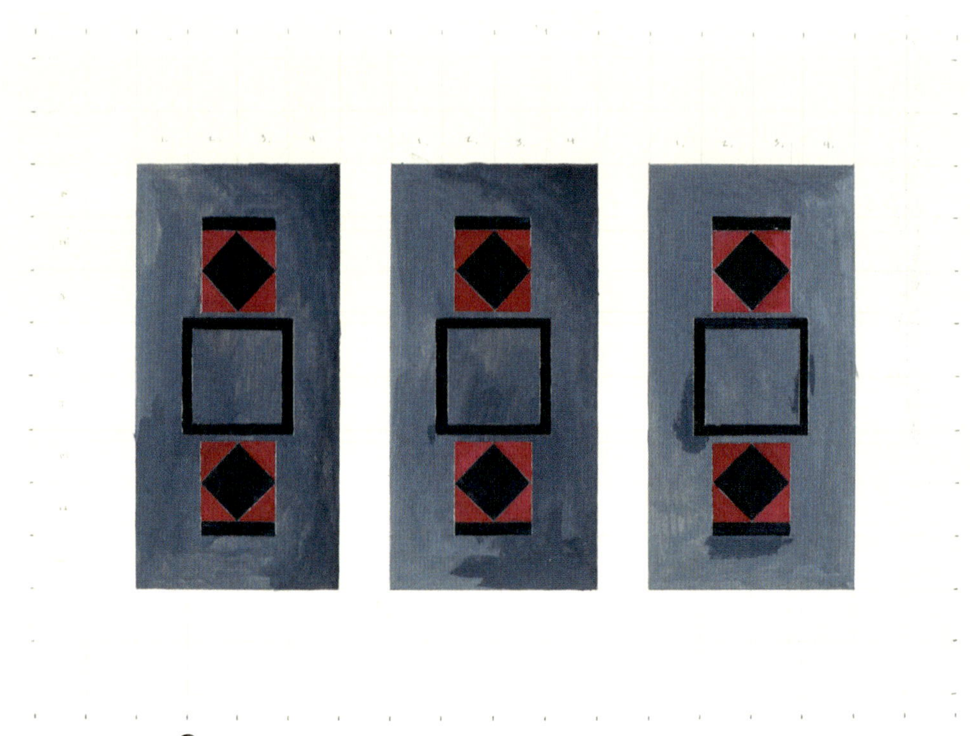

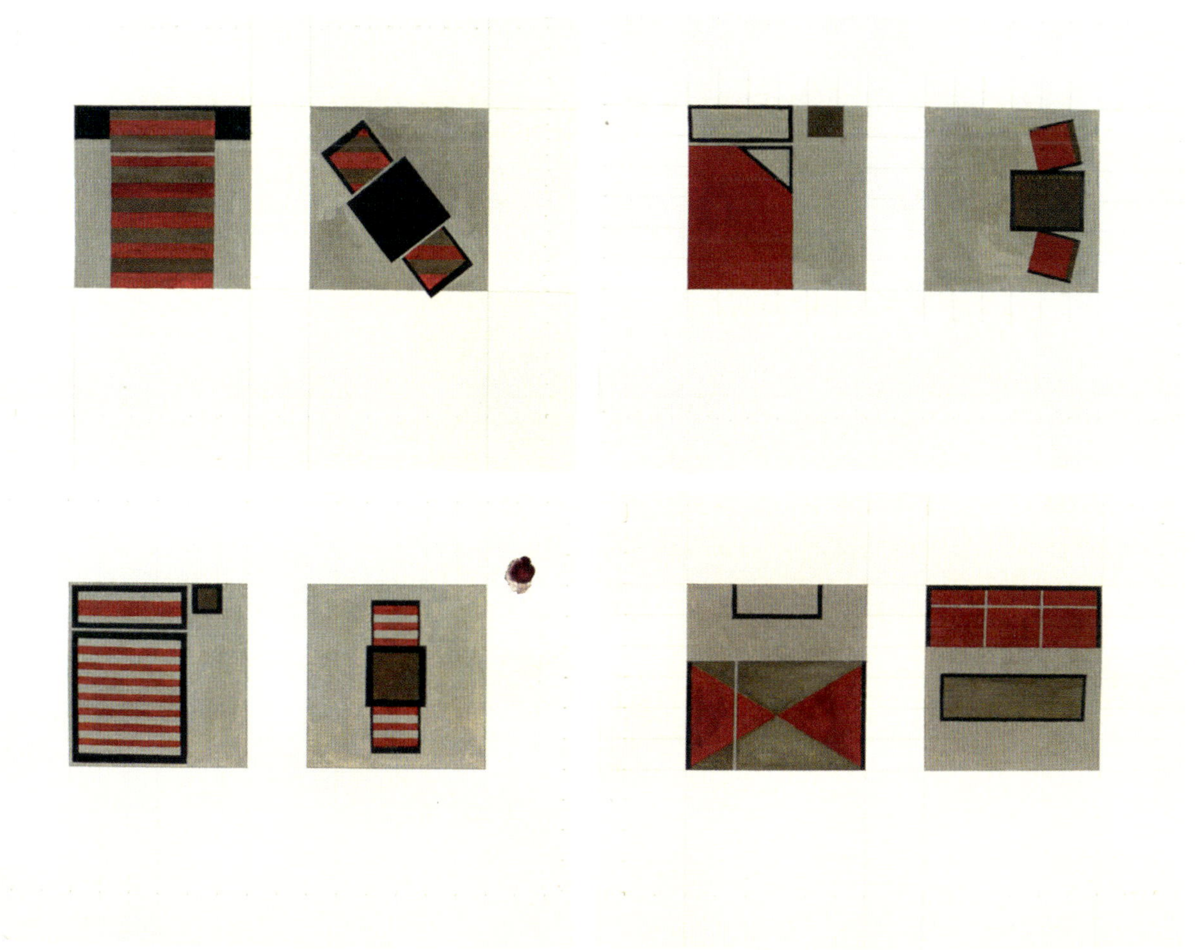

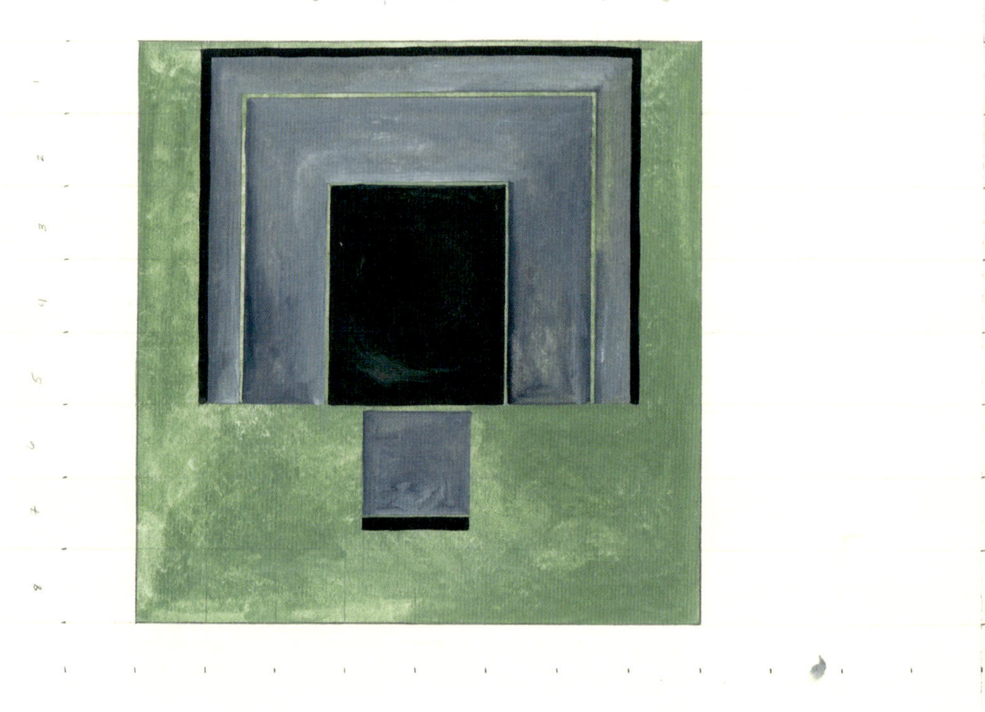

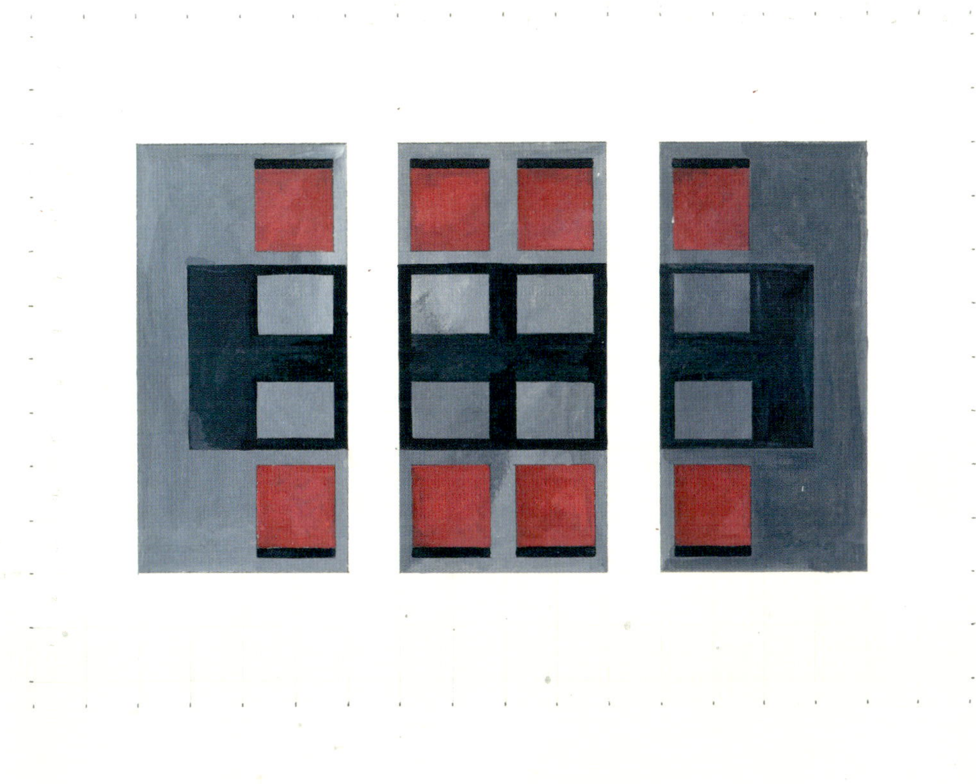

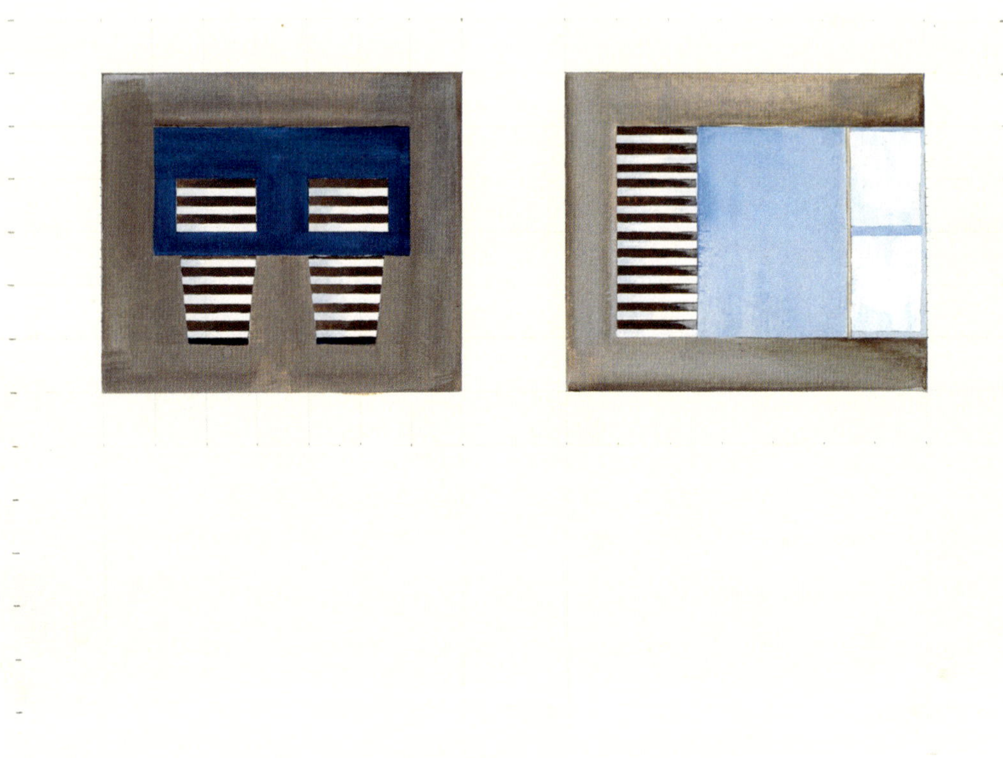

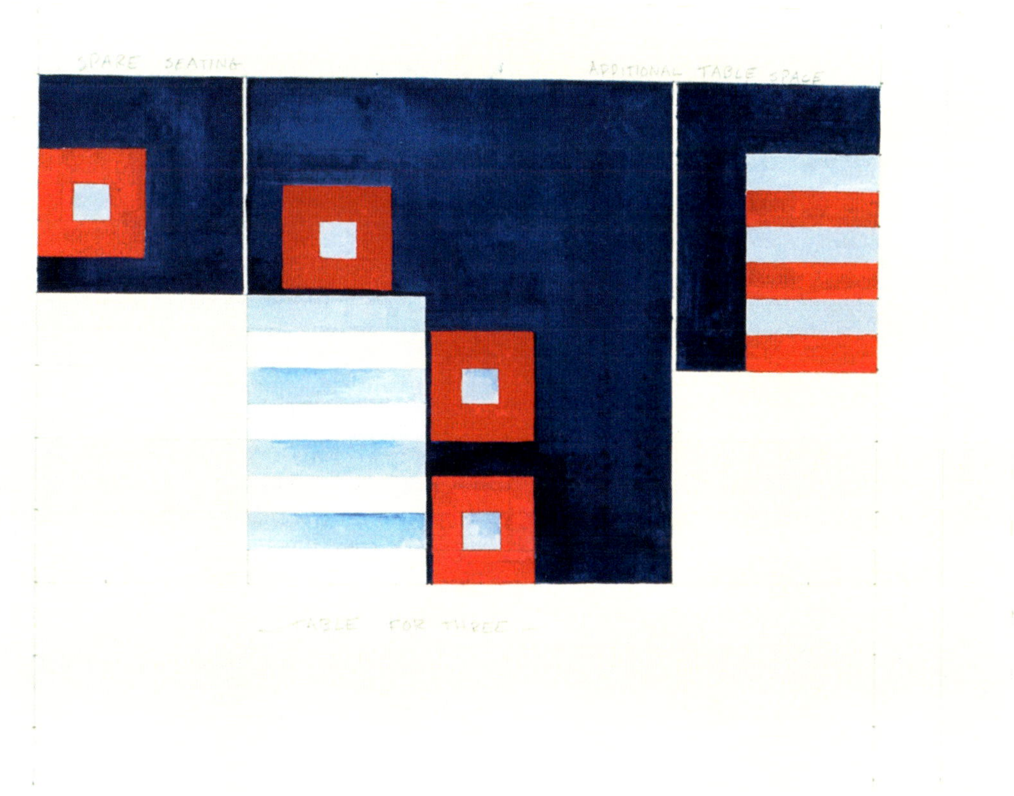

SPARE SEATING
ADDITIONAL TABLE SPACE
TABLE FOR THREE

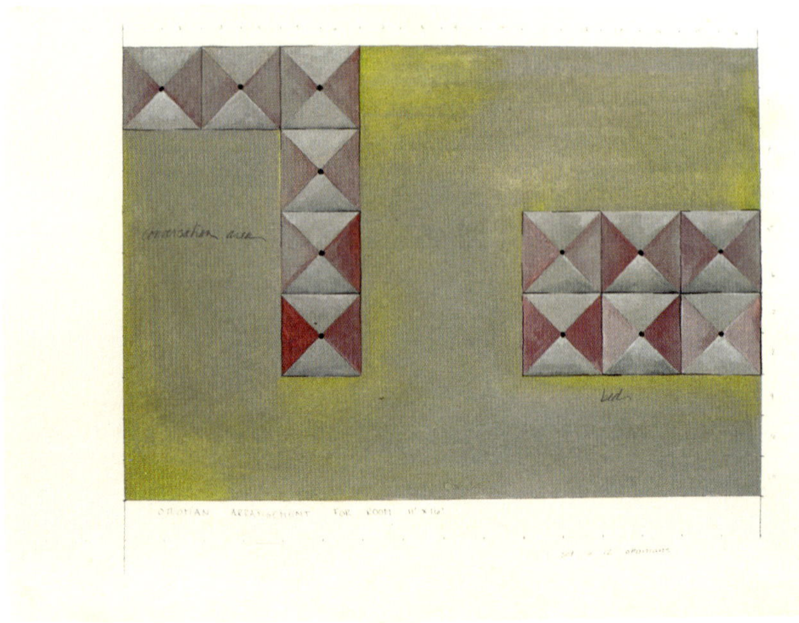

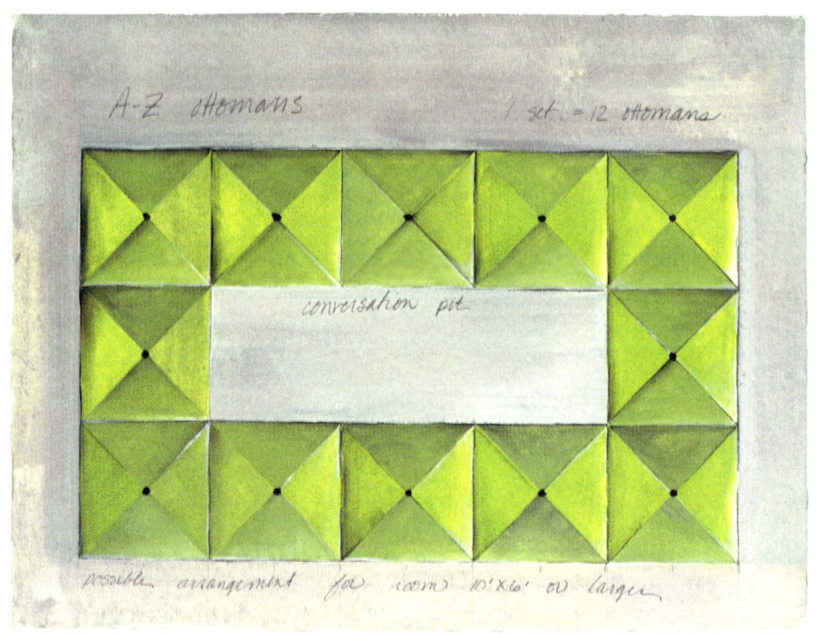
A-Z ottomans
1 set = 12 ottomans
conversation pit
possible arrangement for room 10'x6' or larger

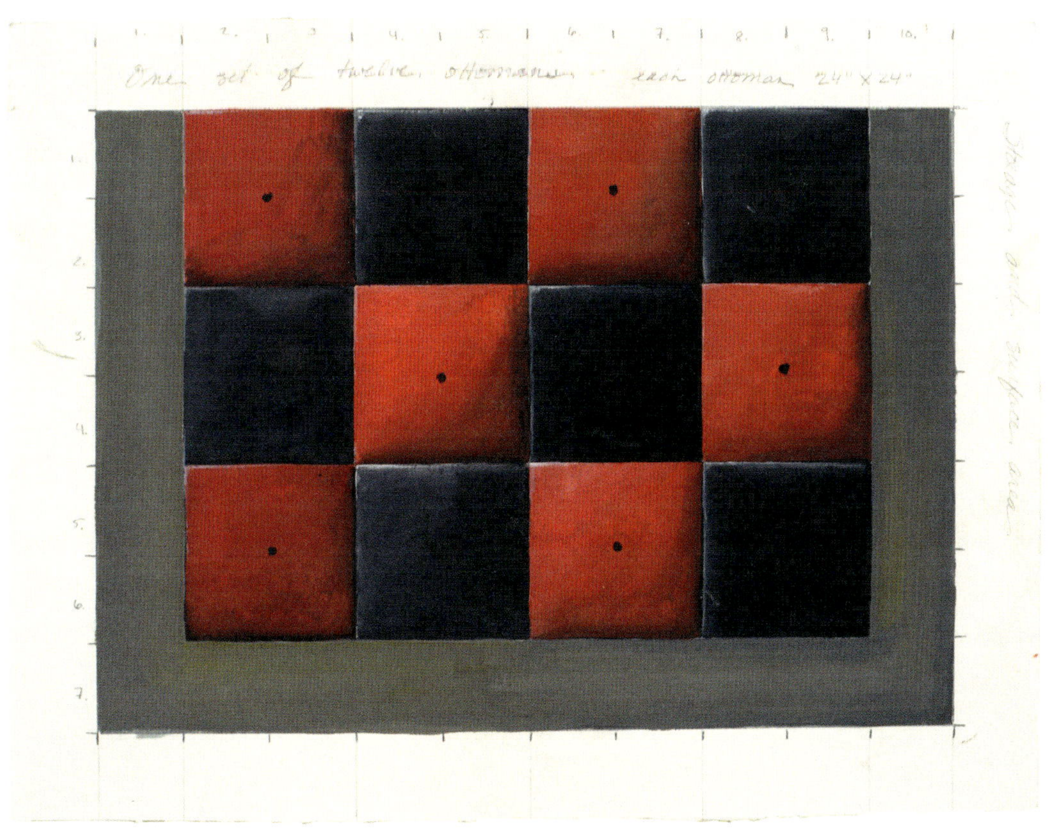
One set of twelve ottomans — each ottoman 24" x 24"

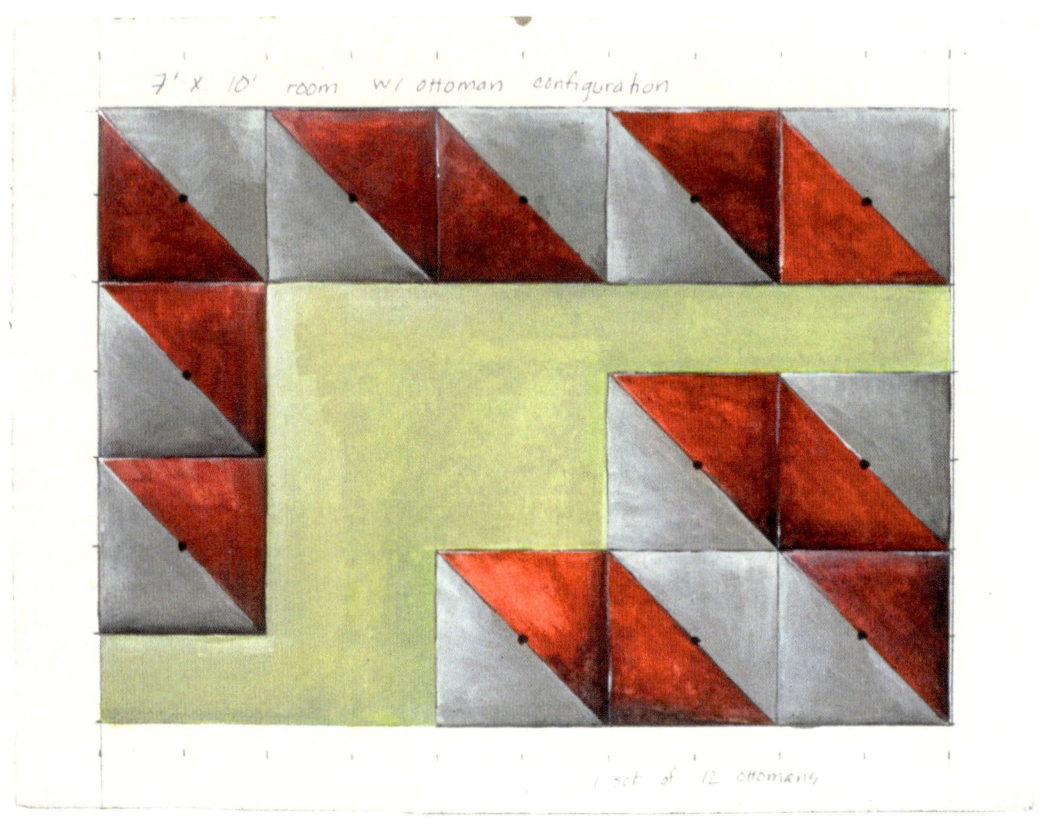
7' x 10' room w/ ottoman configuration
1 set of 12 ottomans

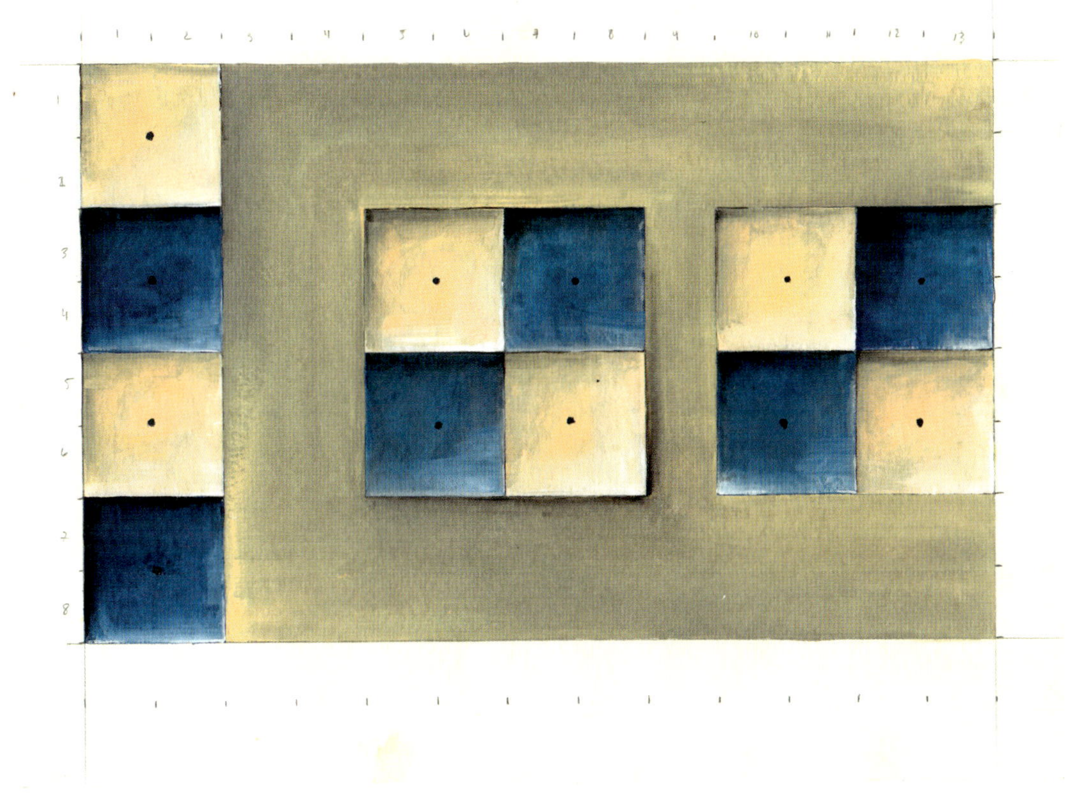

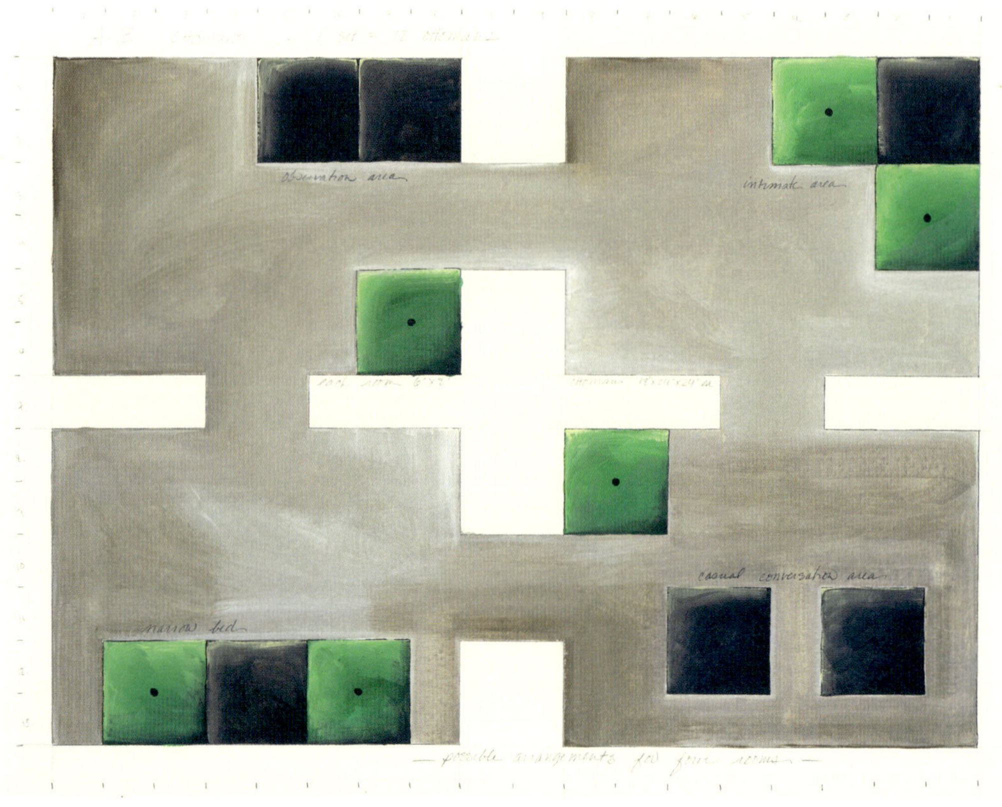
observation area
intimate area
narrow bed
casual conversation area
— possible arrangements for four rooms —

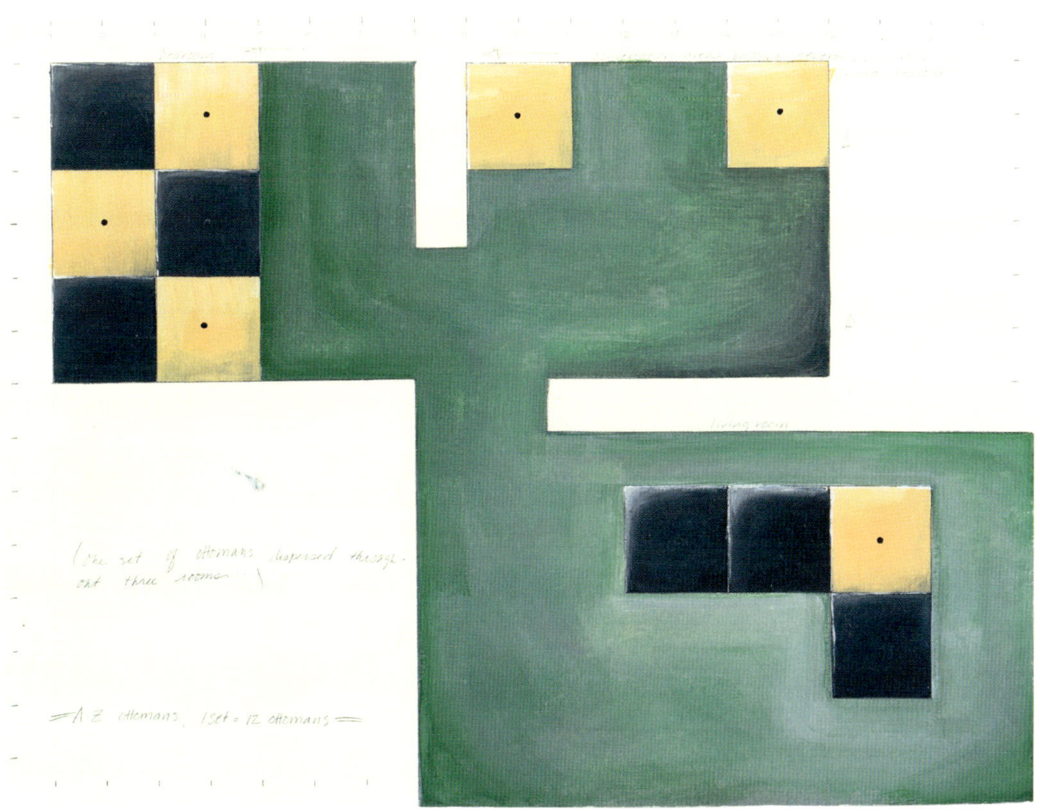
(one set of ottomans dispersed through-
out three rooms)
= A-Z ottomans. 1 set = 12 ottomans =

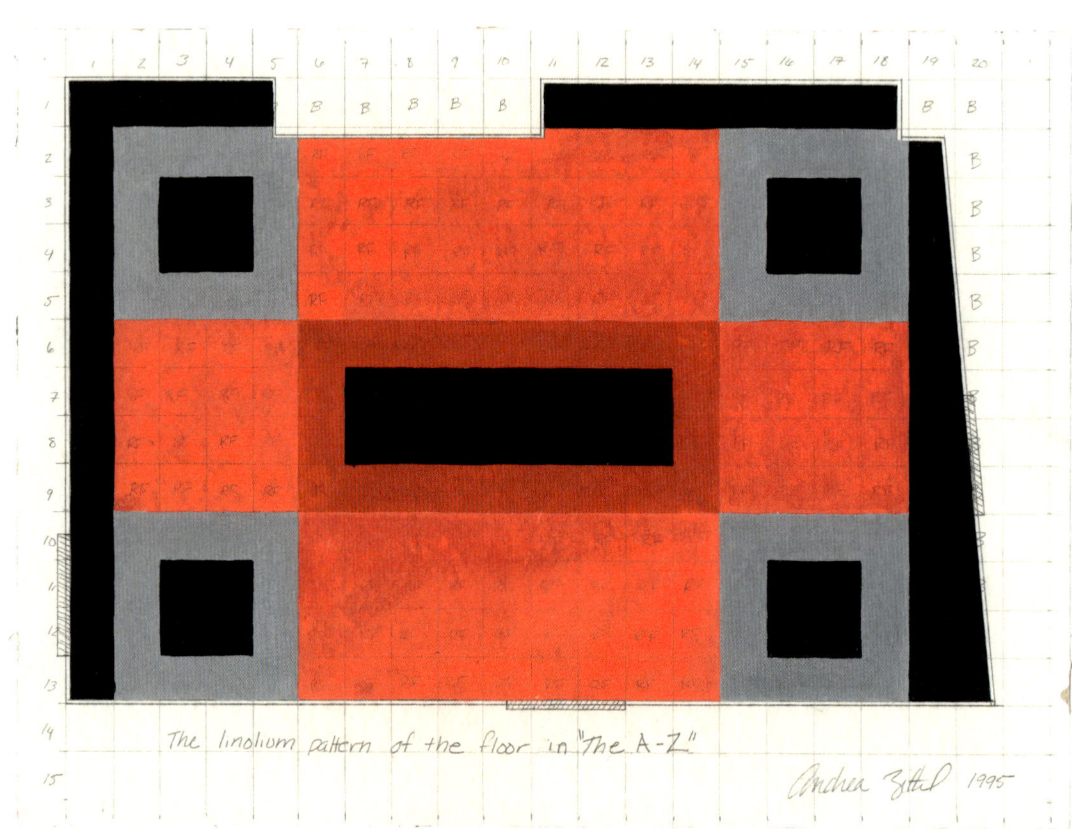

The linolium pattern of the floor in "The A-Z"

Andrea Zittel 1995

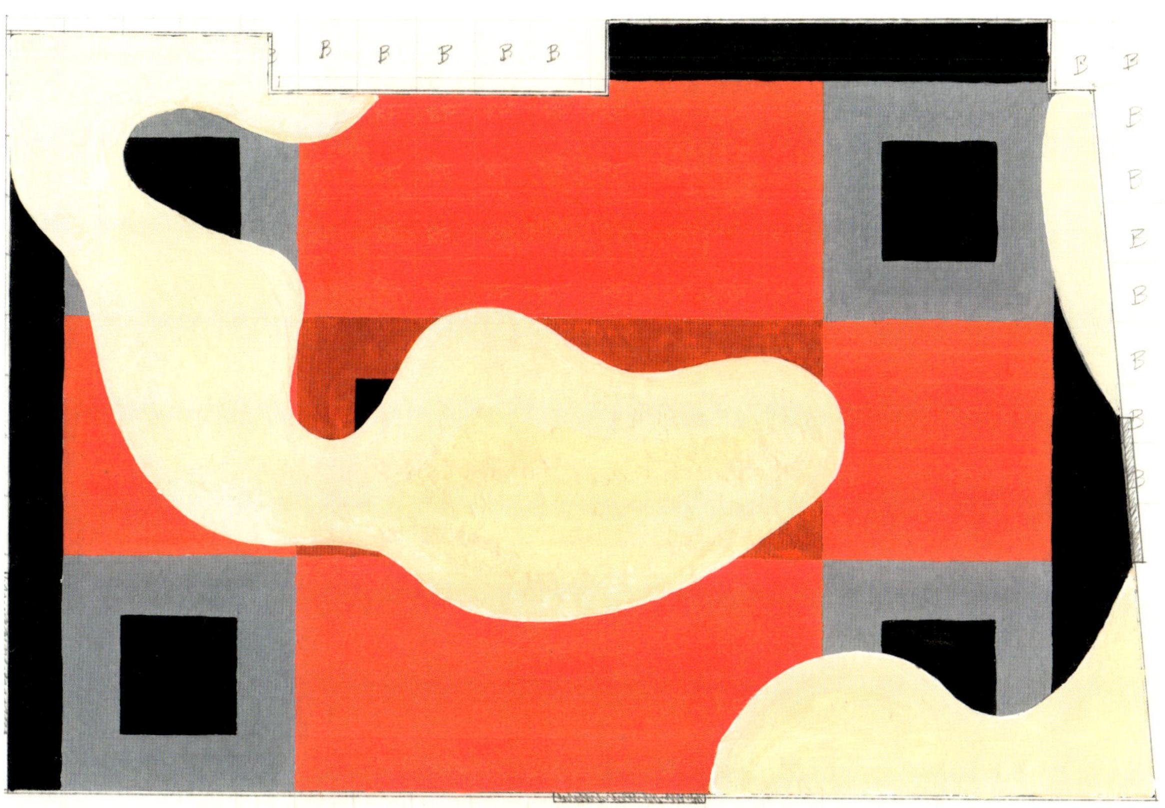

B B B B B
B
B
B
B
B
B
B
B

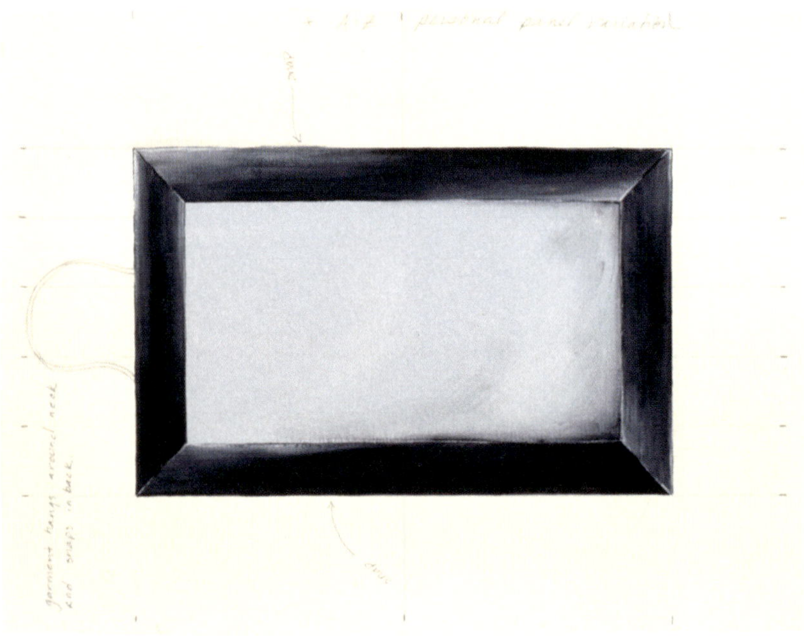

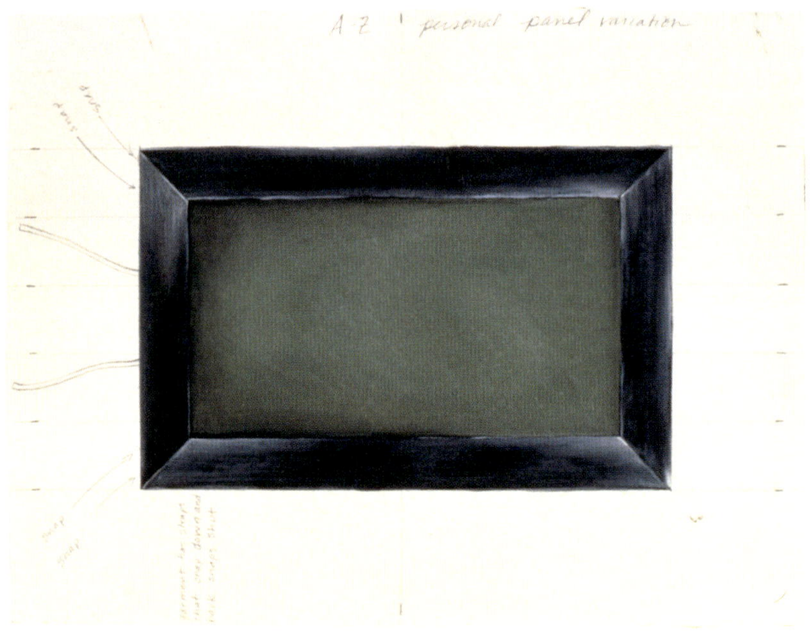

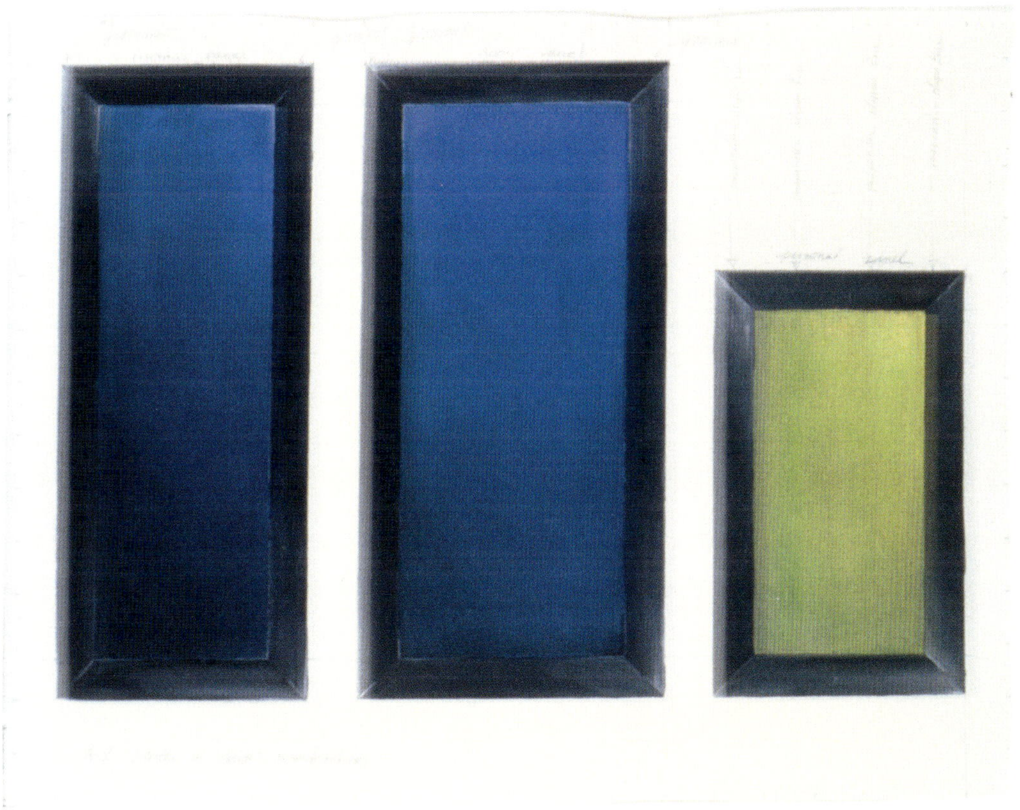

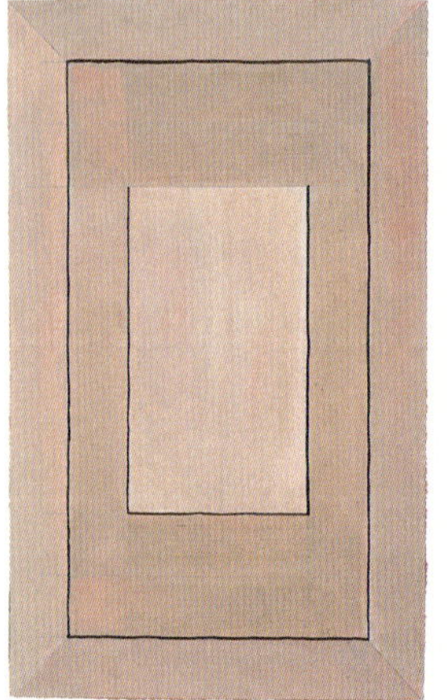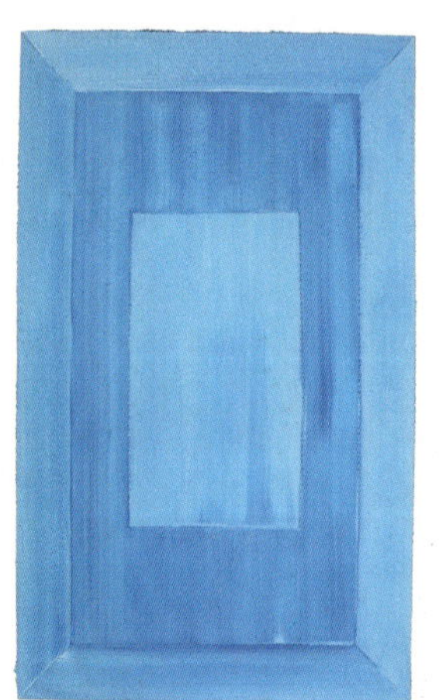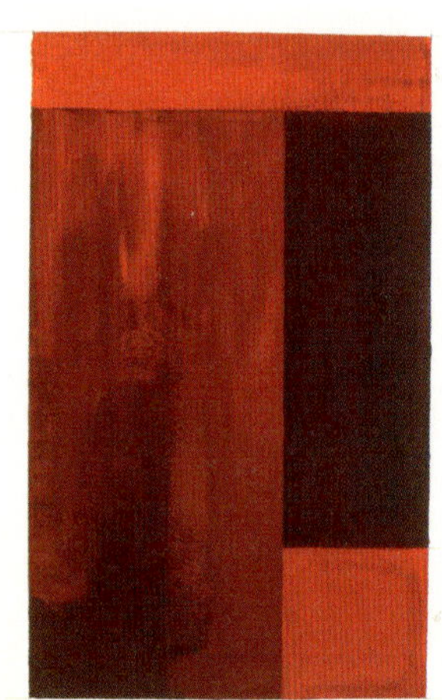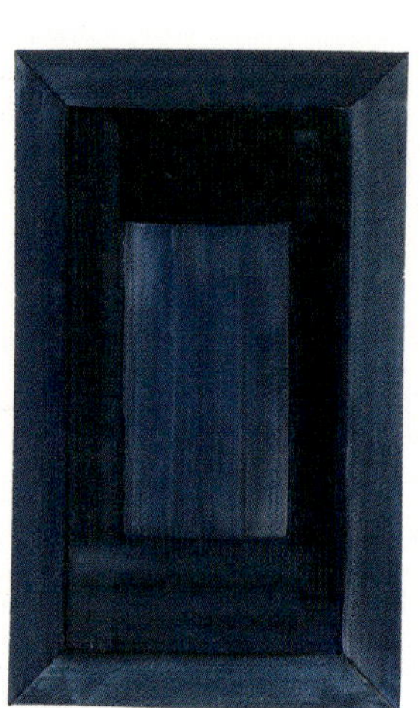

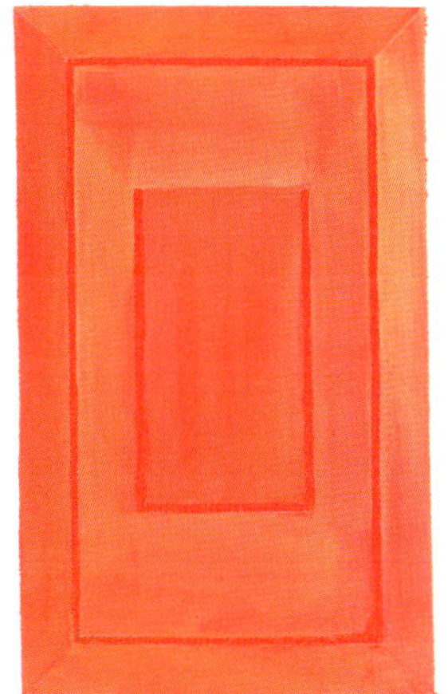 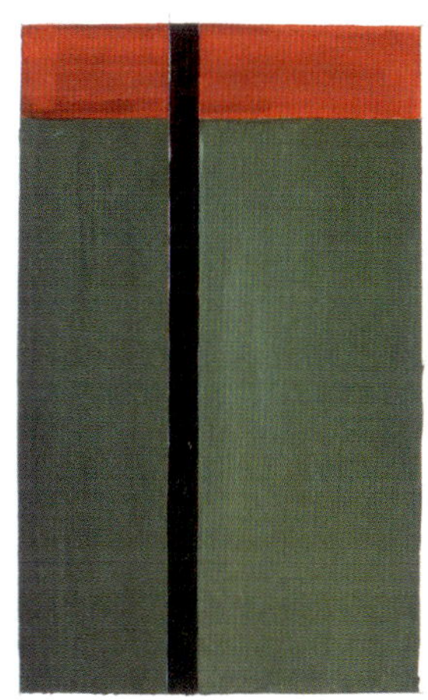 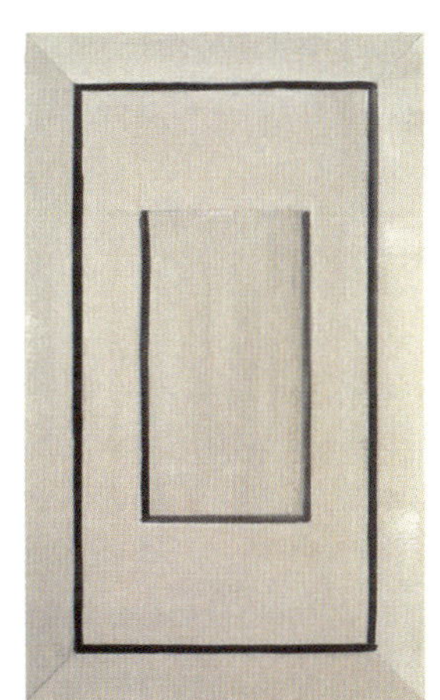 

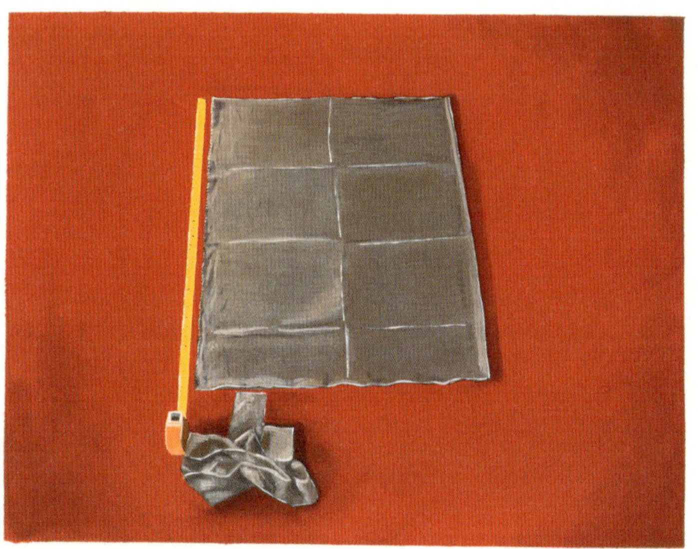

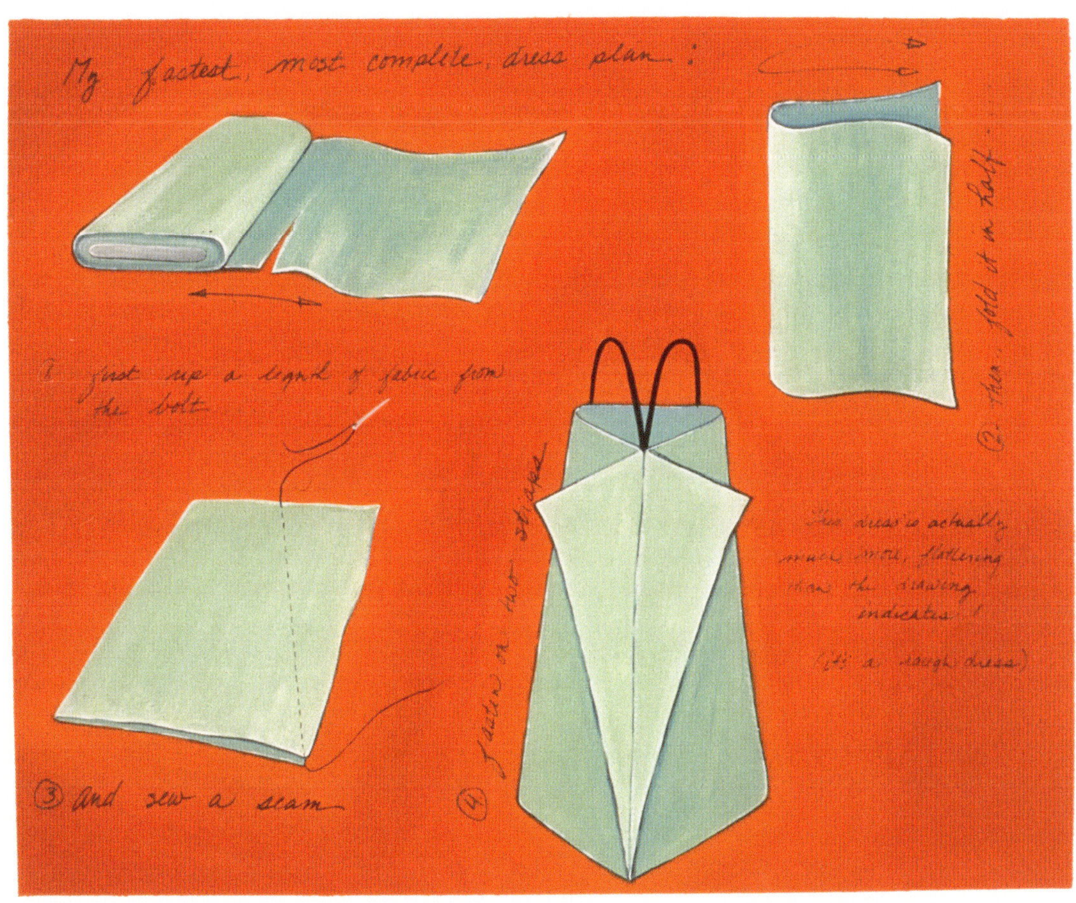
My fastest, most complete, dress plan :
1. just rip a length of fabric from the bolt
2. then fold it in half.
3. and sew a seam.
4. I fasten in two straps.
This dress is actually much more flattering than the drawing indicates !
(it's a rough dress)

When I first started creating images of sculptures I used to think of this kind of painting as a very simple form of 3-D modeling. Most fabricators request CAD drawings in order to construct a piece. Since I have never learned to design on the computer, I would show them the gouache paintings instead. The early designs for the *Escape Vehicle* were influenced by trailers in Berlin, where I was doing a DAAD residency. Later the structure and formal language evolved and began to reflect a Southern California vernacular as I traveled from Germany to Southern California. It is the latter culture that my work constantly refers back to in its exploration of both personal and public boundaries and the construction of individuality.

Ideas about leisure and culture also were a strong factor in the impetus for *Point of Interest*—a public art work that was commissioned for the Doris C. Freedman Plaza at the entrance of Central Park in Manhattan. The intention was to depict a twenty-first-century interpretation of nature (nature as action adventure) to contrast with Frederick Law Olmstead's* nineteenth-century interpretation of nature as pastoral tranquility. Much like my process "imaging" the *Escape Vehicles*, the paintings for the *Point of Interest* are somewhat clunky and simple since I was using the process of painting them as a way to sort out how a rock outcropping could eventually become an expression of cultural values.

In the background of many of these other works is a trail of logos that were usually done just for fun. I have always thought that it is interesting how small companies often strive to appear larger and more anonymous than they really are, while really large companies try equally hard to appear smaller, more intimate, and connected to a single identifiable person. Branding and image design has always fascinated me and as a natural extension of this interest I started sketching ideas for my own branding.

* Frederick Law Olmstead (1822-1903) was an important American landscape architect in the nineteenth century who became famous for designing such important parks as Central Park in Manhattan and Prospect Park in Brooklyn. He also played an important role in the foundation of the first national parks, such as Niagara Falls.

Als ich begann, Bilder von Skulpturen zu machen, betrachtete ich diese Art des Malens als eine ganz einfache Form der 3-D-Modellierung. Die meisten Hersteller verlangen für die Konstruktion eines Werks CAD-Zeichnungen, aber da ich nie gelernt habe, wie man Dinge am Computer entwirft, habe ich ihnen stattdessen die Gouachebilder gezeigt. Die frühen Entwürfe für das „Escape Vehicle" waren von Wohnwagen in Berlin beeinflusst, wo ich ein DAAD-Stipendium hatte. Später entwickelte sich ihre Struktur und Formensprache weiter und bekam einen stärkeren südkalifornischen Einschlag, als ich von Deutschland nach Südkalifornien reiste. Auf diese Kultur bezieht sich mein Werk in seiner Erkundung der persönlichen und öffentlichen Eingrenzungen und in der Konstruktion von Individualität immer wieder.

Ideen, die Freizeit und Kultur betrafen, spielten auch bei der Motivation zu „Point of Interest" eine grosse Rolle; es handelt sich um ein Kunstwerk im öffentlichen Raum, das für die Doris C. Freedman Plaza am Eingang des Central Park in Manhattan in Auftrag gegeben wurde. Meine Absicht war es, eine Interpretation der Natur im 21. Jahrhundert – Natur als Action-Abenteuer – als Kontrast zu Frederick Law Olmsteads* aus dem 19. Jahrhundert stammender Interpretation der Natur als pastoraler Landschaft darzustellen. Ähnlich wie bei meinem Prozess der Bildentwicklung für die „Escape Vehicles" sind die Gemälde für „Point of Interest" ein bisschen klobig und schlicht, da ich den Malprozess dazu benutzte, herauszufinden, wie aus einem Felsvorsprung schliesslich ein Ausdruck kultureller Werte werden kann.

Im Hintergrund vieler dieser anderen Werke findet sich eine Reihe von Logos, die ich in der Regel einfach nur so zum Spass gemacht habe. Ich habe mir häufig gedacht, es ist interessant, dass kleine Unternehmen sich oft bemühen, grösser und anonymer zu wirken, als sie tatsächlich sind, und dass wirklich grosse Unternehmen sich genauso stark bemühen, kleiner und intimer zu erscheinen und so, als seien sie mit einer einzigen identifizierbaren Person verknüpft. Branding und Image Design haben mich schon immer fasziniert und als natürliche Erweiterung dieses Interesses habe ich begonnen, Ideen für meine eigene Markenbildung zu skizzieren.

* Frederick Law Olmstead (1822-1903) war ein bedeutender amerikanischer Landschaftsarchitekt im 19. Jahrhundert, der für die Gestaltung von wichtigen Parks wie Central Park und Prospect Park in New York bekannt geworden ist. Darüber hinaus spielte er bei der Gründung der ersten Nationalparks wie den Niagara Falls eine wichtige Rolle.

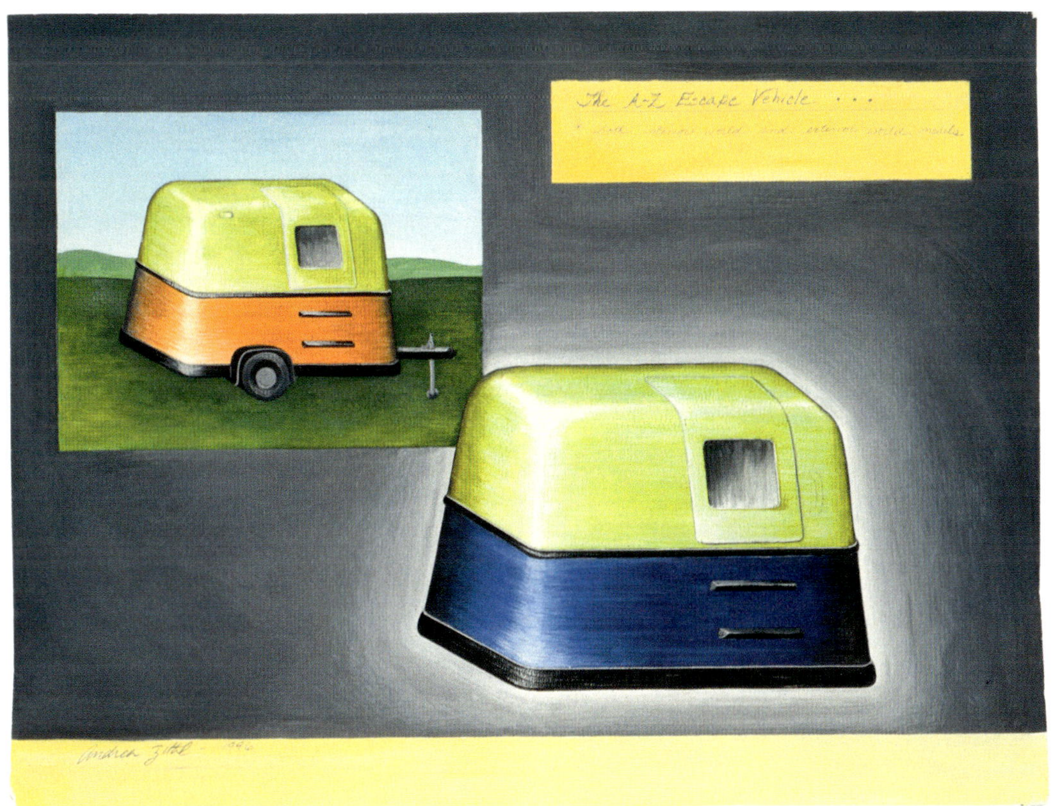
The A-Z Escape Vehicle . . .
Andrea Zittel - '96

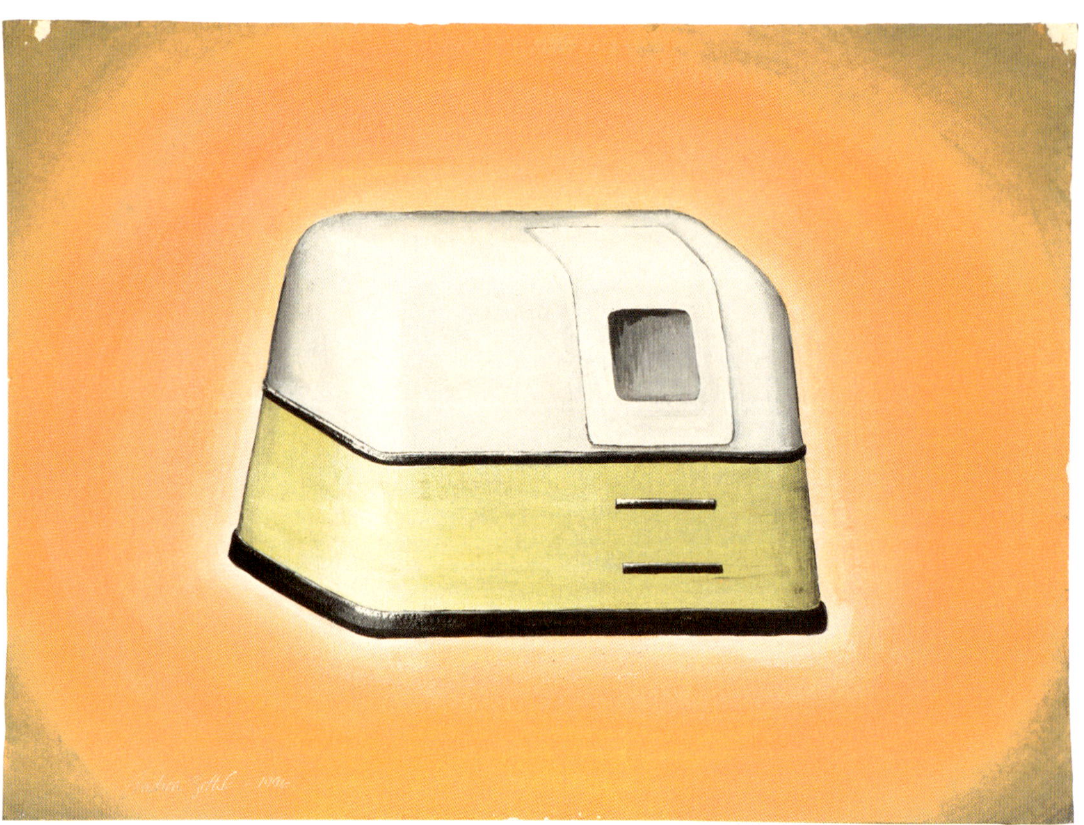

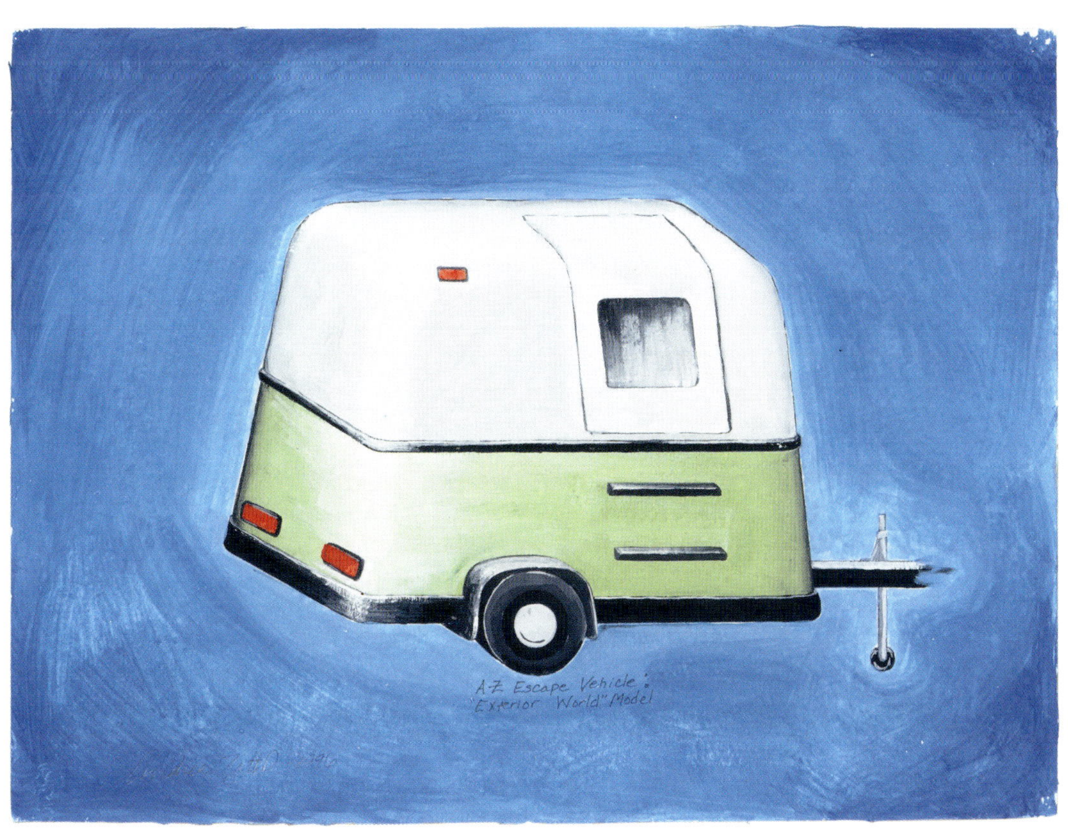

A-Z Escape Vehicle:
"Exterior World" Model

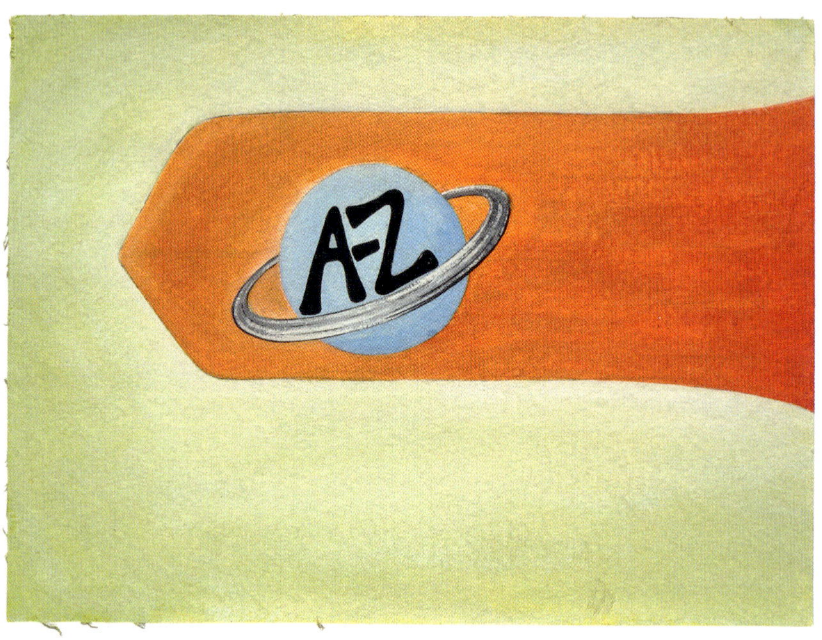
A-Z

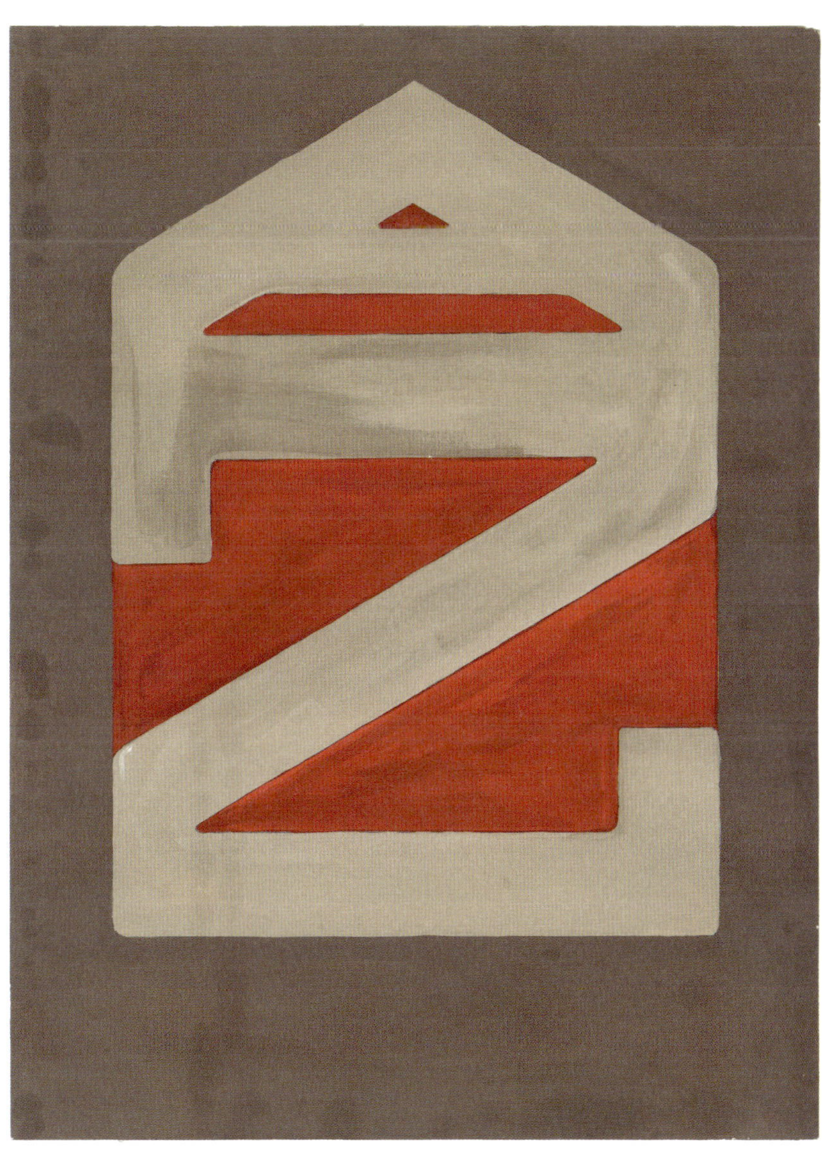

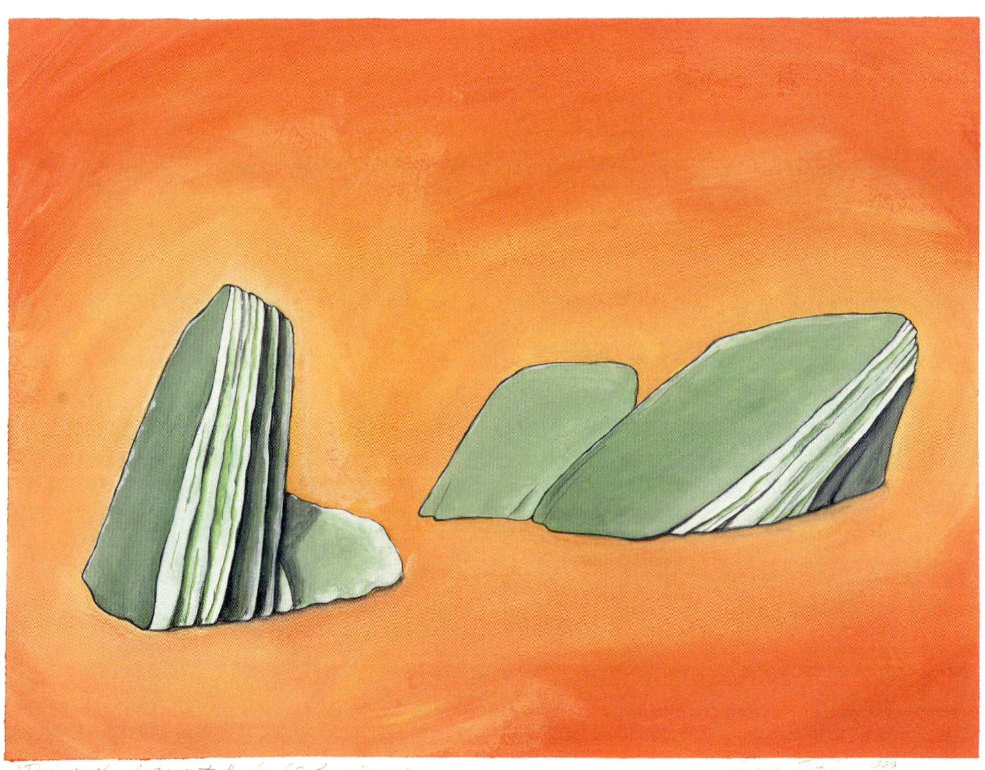

"Point of Interest" in 6.8 Lava Brand

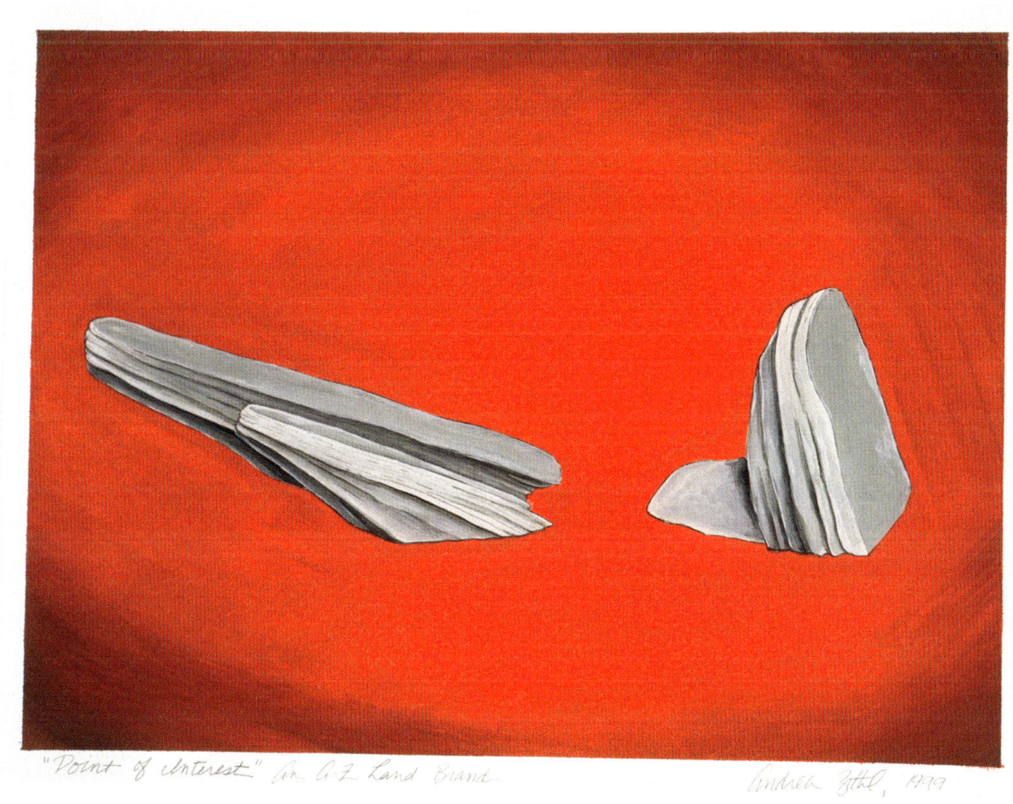
"Point of Interest" for A-Z Land Brand
Andrea Zittel, 1999

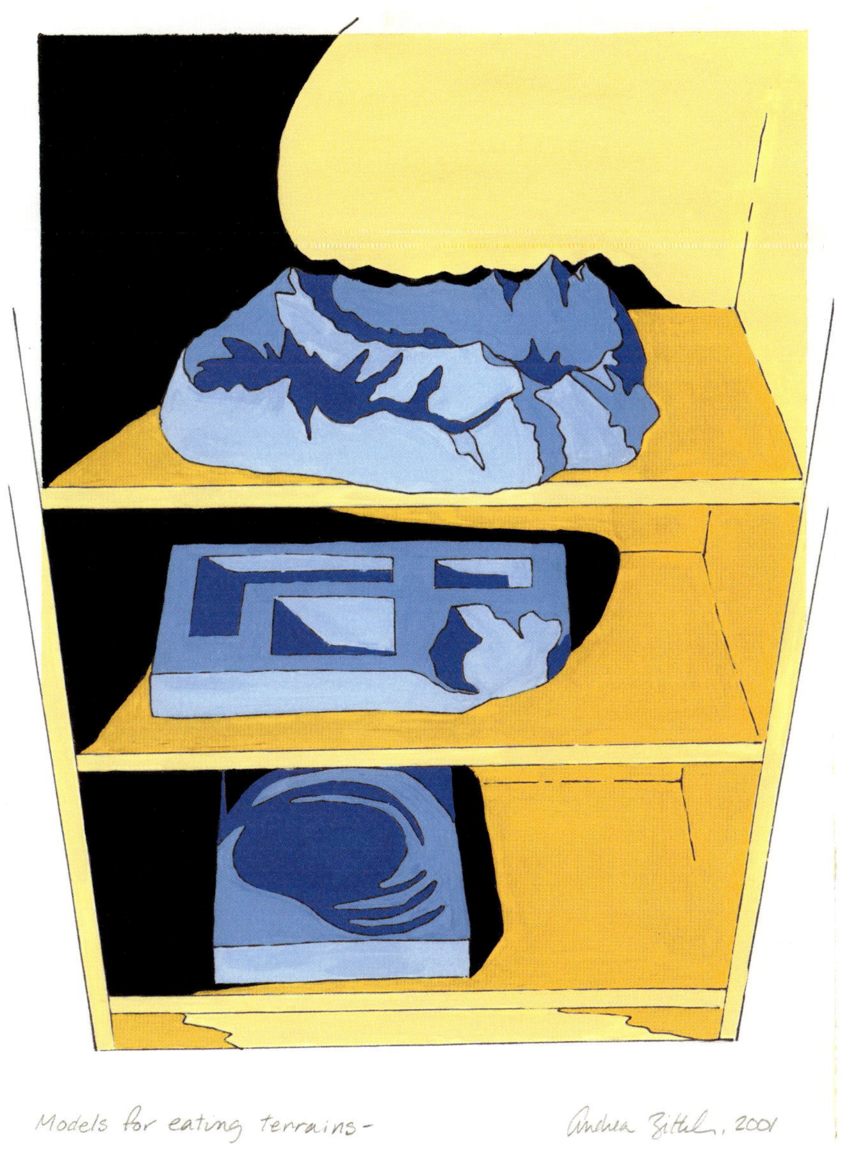

Models for eating terrains—
Andrea Zittel, 2001

Most of the following paintings were made while living for a year in Altadena, California—a Los Angeles suburb in the foothills of the San Gabriel Mountains. Although I was far from Brooklyn and the A–Z, I was again working with panels—this time they were modeled into garments called *Personal Panels*. I had come up with this format for clothing because I felt that it was increasingly difficult to decide what to wear when all options were open. The Russian Constructivist idiom of maintaining the integrity of the rectilinear nature of fabric (hence their geometric style clothing) was the inspiration for the panels. I remember thinking that they had a certain affinity with the nature of painting because being limited to a rectangle actually opened up such a flood of creative possibilities. I made and wore *Personal Panels* exclusively for many years. Some of these gouaches were attempts to show the vast myriad of functions that the panel could potentially facilitate.

Suburbane Gebirgsausläufer   Suburban Foothills

Die meisten der folgenden Arbeiten entstanden während meines einjährigen Aufenthalts in Altadena (Kalifornien), einer Vorstadt von Los Angeles in den Ausläufern des San Gabriel-Gebirges. Obwohl ich weit weg von Brooklyn und dem A–Z war, arbeitete ich erneut mit *panels*. Diesmal wurden daraus Kleidungsstücke hergestellt, die ich „Personal Panels" nannte. Ich war auf dieses Format für Kleidung gekommen, weil ich das Gefühl hatte, dass es zunehmend schwierig ist, zu entscheiden, was man tragen soll, wenn einem alle Optionen offen stehen. Die Sprache des Russischen Konstruktivismus, bei der die Unversehrtheit der Rechteckigkeit des Stoffes – daher ihr geometrischer Stil der Kleidung – gewahrt wird, inspirierte mich zu meinen *panels*. Ich erinnere mich daran, das sie für mich eine gewisse Affinität zum Wesen der Malerei hatten, weil sie wie diese auf ein Rechteck beschränkt sind, und mir so eine Fülle kreativer Möglichkeiten eröffnete. Viele Jahre lang trug ich ausschliesslich „Personal Panels". Einige dieser Gouachen entstanden als Versuch, die gewaltige Menge von Funktionen zu veranschaulichen, die das *panel* potentiell annehmen könnte.

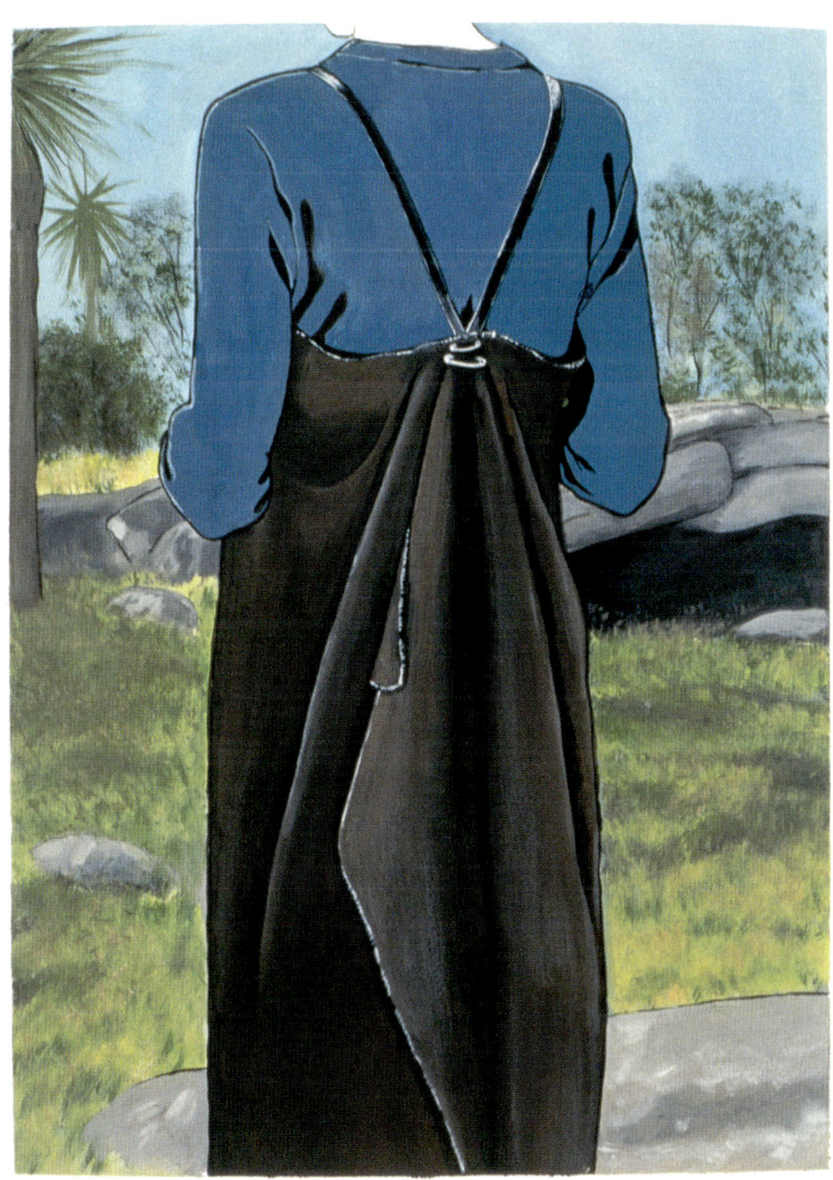

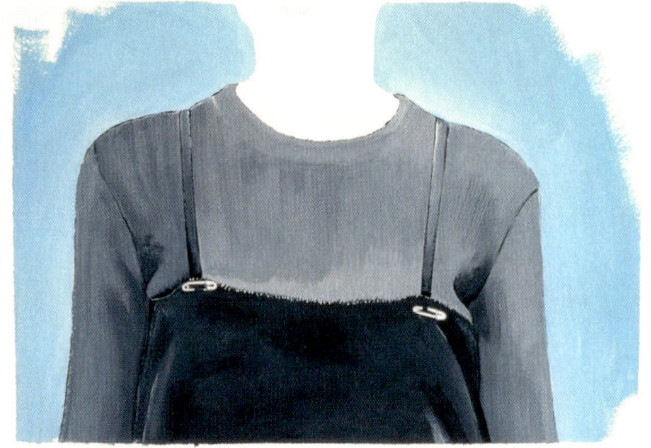

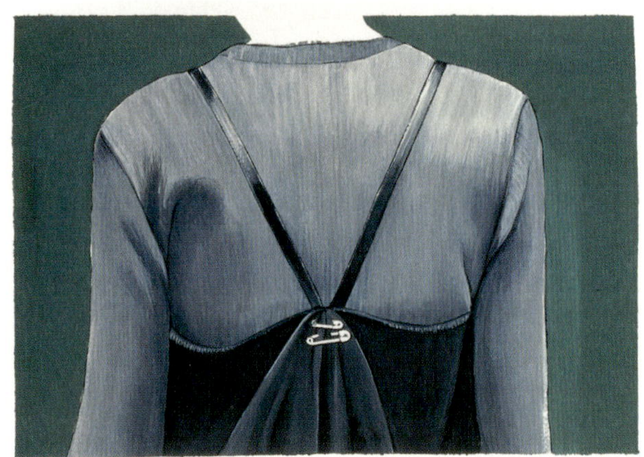

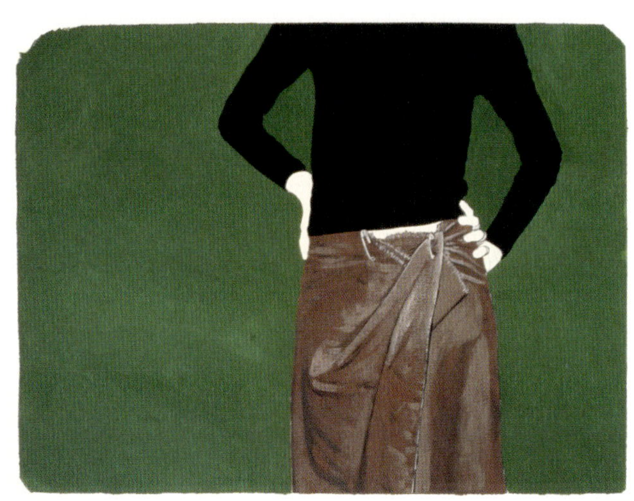

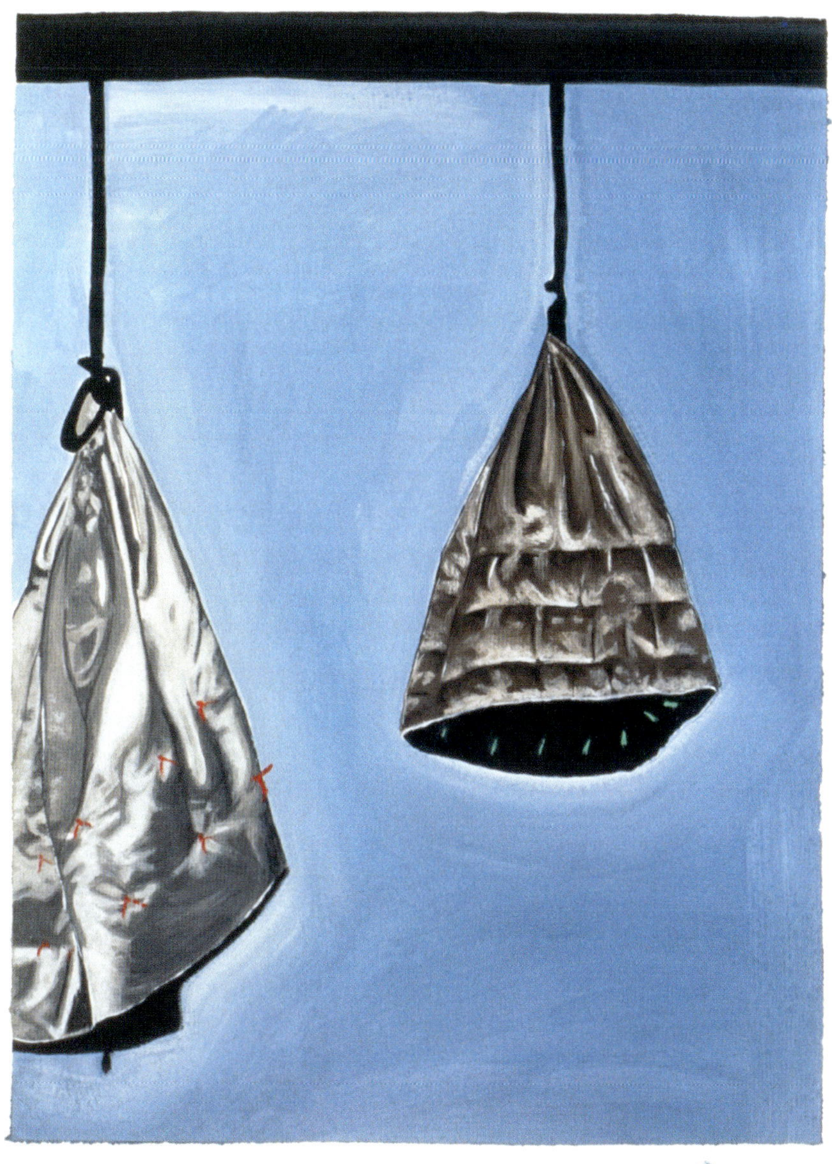

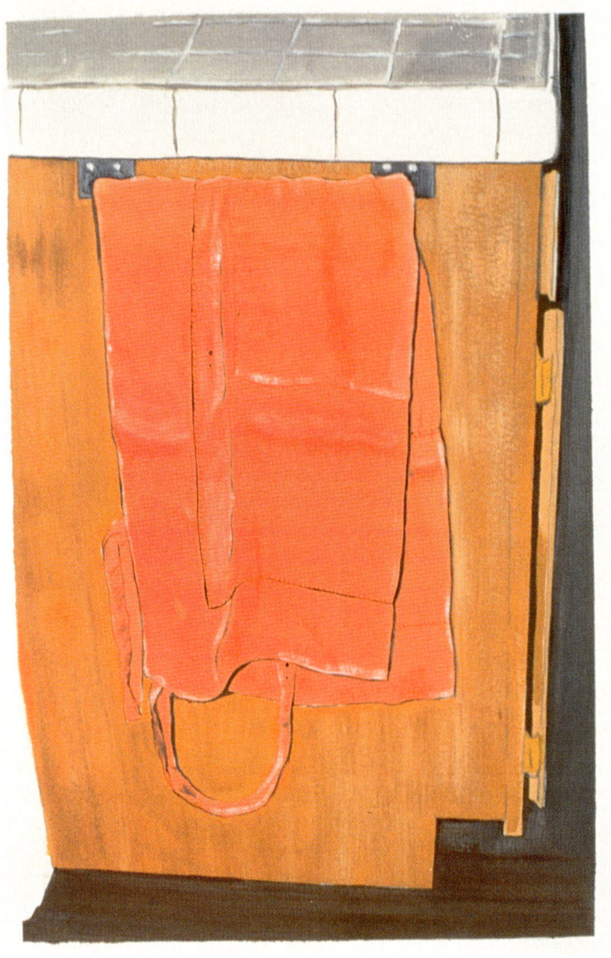

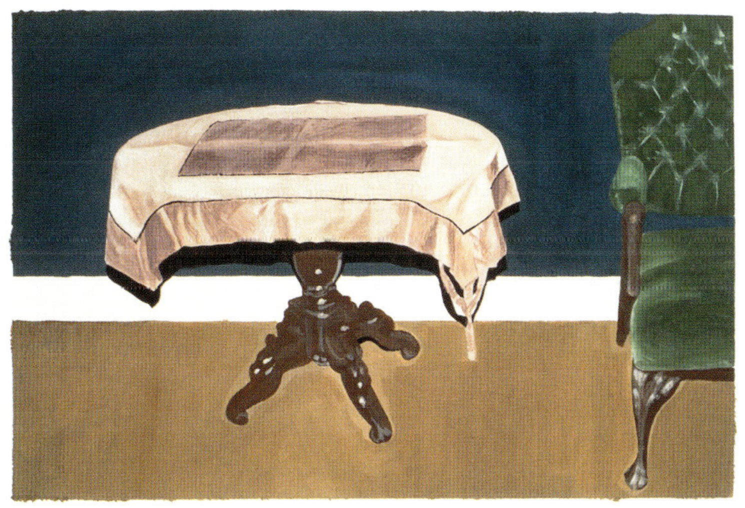

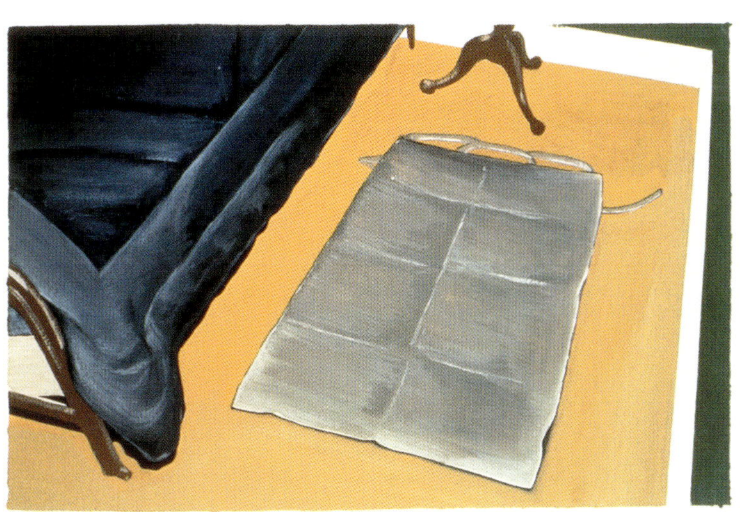

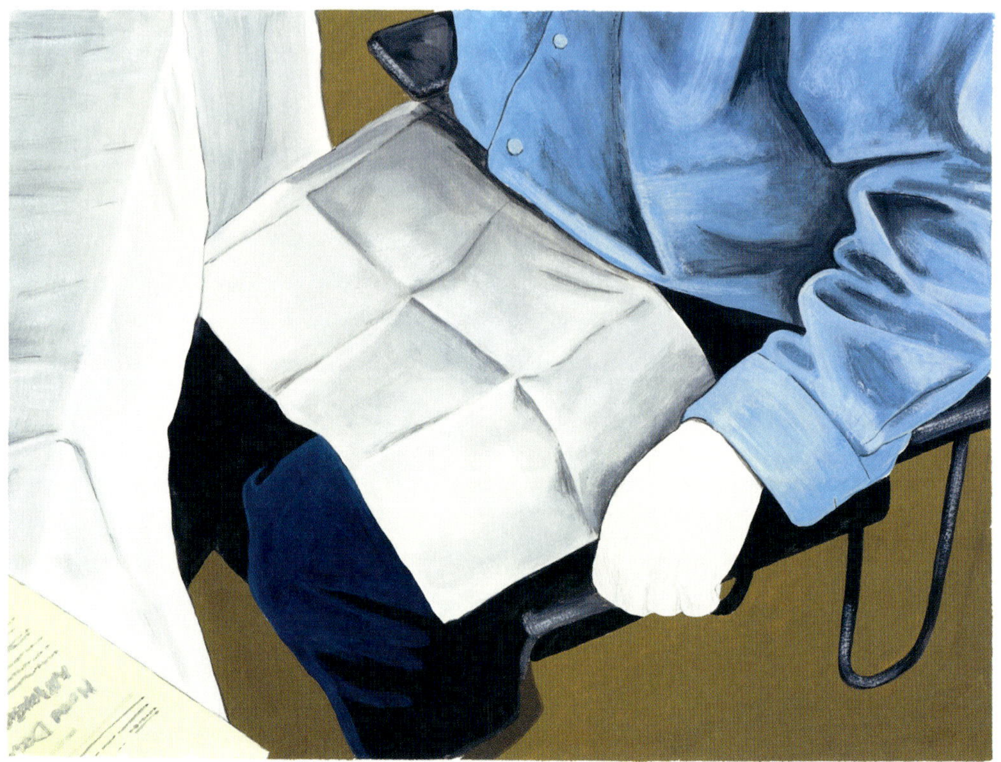

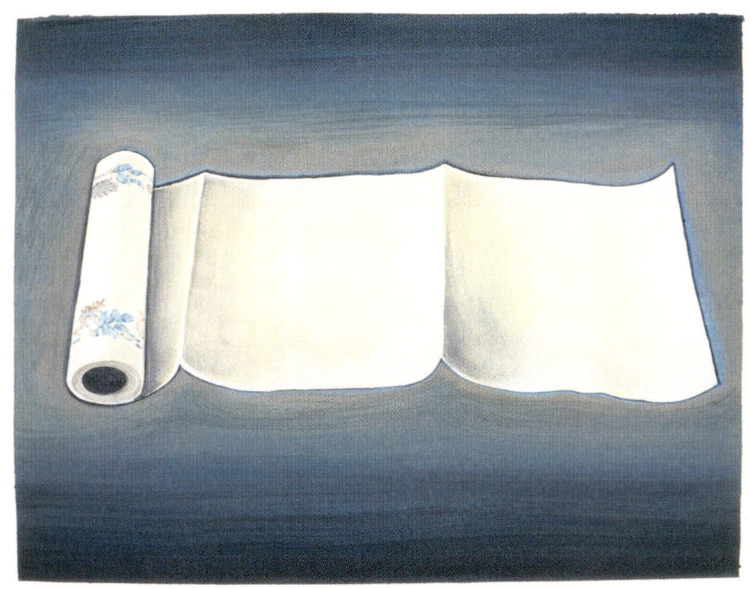

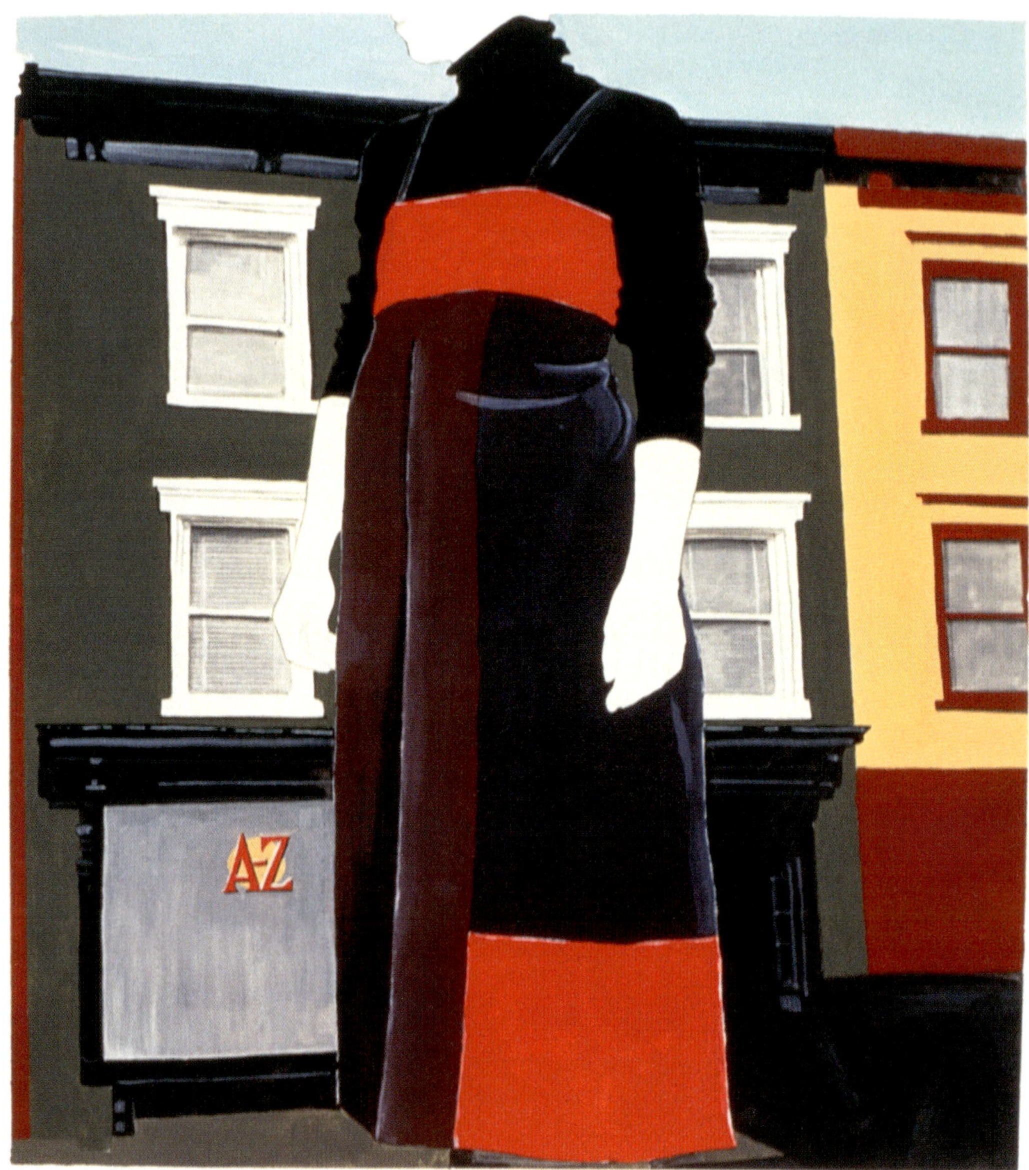
A-Z

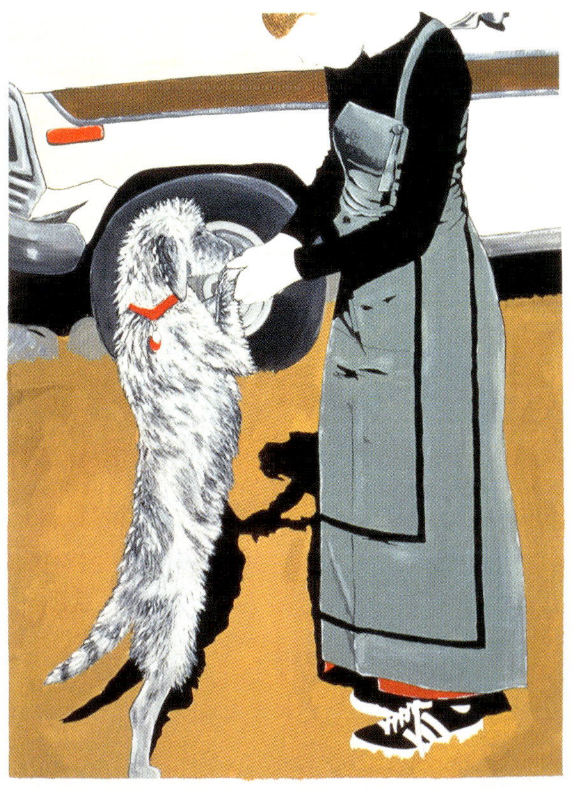
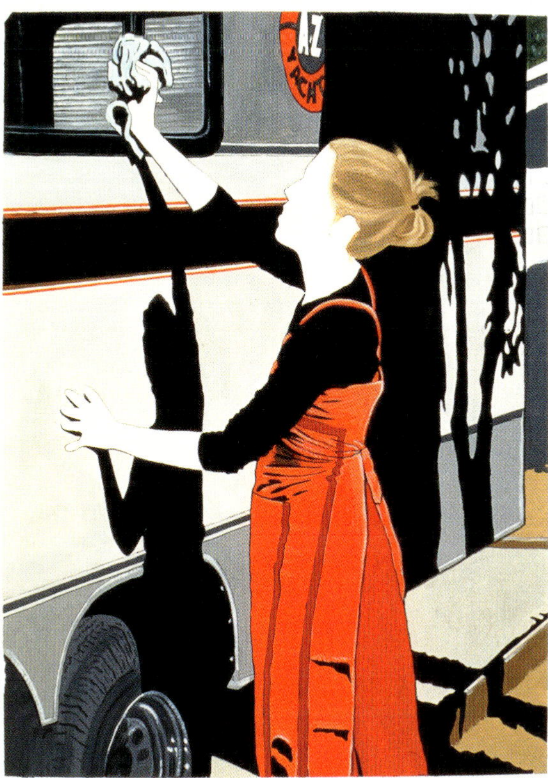

AZ
YACHT

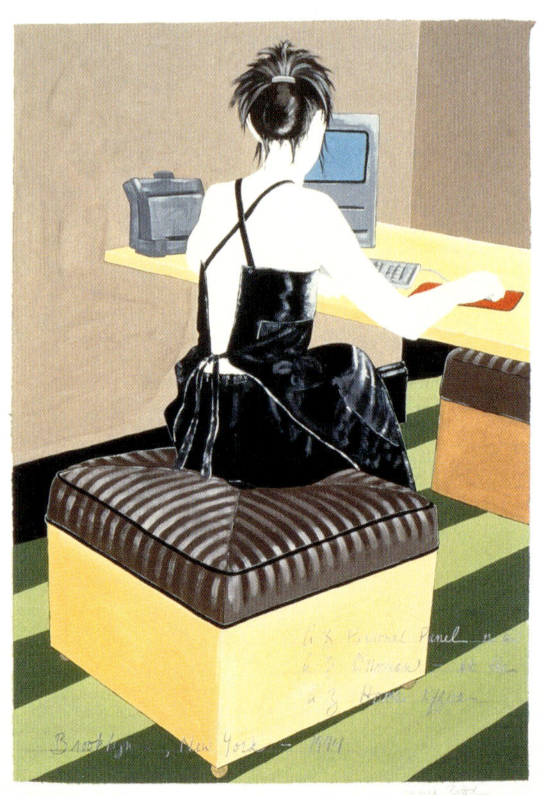

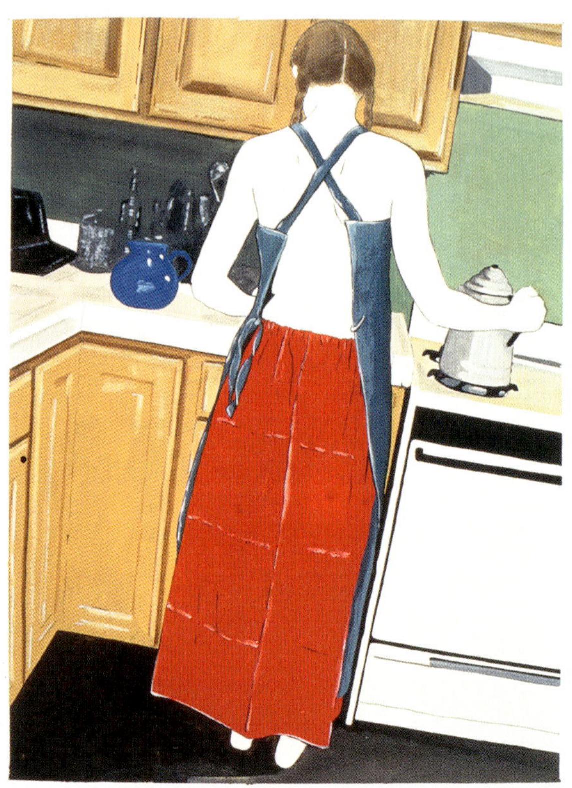

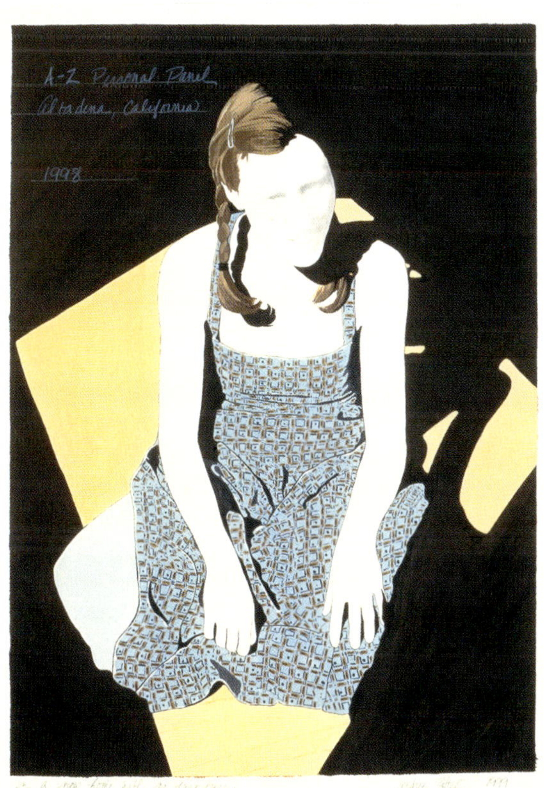

A-Z Personal Panel
Altadena, California

1998

I have always been deeply interested in the crossover between fine art and commercial art, from the paintings of Toulouse-Lautrec to the social utopian posters of Europe to the New Deal—era* murals and illustrations in the United States. This space between advertising and painting is similar to the space between sculpture and design. There are perceived conventions of high and low—but ultimately the hierarchies are not as interesting as the ability of both fields to reveal social codes and norms.
Even early on, starting to paint in a more commercial and illustrative manner felt completely liberating, as I was no longer struggling with the ideological weight of representation in fine art. Because we already understand images to serve a function of persuasion in advertising they are already read as a potential "fraud" or "lie" that somehow makes them feel more truthful since their role as propaganda is so transparent.
I realized that I could say something that I believed in the form of an advertisement even if it might not possibly be true. This idea is based on one of the theories fundamental to my work that what we "believe" and what we "know" can in fact sometimes be two different things.

 * New Deal refers to a series of economic and social reforms launched in the United States of America in the 1930s under President Franklin Delano Roosevelt to stimulate the economy during the Depression and to fight mass unemployment and poverty.

Ich habe mich schon immer extrem für den Crossover zwischen sogenannter schöner Kunst und kommerzieller Kunst interessiert, von den Gemälden Toulouse-Lautrecs über die sozial-utopischen Plakate Europas bis zu den Wandgemälden und Illustrationen der *New Deal*-Ära* in den USA. Dieser Raum zwischen Werbung und Malerei ähnelt dem zwischen Skulptur und Design. Es handelt sich um anerkannte Konventionen des Hohen und des Trivialen, doch letztlich interessieren weniger diese Hierarchien als die Fähigkeit beider Felder, soziale Codes und Normen zu offenbaren.

Schon von früh an empfand ich das Malen in einer eher kommerziellen und illustrativen Weise als grosse Befreiung, da ich mich nicht mehr mit dem ideologischen Gewicht der Repräsentation in der bildenden Kunst herumschlagen musste. Da wir ja wissen, dass Bilder in der Werbung Überzeugungszwecken dienen, werden sie von vornherein als potentieller ‚Betrug‘ oder als ‚Lüge‘ wahrgenommen, und das macht sie irgendwie wahrhaftiger, da ihre Rolle als Propaganda so durchsichtig ist.

Ich merkte, dass ich etwas, das ich glaube, in Form einer Werbung sagen konnte, selbst wenn es möglicherweise gar nicht wahr ist. Diese Idee beruht auf einer, der für mein Werk grundlegenden Theorien, dass das, was wir ‚glauben‘ und das, was wir ‚wissen‘, manchmal zwei unterschiedliche Dinge sein können.

* *New Deal* bezeichnet eine Reihe von Wirtschafts- und Sozialreformen, die in den USA in den 1930er Jahren unter dem Präsidenten Franklin Delano Roosevelt lanciert wurden, um die Wirtschaft wieder anzukurbeln und die Massenarbeitslosigkeit und -armut zu bekämpfen.

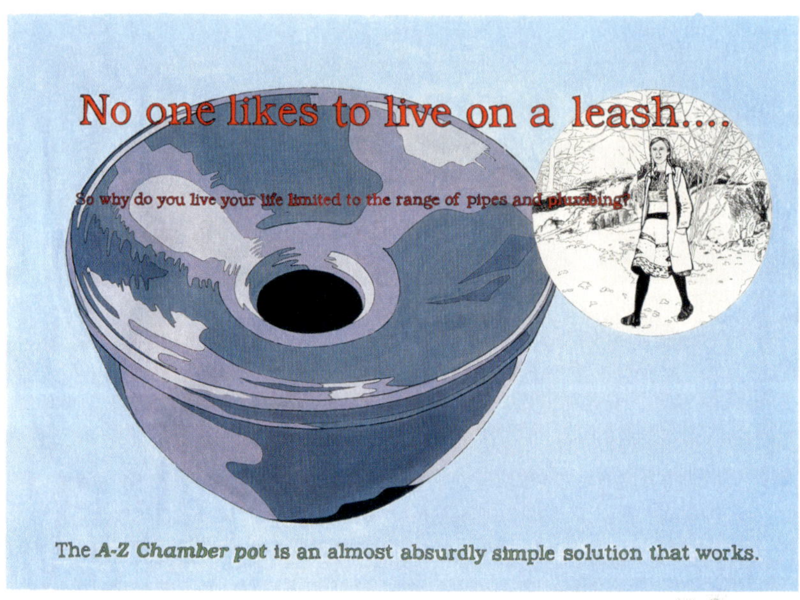
No one likes to live on a leash....
So why do you live your life limited to the range of pipes and plumbing?
The A-Z Chamber pot is an almost absurdly simple solution that works.

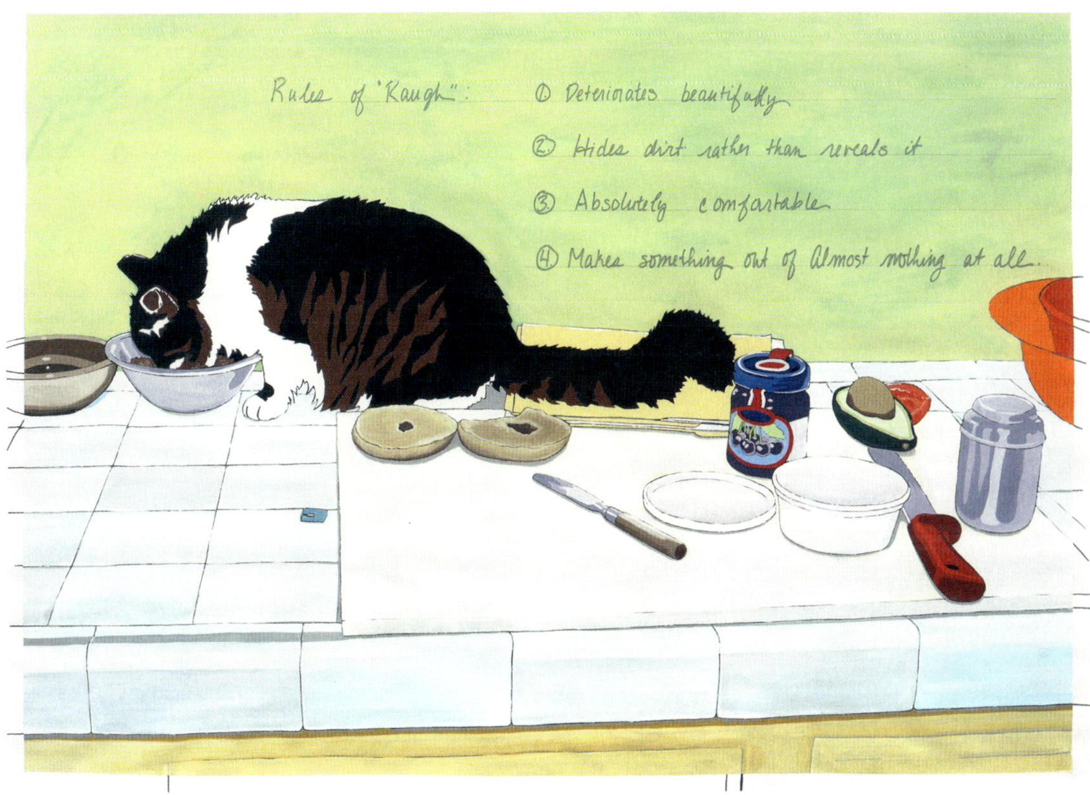

Rules of "Kaugh":
① Deteriorates beautifully
② Hides dirt rather than reveals it
③ Absolutely comfortable
④ Makes something out of Almost nothing at all.

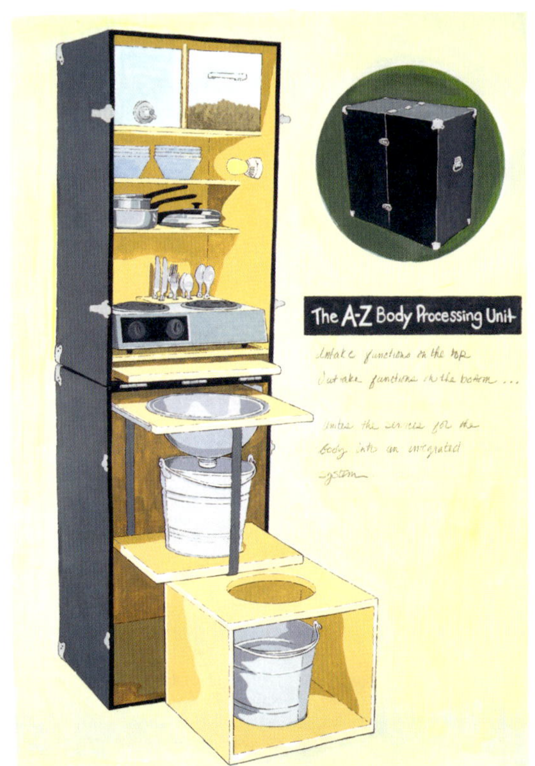

The A-Z Body Processing Unit
Intake functions on the top
Outtake functions on the bottom ...
unites the services for the
body into an integrated
system

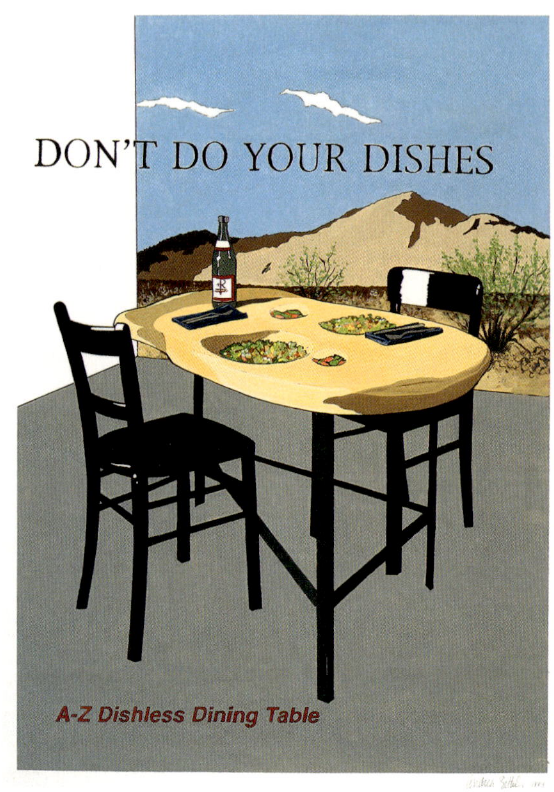

DON'T DO YOUR DISHES
A-Z Dishless Dining Table

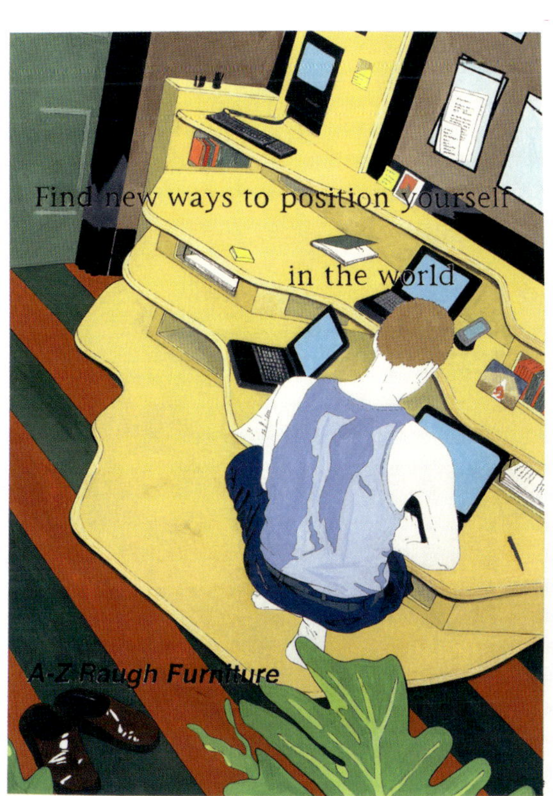
Find new ways to position yourself
in the world
A-Z Raugh Furniture

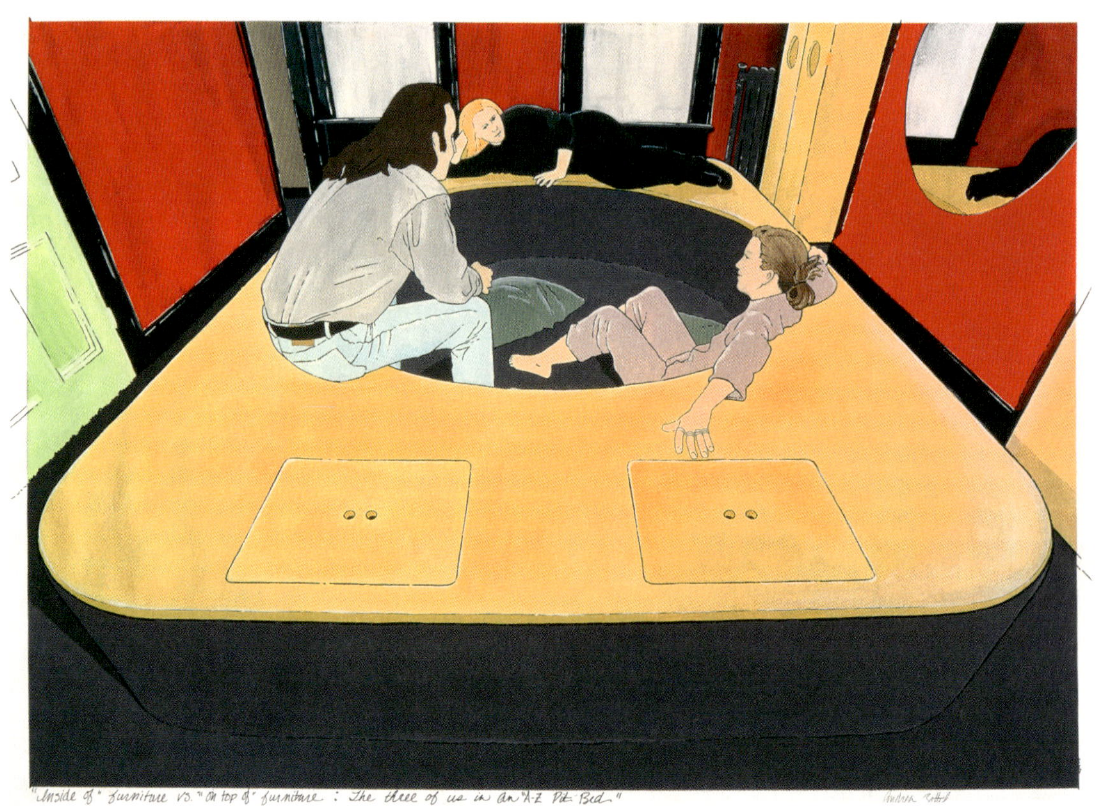

"Inside of" furniture vs. "On top of" furniture : The three of us in an "A-Z Pit Bed."
Andrea Zittel

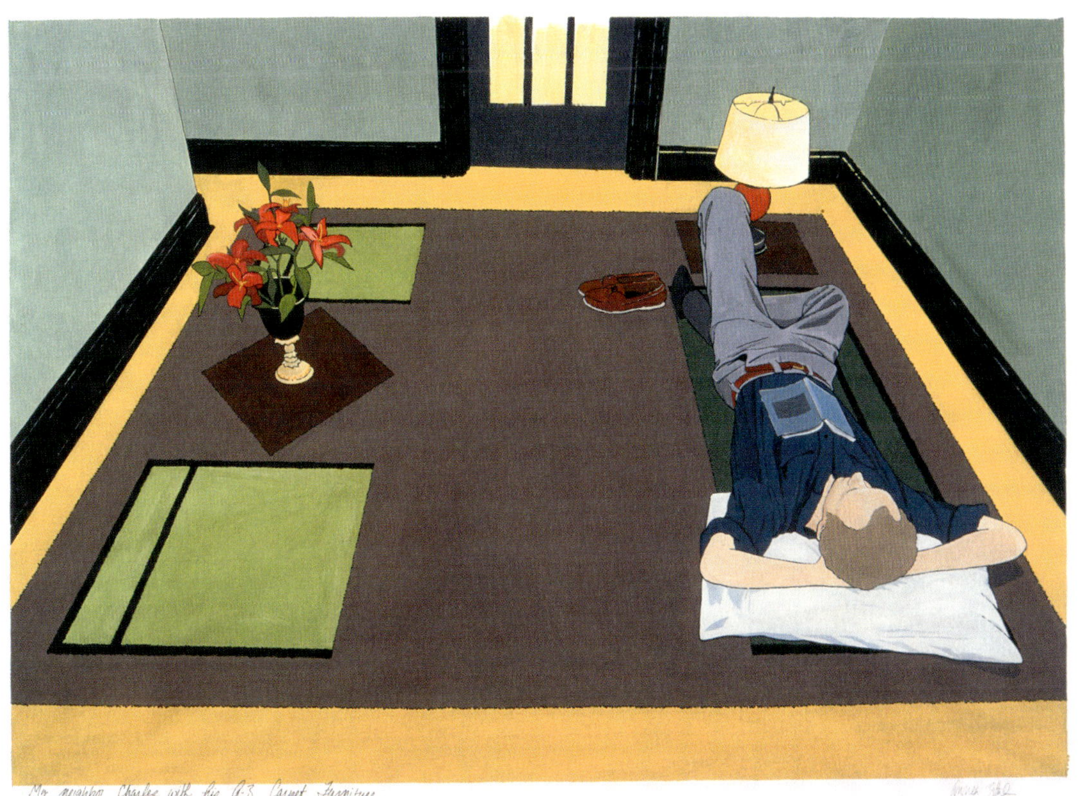

My neighbor Charles with his A-Z Carpet Furniture

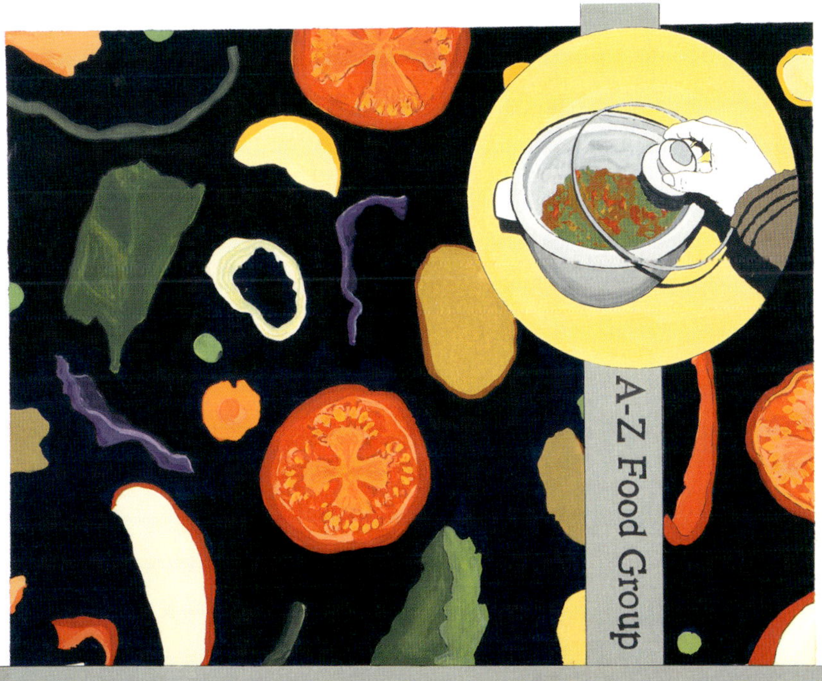

Eat it raugh, cook it as a patty, or even into stew...

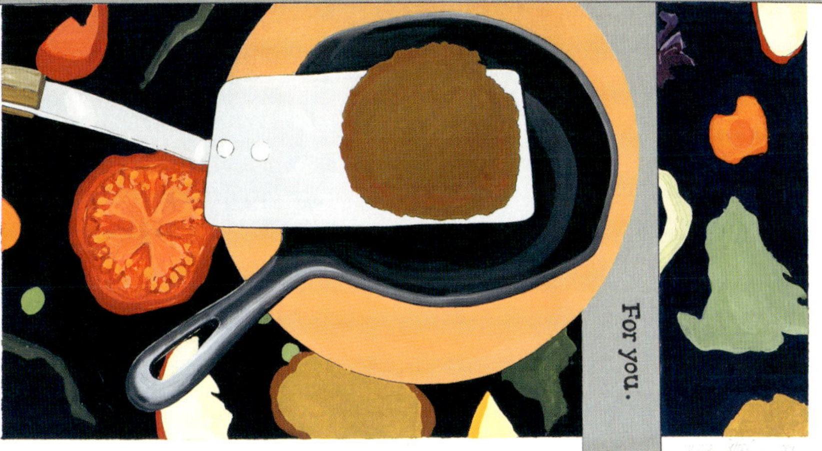

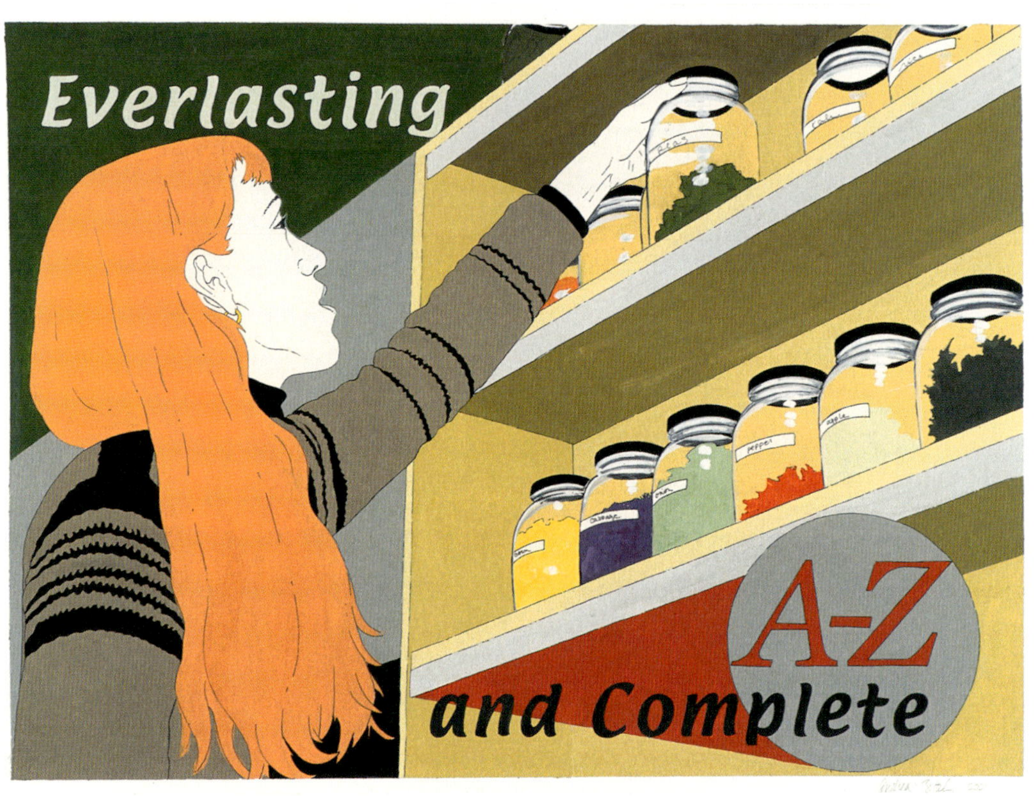

Everlasting
A-Z
and Complete

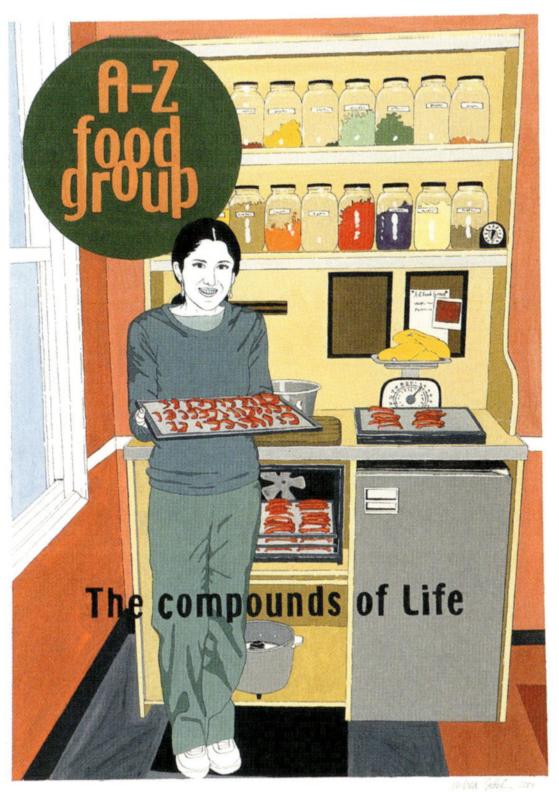
A–Z
food
group
The compounds of Life

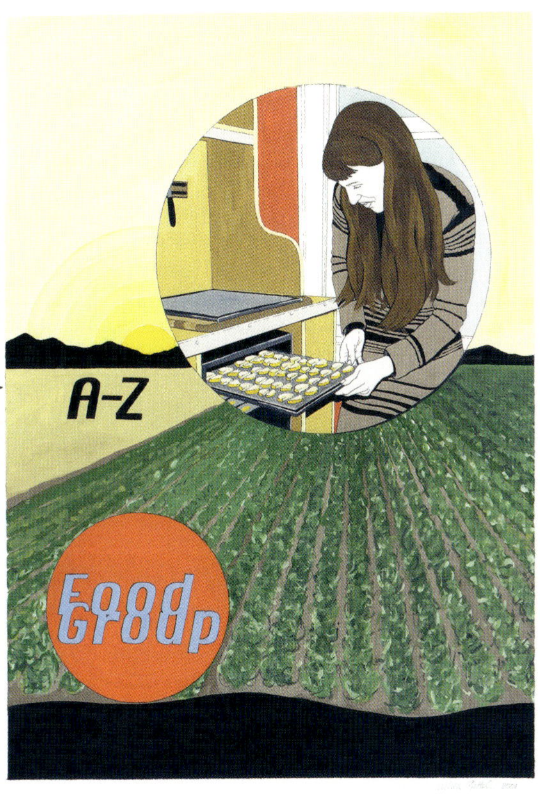
A–Z
Food
Group

The images of the *Suburban Sprawls* were prototypes for a series of lithographs. This was my first foray into printmaking, and I remember wondering why I would possibly want to reproduce the same image over and over again. It seemed to me that there should be some fundamental aspect of the image itself that might compel its multiplication. The sprawling suburban growth in my native state of California provided just the kind of viral expansion that seemed appropriate for print, which likewise populated many identical replicas of my original image. Suburban expansion was again the inspiration for the project called *Cellular Compartment Units*, which offered a response to the historic increasing compartmentalization of domestic living spaces.

If physical structures are an identifiable form of social control, the more invisible invention of time is an even more pervasive one. I have always been interested in the invention of time. For the *A–Z Time Trials*, or *Free Running Rhythms and Patterns*, I wanted to ask if it was truly possible to escape the regulatory system of the clock. The experiment entailed living in a basement apartment which had been sealed off from all sound and light for the period of a week. It was one of the most profound experiences in my life (and hence one of my favorite artworks), yet one of the most difficult to resolve as a finished work. This project raised questions about the representation of experience, and if having a truly unique and important experience is enough to qualify as a good artwork, or if this experience must be communicable or presentable to a larger audience. Most current lines of thinking would assert that art must be a form of communication; I would argue that this is the point where art as communication tends to become a mediated and "packaged" public presentation compared to a more unknowable first-hand experience.

Although I do not feel that I have solved this larger issue of representation, my resolution of the project at that time included a timeline in which I painted the "patterns and rhythms" of my week without time. Each color in the painting represents a different activity. Images and "color keys" that reveal these codes punctuate the overall work. This is the first time that the paintings have intertwined with the more experiential and structural side of my practice.

Mass und Markierung   Measure and Marking

Die Bilder der „Suburban Sprawls" waren Prototypen für eine Serie von Lithografien. Dies war mein erster Ausflug ins Gebiet der Druckgrafik, und ich erinnere mich daran, dass ich mich fragte, warum ich eigentlich dasselbe Bild immer wieder reproduzieren sollte. Ich hatte den Eindruck, es müsse eine grundlegende Seite des Bildes selbst geben, die seine Vervielfältigung erzwingt. Das stete Anwachsen der riesigen Vorstädte in meinem Heimatstaat Kalifornien stellte genau jene Form virusartiger Ausbreitung bereit, die mir für den Druck angemessen schien, durch den ja ebenfalls viele identische Repliken meines ursprünglichen Bildes in die Welt gesetzt wurden. Die Ausbreitung der Vorstädte war auch die Inspiration für mein Projekt „Cellular Compartment Units", das eine Antwort auf die historisch belegte zunehmende Aufteilung des häuslichen Wohnraums bot.

Wenn physische Strukturen eine identifizierbare Form sozialer Kontrolle sind, dann ist die weniger sichtbare Erfindung der Zeit eine noch durchdringendere. Die Erfindung der Zeit hat mich schon immer interessiert. Bei den „A–Z Time Trials" oder „Free Running Rhythms and Patterns" wollte ich die Frage stellen, ob es wirklich möglich ist, dem regulativen System der Uhr zu entkommen. Bei diesem Experiment lebte ich eine Woche lang in einer Kellerwohnung, in die keinerlei Geräusche oder Licht eindrangen. Es war eine der tiefgründigsten Erfahrungen meines Lebens – und daher auch eines meiner Lieblingswerke – und dennoch eine, aus der sich nur äusserst schwer ein fertiges Werk machen liess. Dieses Projekt warf Fragen nach der Darstellung von Erfahrung auf, aber auch die, ob es, damit es ein gutes Kunstwerk ist, ausreicht, eine wirklich einzigartige und wichtige Erfahrung gemacht zu haben, oder ob diese Erfahrung gegenüber einem grösseren Publikum kommunizierbar oder darstellbar sein muss. Den meisten aktuellen Auffassungen zufolge muss Kunst eine Form der Kommunikation sein, doch mein Gegenargument lautet, dass genau dies der Punkt ist, an dem Kunst als Kommunikation eine vermittelte und ‚abgepackte' öffentliche Präsentation wird, im Vergleich zu einer eher unfassbaren Erfahrung aus erster Hand.

Obwohl ich nicht das Gefühl habe, diese grössere Repräsentationsfrage gelöst zu haben, beinhaltete meine Lösung des Projekts damals eine Zeitachse, auf der ich die ‚Muster und Rhythmen' meiner Woche ohne Zeit malte. Jede Farbe auf dem Gemälde repräsentiert eine andere Aktivität. Bilder und ‚Farbschlüssel', die diese Codes offenlegen, durchziehen das ganze Werk. Dies ist das erste Mal, dass sich meine Bilder mit der eher erfahrungsmässigen und strukturellen Seite meiner künstlerischen Praxis verflochten haben.

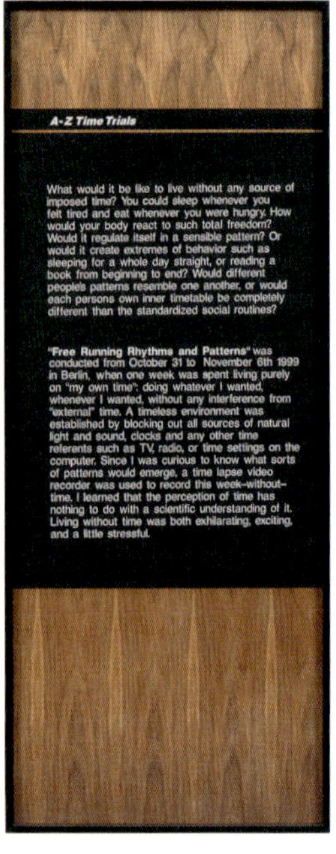

A-Z Time Trials

What would it be like to live without any source of imposed time? You could sleep whenever you felt tired and eat whenever you were hungry. How would your body react to such total freedom? Would it regulate itself in a sensible pattern? Or would it create extremes of behavior such as sleeping for a whole day straight, or reading a book from beginning to end? Would different people's patterns resemble one another, or would each persons own inner timetable be completely different than the standardized social routines?

"Free Running Rhythms and Patterns" was conducted from October 31 to November 6th 1999 in Berlin, when one week was spent living purely on "my own time": doing whatever I wanted, whenever I wanted, without any interference from "external" time. A timeless environment was established by blocking out all sources of natural light and sound, clocks and any other time referents such as TV, radio, or time settings on the computer. Since I was curious to know what sorts of patterns would emerge, a time lapse video recorder was used to record this week–without–time. I learned that the perception of time has nothing to do with a scientific understanding of it. Living without time was both exhilarating, exciting, and a little stressful.

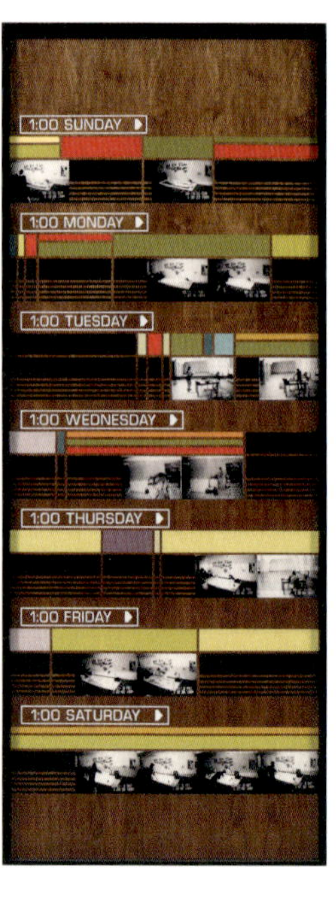
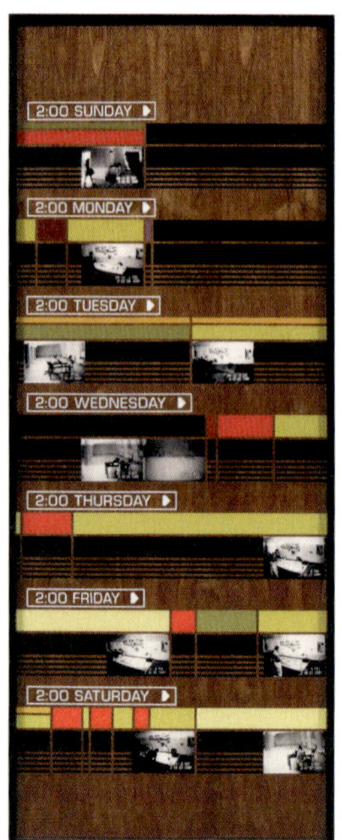
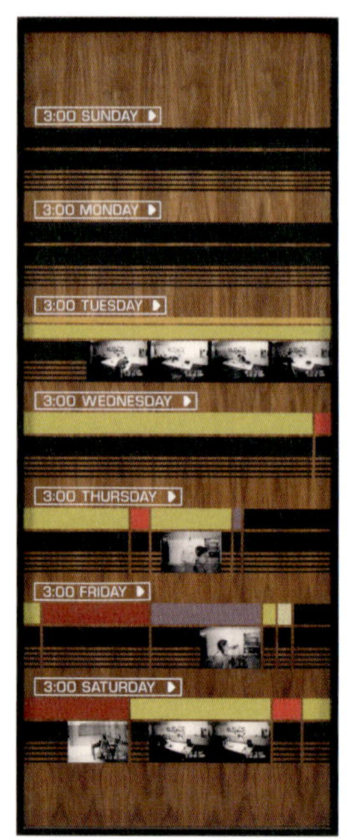
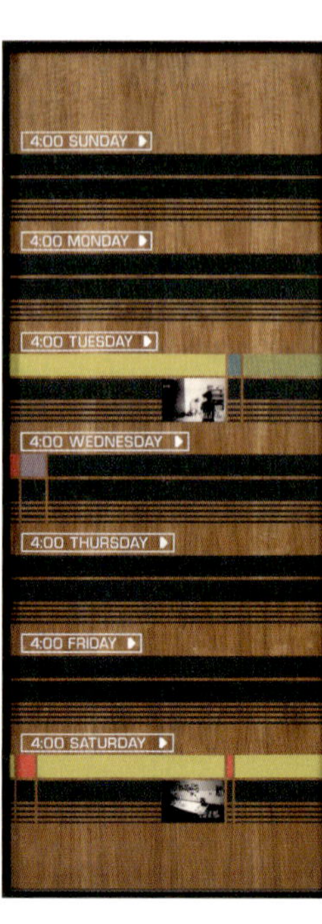

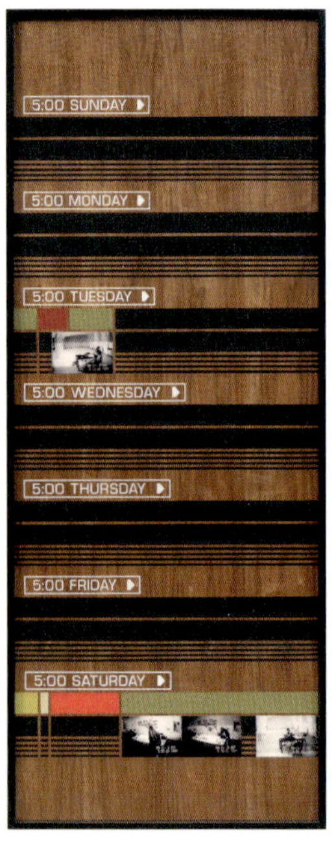
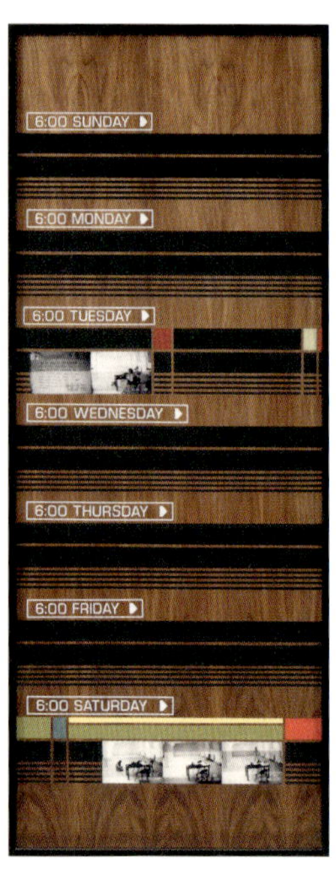
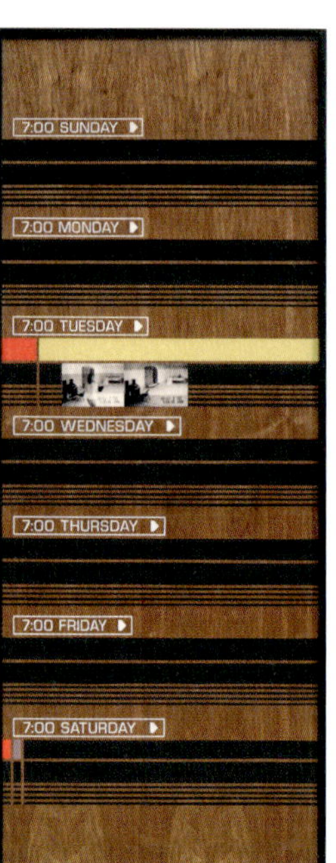
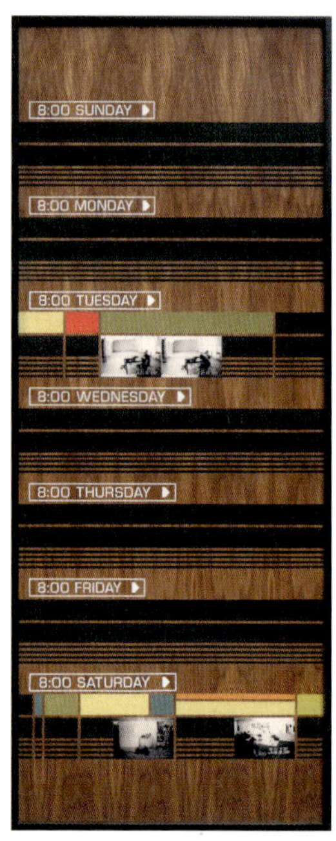
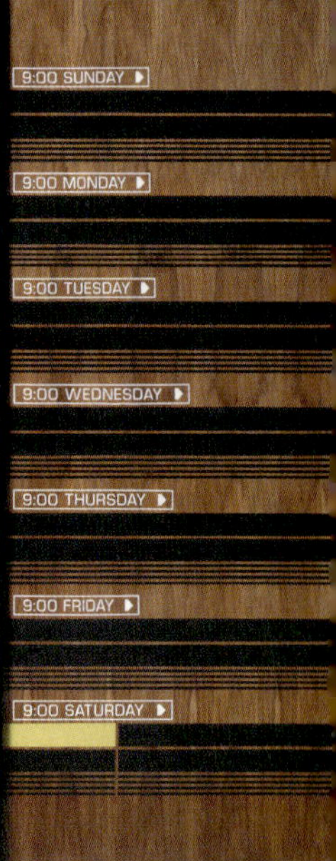

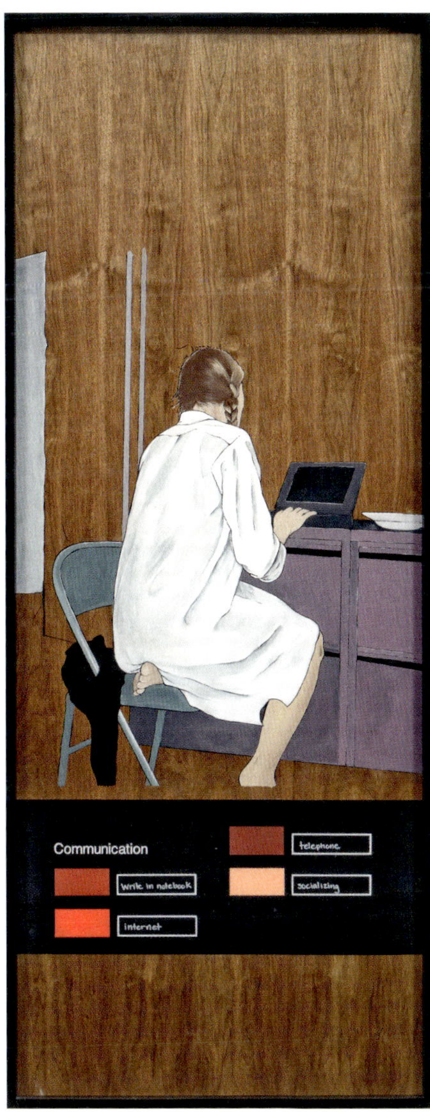

Communication
Write in notebook
internet
telephone
socializing

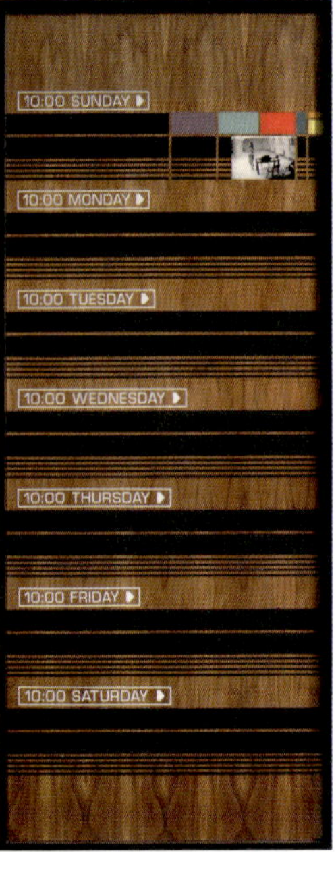
10:00 SUNDAY
10:00 MONDAY
10:00 TUESDAY
10:00 WEDNESDAY
10:00 THURSDAY
10:00 FRIDAY
10:00 SATURDAY

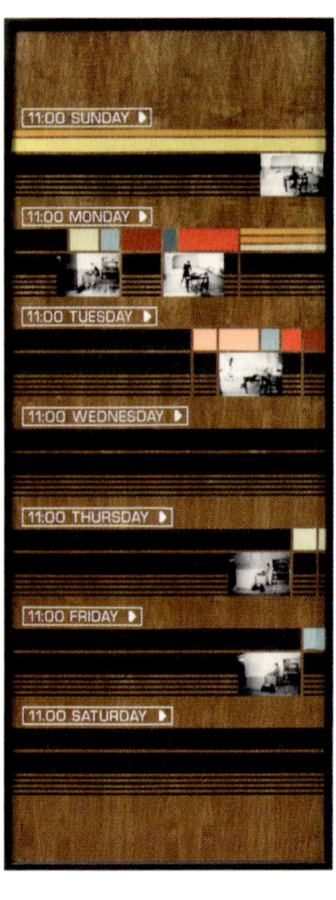
11:00 SUNDAY
11:00 MONDAY
11:00 TUESDAY
11:00 WEDNESDAY
11:00 THURSDAY
11:00 FRIDAY
11:00 SATURDAY

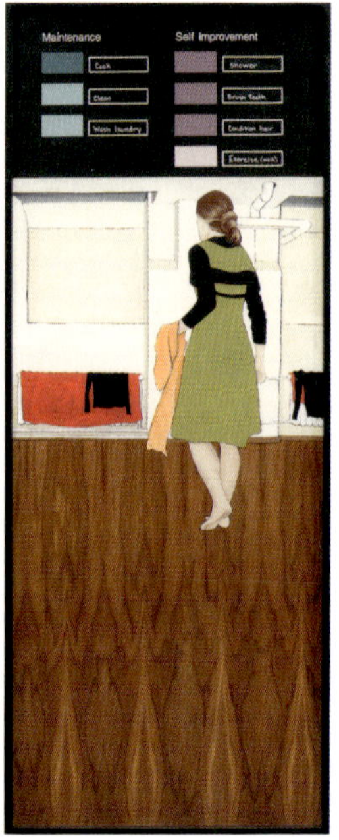
Maintenance
Cook
Clean
Wash laundry
Self Improvement
Shower
Brush Teeth
Condition hair
Exercise (walk)

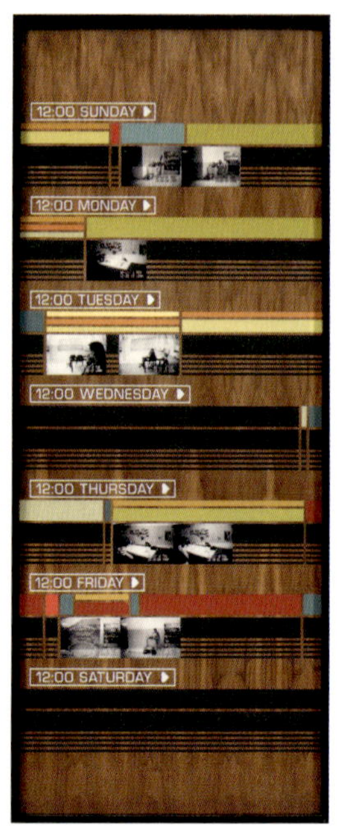
12:00 SUNDAY
12:00 MONDAY
12:00 TUESDAY
12:00 WEDNESDAY
12:00 THURSDAY
12:00 FRIDAY
12:00 SATURDAY

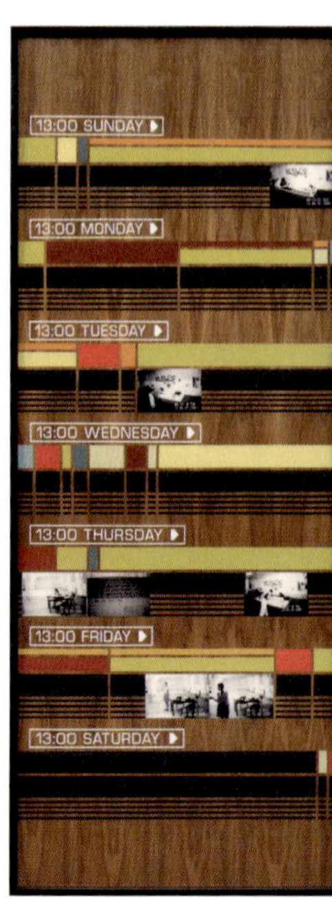
13:00 SUNDAY
13:00 MONDAY
13:00 TUESDAY
13:00 WEDNESDAY
13:00 THURSDAY
13:00 FRIDAY
13:00 SATURDAY

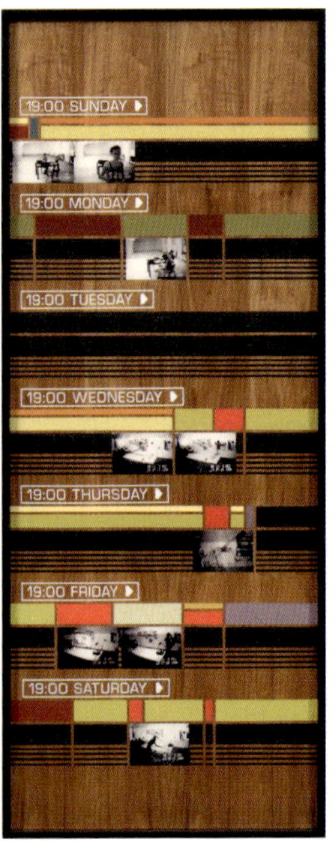
19:00 SUNDAY
19:00 MONDAY
19:00 TUESDAY
19:00 WEDNESDAY
19:00 THURSDAY
19:00 FRIDAY
19:00 SATURDAY

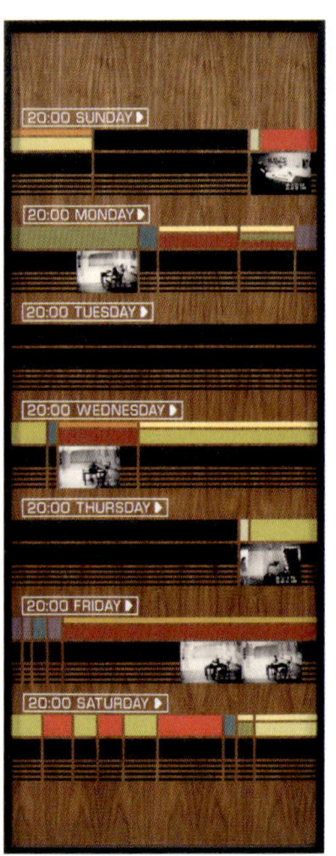
20:00 SUNDAY
20:00 MONDAY
20:00 TUESDAY
20:00 WEDNESDAY
20:00 THURSDAY
20:00 FRIDAY
20:00 SATURDAY

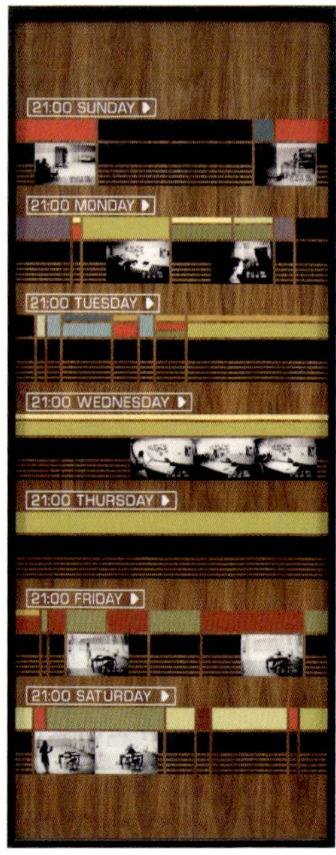
21:00 SUNDAY
21:00 MONDAY
21:00 TUESDAY
21:00 WEDNESDAY
21:00 THURSDAY
21:00 FRIDAY
21:00 SATURDAY

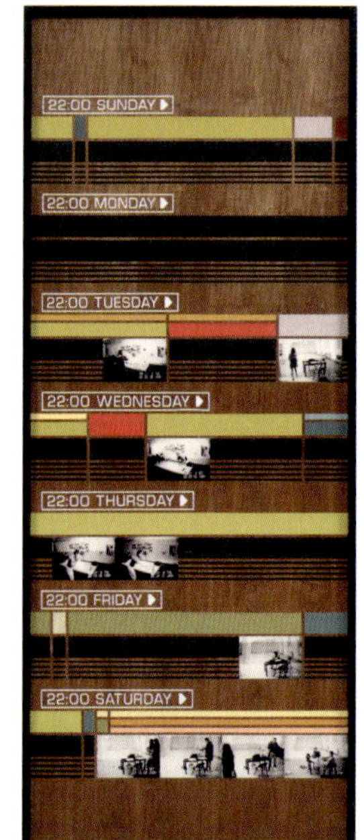
22:00 SUNDAY
22:00 MONDAY
22:00 TUESDAY
22:00 WEDNESDAY
22:00 THURSDAY
22:00 FRIDAY
22:00 SATURDAY

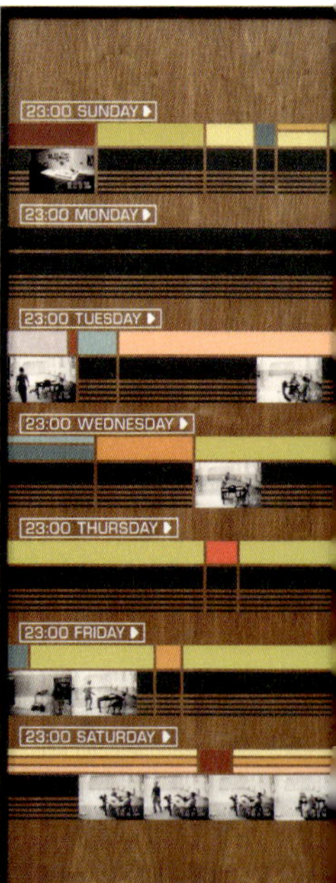
23:00 SUNDAY
23:00 MONDAY
23:00 TUESDAY
23:00 WEDNESDAY
23:00 THURSDAY
23:00 FRIDAY
23:00 SATURDAY

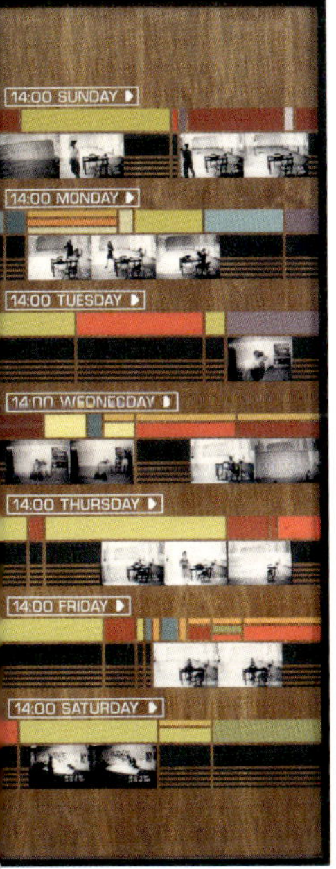

14:00 SUNDAY
14:00 MONDAY
14:00 TUESDAY
14:00 WEDNESDAY
14:00 THURSDAY
14:00 FRIDAY
14:00 SATURDAY

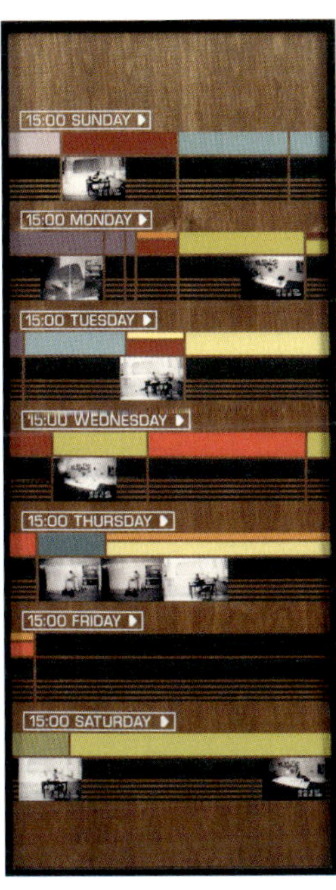

15:00 SUNDAY
15:00 MONDAY
15:00 TUESDAY
15:00 WEDNESDAY
15:00 THURSDAY
15:00 FRIDAY
15:00 SATURDAY

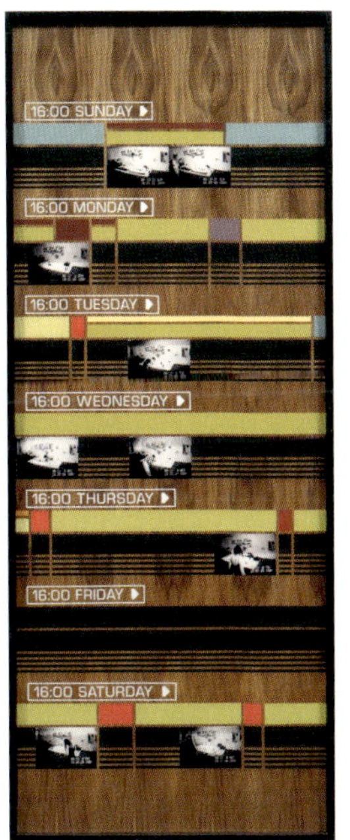

16:00 SUNDAY
16:00 MONDAY
16:00 TUESDAY
16:00 WEDNESDAY
16:00 THURSDAY
16:00 FRIDAY
16:00 SATURDAY

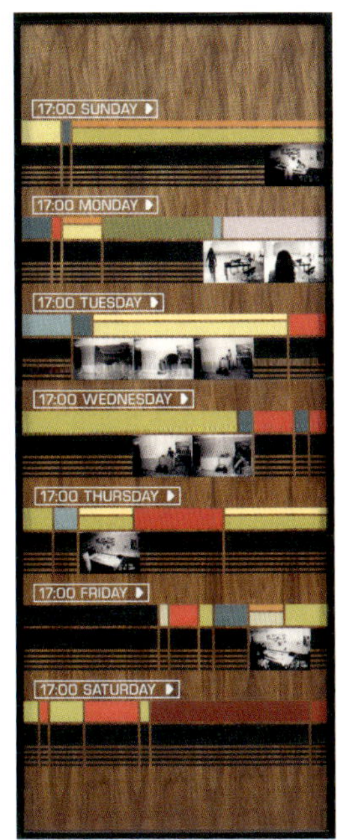

17:00 SUNDAY
17:00 MONDAY
17:00 TUESDAY
17:00 WEDNESDAY
17:00 THURSDAY
17:00 FRIDAY
17:00 SATURDAY

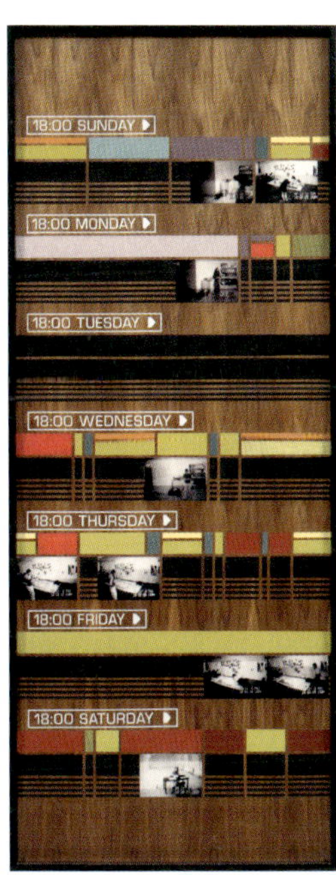

18:00 SUNDAY
18:00 MONDAY
18:00 TUESDAY
18:00 WEDNESDAY
18:00 THURSDAY
18:00 FRIDAY
18:00 SATURDAY

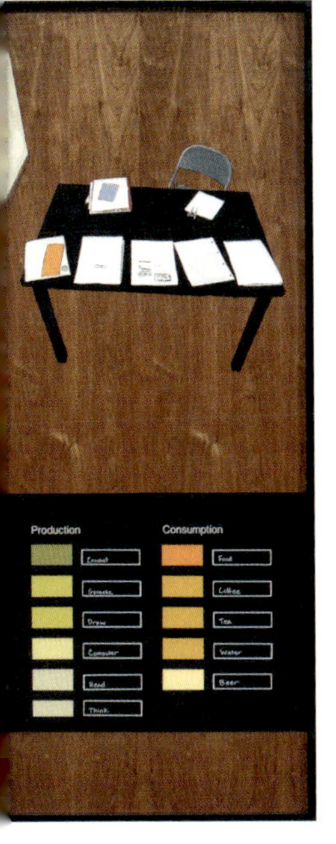

Production
Errand
Errands
Draw
Computer
Read
Think
Consumption
Food
Coffee
Tea
Water
Beer

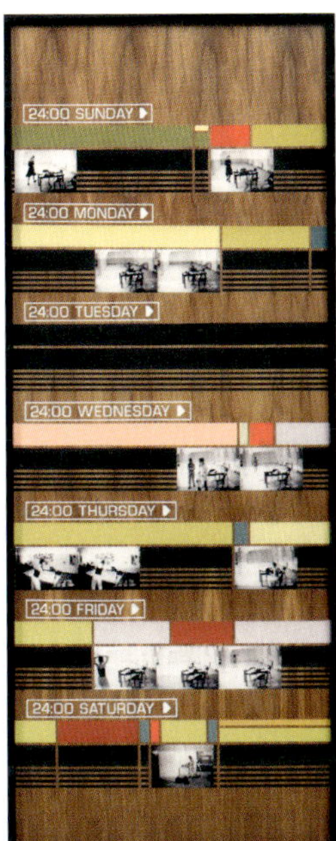

24:00 SUNDAY
24:00 MONDAY
24:00 TUESDAY
24:00 WEDNESDAY
24:00 THURSDAY
24:00 FRIDAY
24:00 SATURDAY

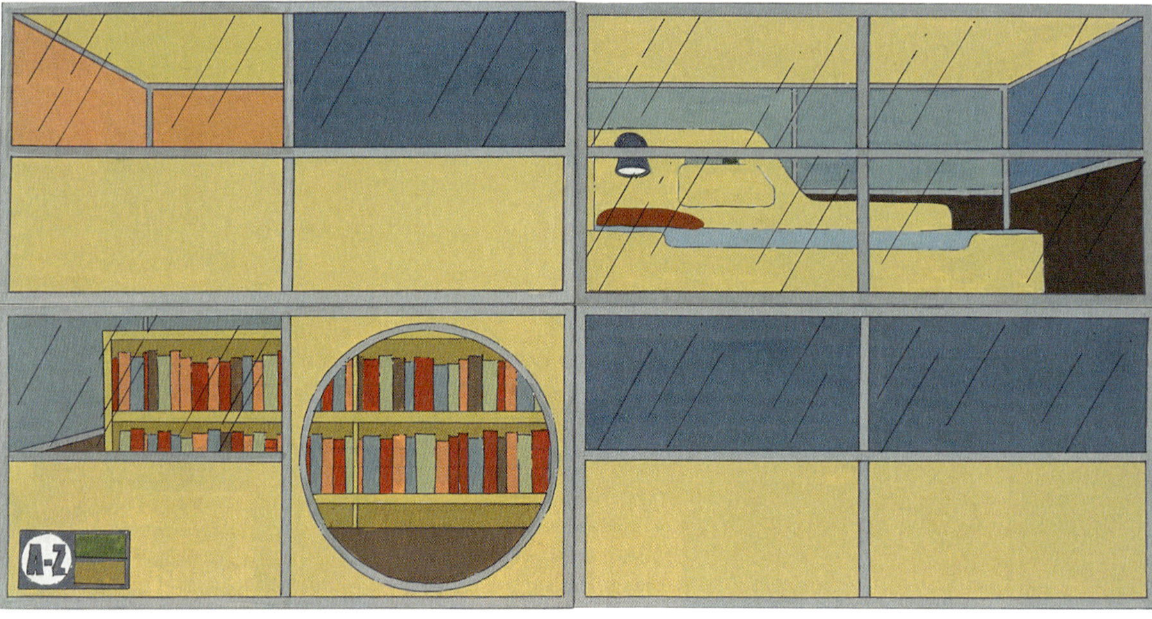
A-Z

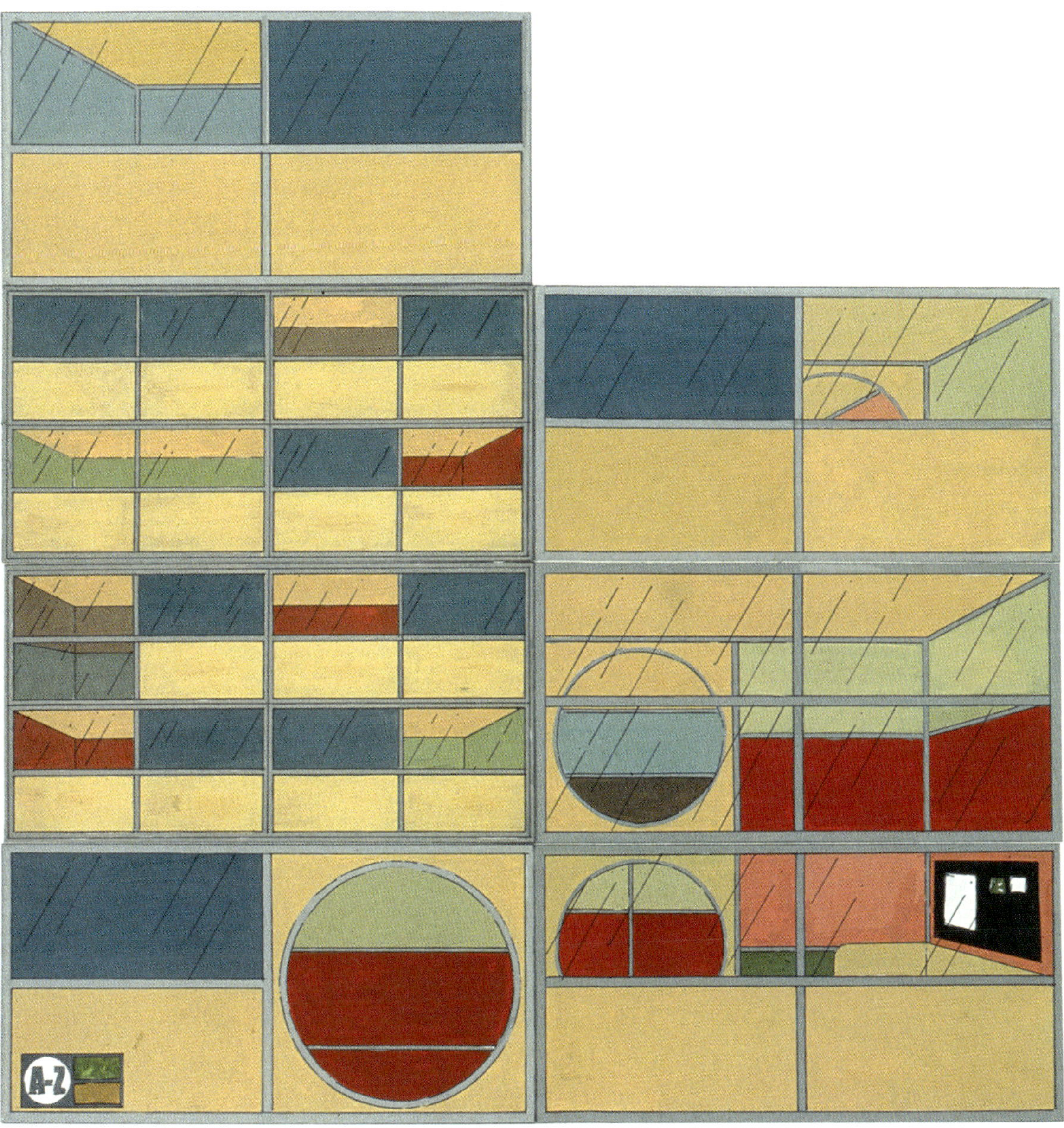
A-Z

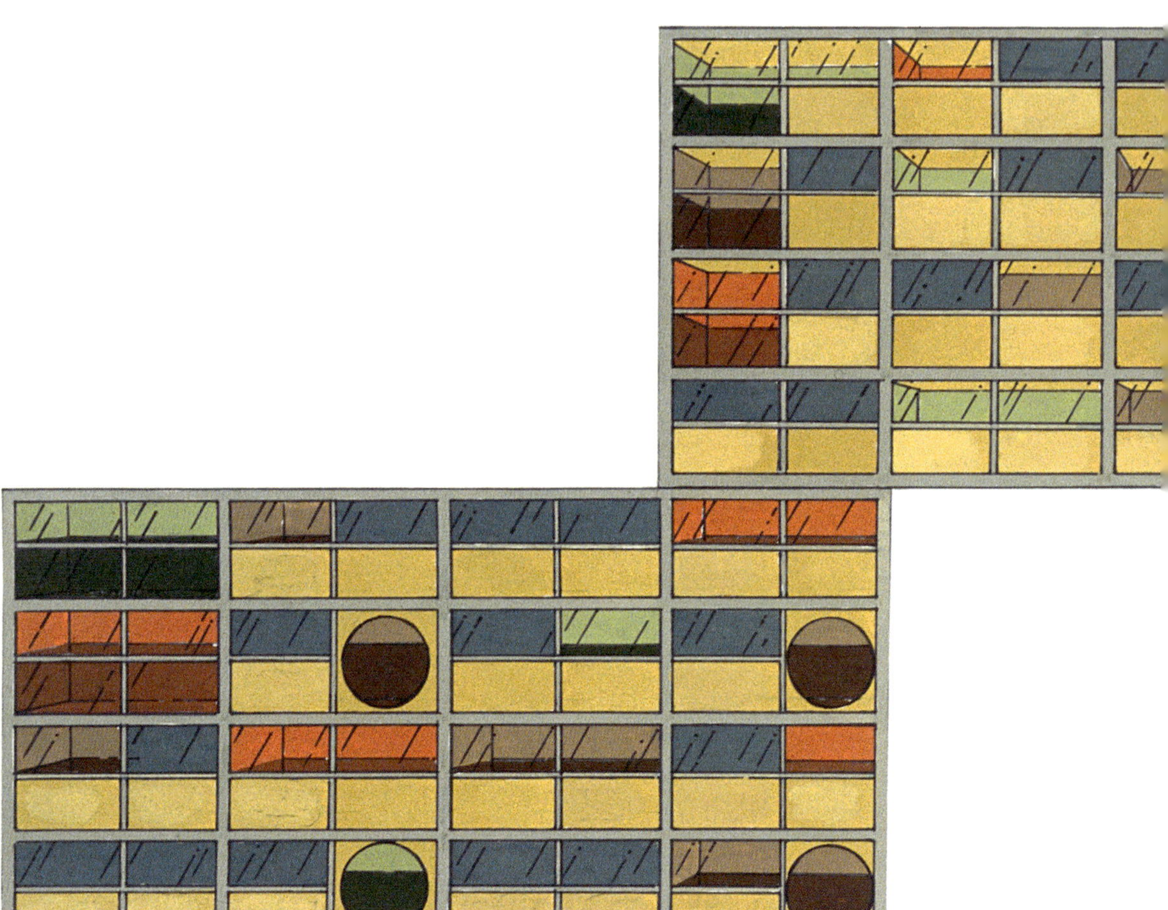

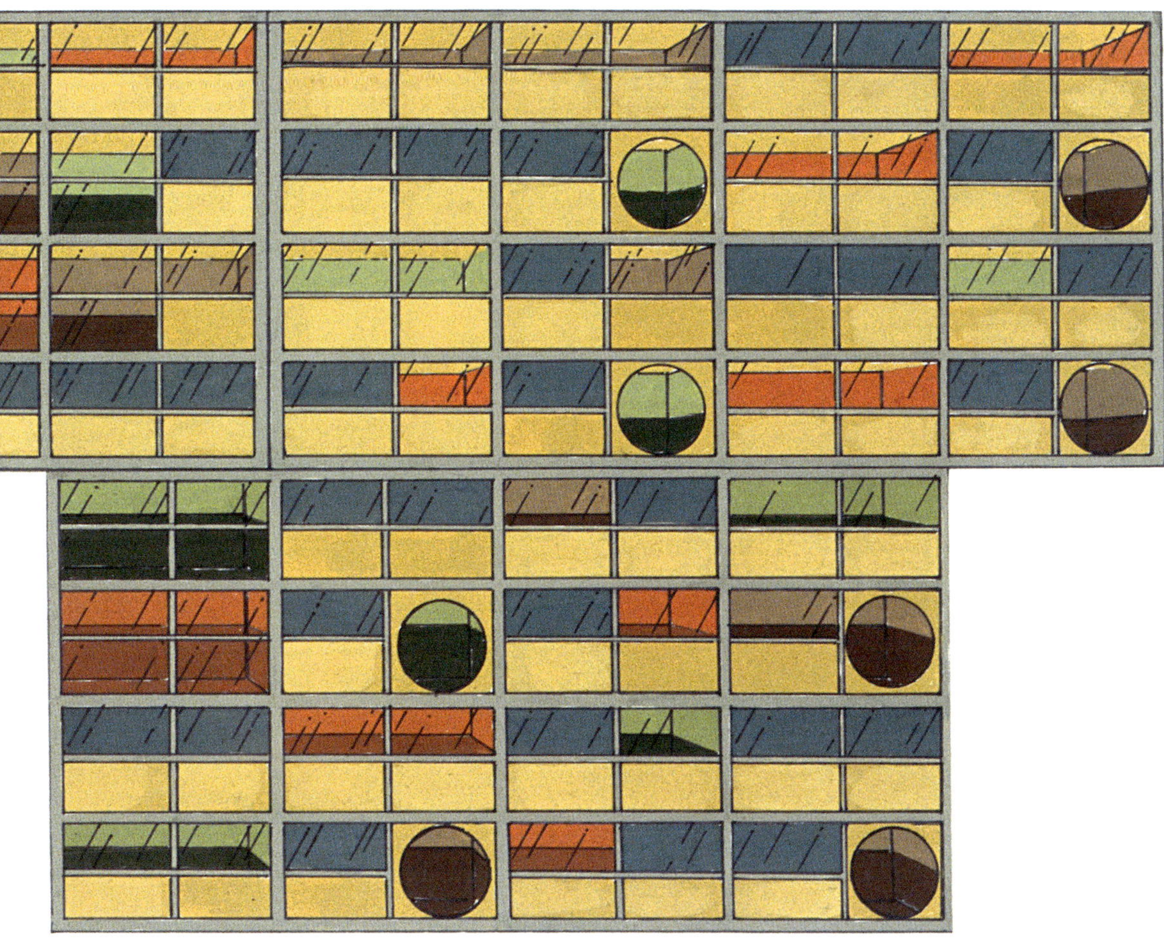

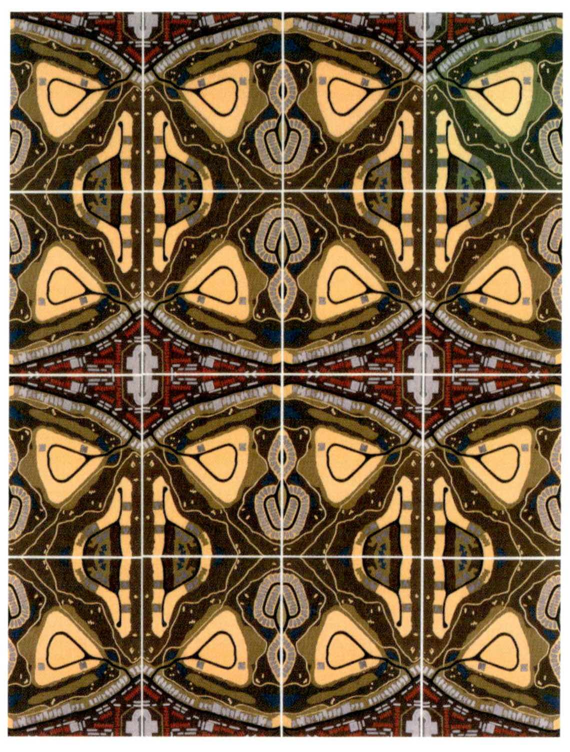

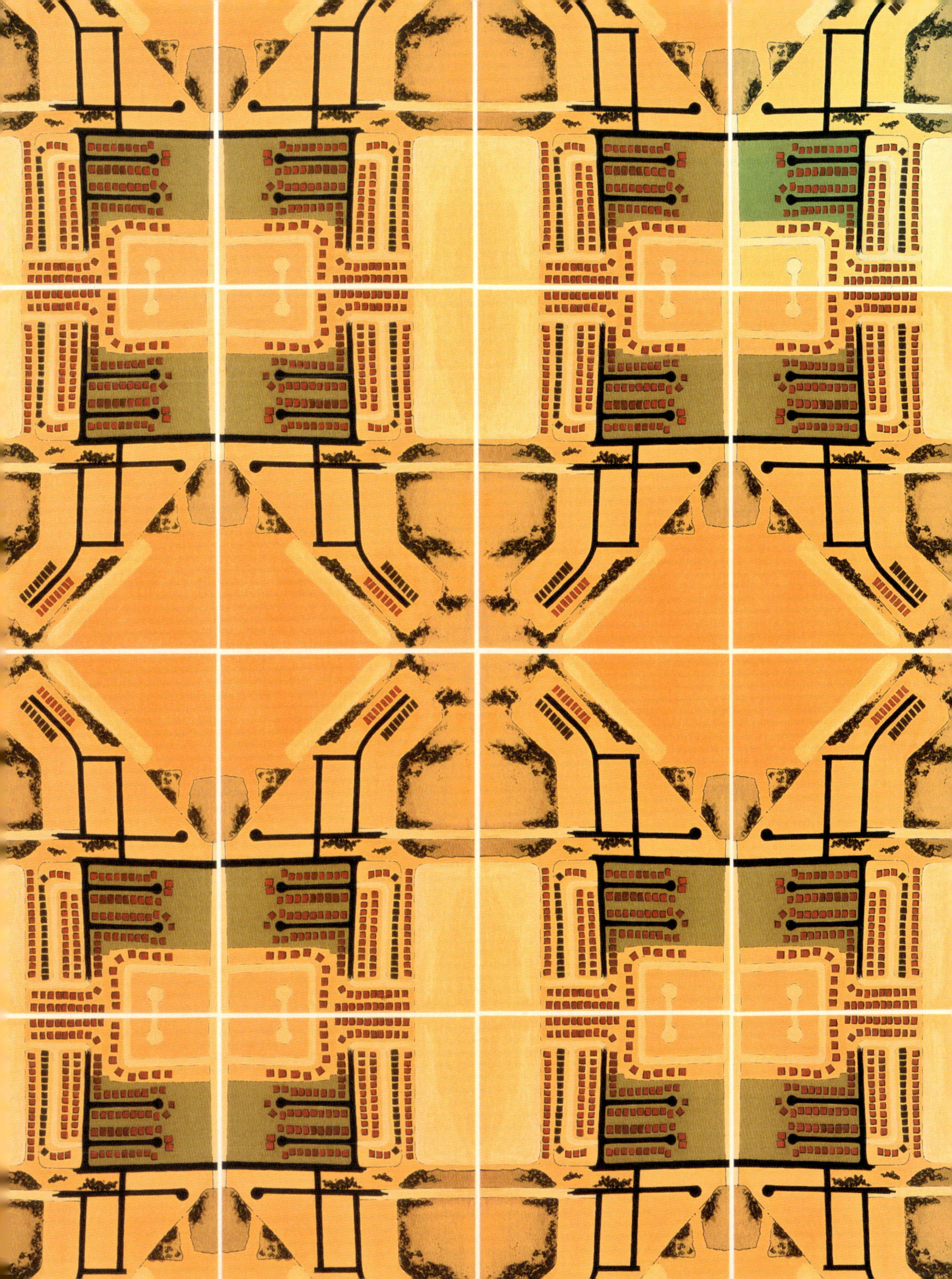

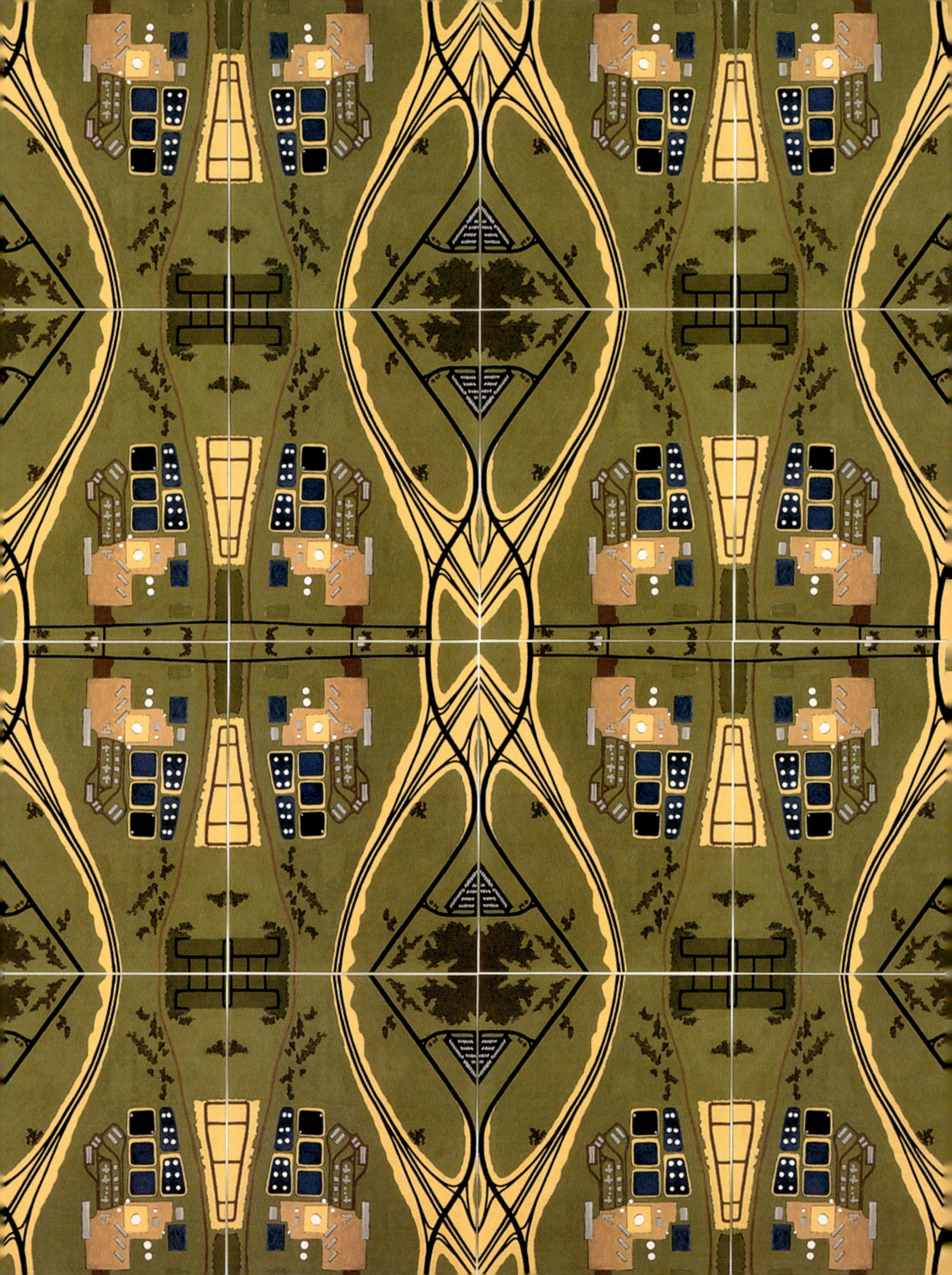

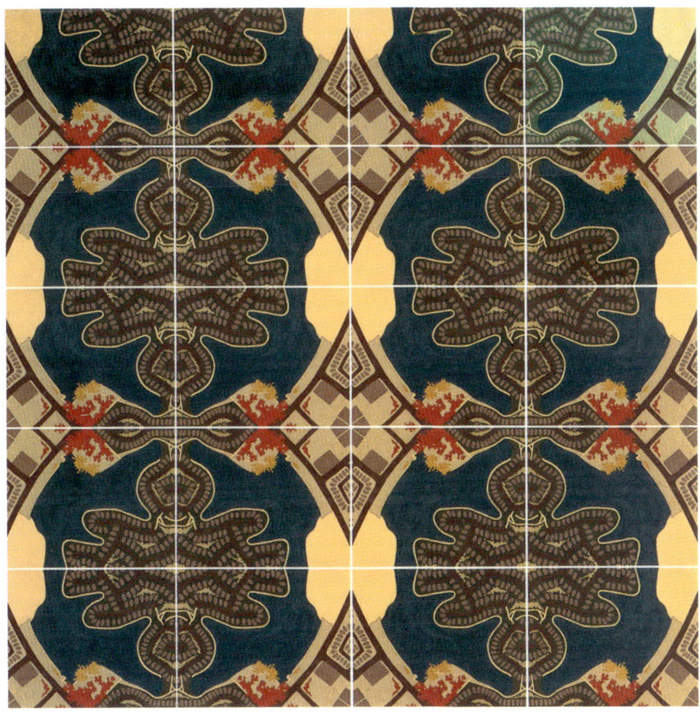

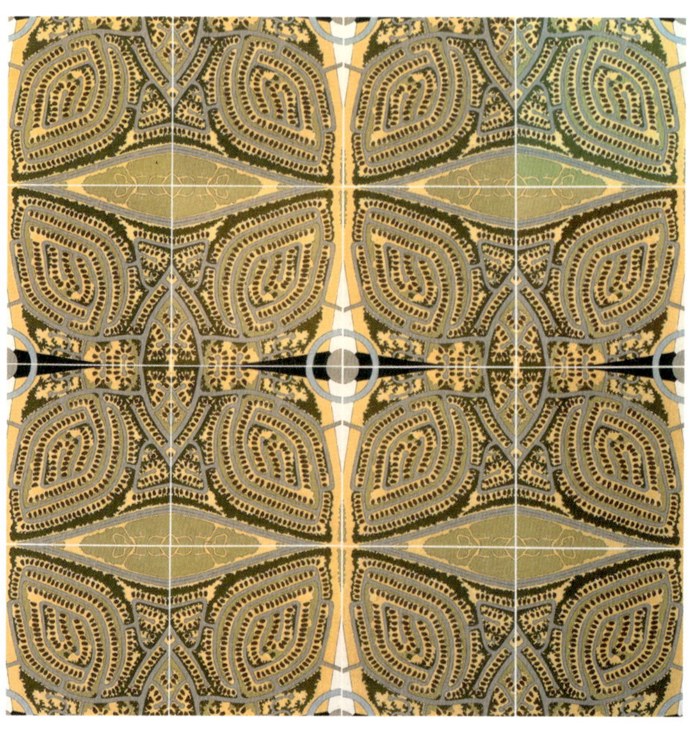

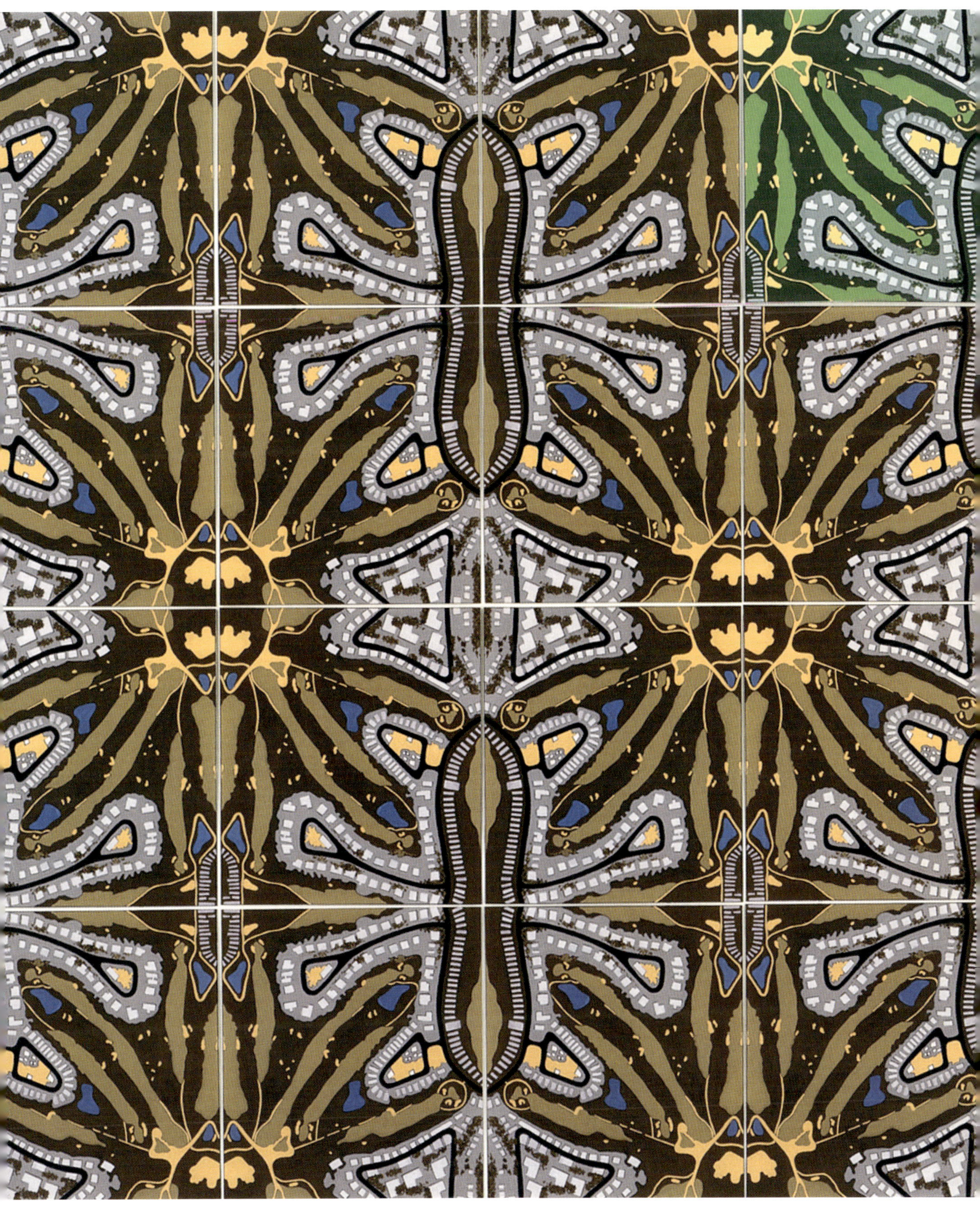

After moving to live in the California desert at A–Z West, my first endeavor was to invent a new building technology that made more sense in the desert heat, and where the usual building materials were hard to come by and difficult to work with in the hot, sandy environment. I ended up finding a way to pulp my junk mail (I figured that this was my most plentiful natural resource) and to cast it into decorative wall panels. I liked to think of this practice almost as if I were farming my art. My grandparents were ranchers a bit south of this area, and it was a lifestyle that has always greatly appealed to me. The gouaches *sfnwvlei (Something for Nothing with Very Little Effort Involved)* are painted in the manner of the social utopian posters of people working in the fields or carrying fruit out to dry in the sun.

Later when we started producing Homestead Units, I also wanted to paint images of them as advertisements. I started using an airbrush, and the work referenced ads for locales and lifestyles as they used to be pictured in *Arizona Highways* magazine. The *Advanced Technologies* and *Fiber Form* images are also painted as advertisements for products—using my own body as a model but trying to keep my identity rather posed and generic as if a standard citizen living a romanticized lifestyle.

Some of my most diaristic works began at a time when I started to feel that small observations, events, and realities that emerge through day-to-day living are in many ways more profound than any of the larger premises that substantiate art. I have been looking for a way to record an observation or event that might otherwise be forgotten twenty minutes later. These paintings and my videos have felt like some of the most fluid outcroppings from my life at A–Z West.

Nach meinem Umzug in die kalifornische Wüste, um dort in A–Z West zu leben, war es mein erstes Bestreben, eine neue Gebäudetechnologie zu erfinden, die sich besser für die Wüstenhitze eignete. Die üblichen Baumaterialien waren schwer erhältlich und man konnte in dieser heissen sandigen Umgebung auch nur schwer mit ihnen arbeiten. Schliesslich fand ich eine Methode, wie ich den ganzen Papierabfall – der vermutlich meine ergiebigste natürliche Ressource war – zu einem Papierbrei verarbeiten und dann zu dekorativen Wandpaneelen giessen konnte. Für mich war diese Praxis ein bisschen so, als würde ich meine Kunst wie Landwirtschaft betreiben. Meine Grosseltern hatten etwas weiter südlich eine Ranch, und dieser Lebensstil gefiel mir schon immer ausgesprochen gut. Die Gouachen „sfnwvlei (Something for Nothing with Very Little Effort Involved)" sind im Stil jener sozialutopischen Plakate gemalt, die Leute bei der Feldarbeit oder beim Heraustragen von Früchten zeigen, damit diese in der Sonne trocknen können.

Später, als wir begannen, „Homestead Units" zu produzieren, wollte ich auch Bilder von ihnen als Reklame malen. Ich begann einen *Airbrush* zu verwenden und bezog mich auf Anzeigen für Schauplätze und Lebensstile, wie man sie früher in der Zeitschrift „Arizona Highways" fand. Auch die „Advanced Technologies" und „Fiber Form"-Bilder sind wie Produktwerbung gemalt – ich benutzte meinen eigenen Körper als Modell, versuchte aber ziemlich gestellt und unspezifisch zu erscheinen, wie eine Durchschnittsbürgerin mit einem romantischen Lebensstil. Einige meiner tagebuchartigsten Werke begannen zu einem Zeitpunkt, als ich den Eindruck gewann, dass kleine Beobachtungen, Ereignisse und Wirklichkeiten, die sich im Alltagsleben bemerkbar machen, in vieler Hinsicht wesentlich tiefgründiger sind als irgendeine jener grösseren Prämissen, die der Kunst zugrunde liegen. Ich suchte nach einer Möglichkeit, eine Beobachtung oder ein Ereignis festzuhalten, die bzw. das andernfalls zwanzig Minuten später vergessen wäre. Diese Gemälde und meine Videos zählen meinem Gefühl nach zu den selbstverständlichsten Hervorbringungen meines Lebens in A–Z West.

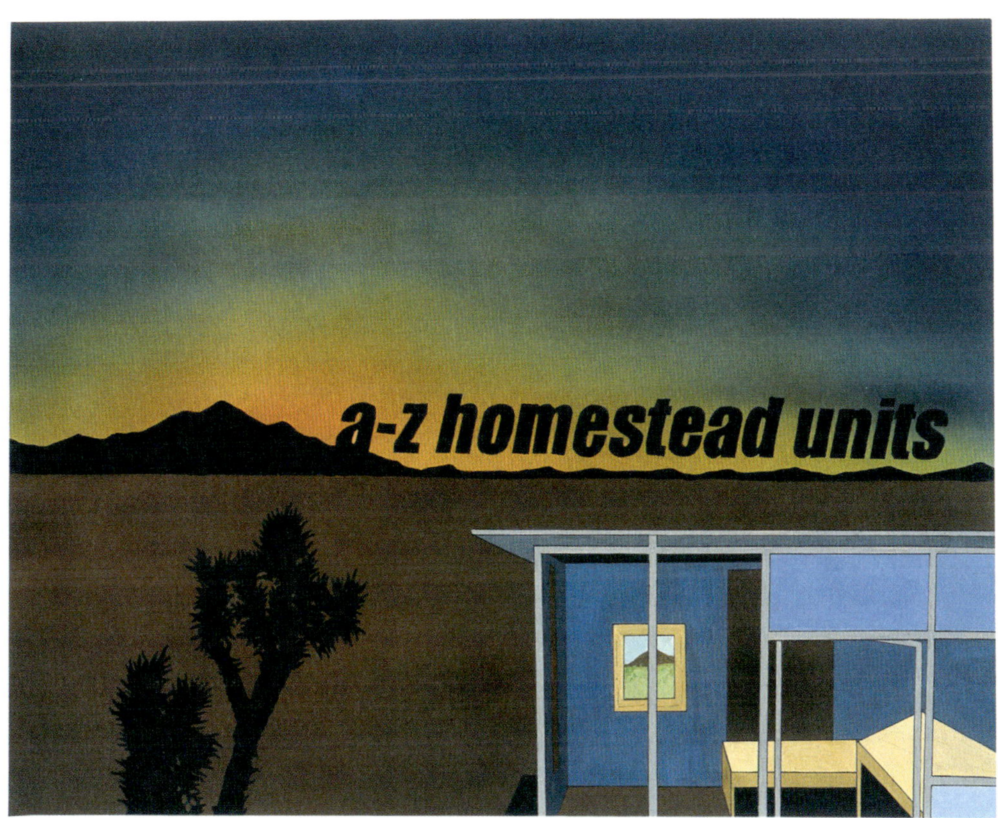
a-z homestead units

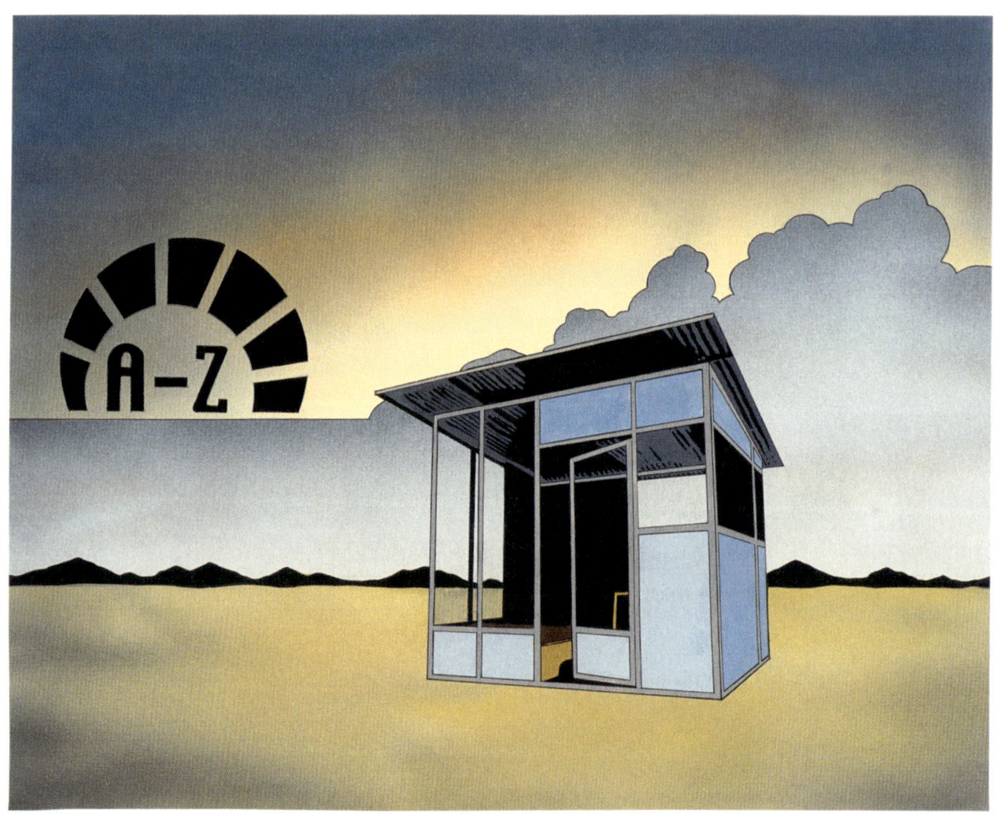
A-Z

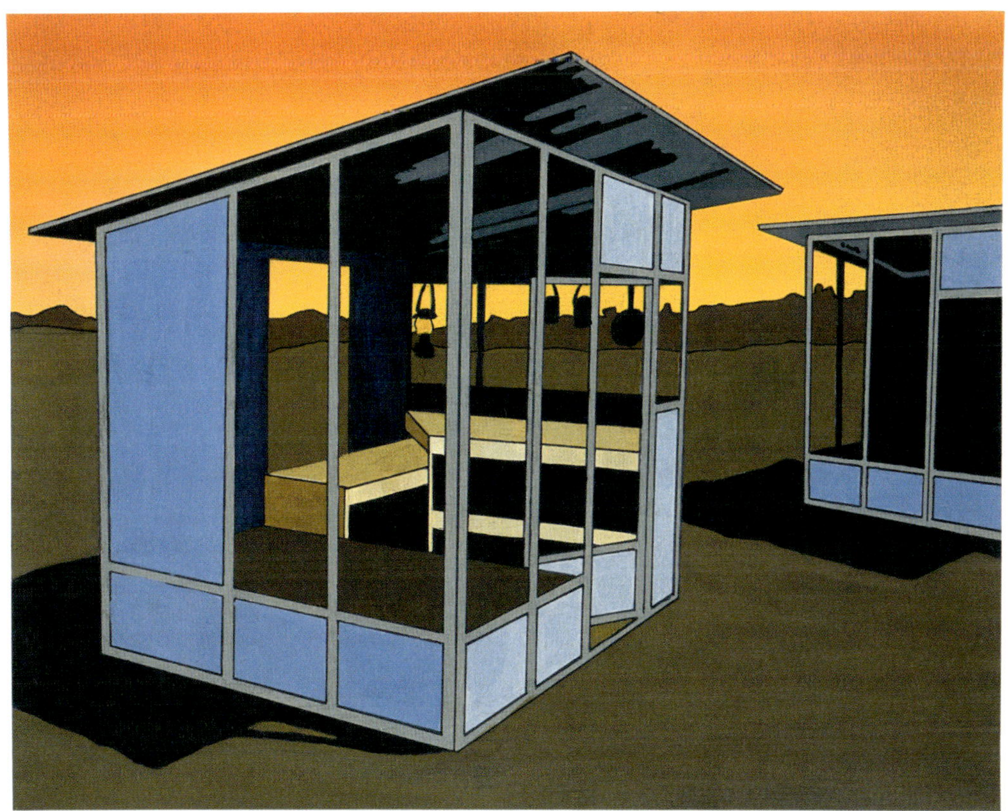

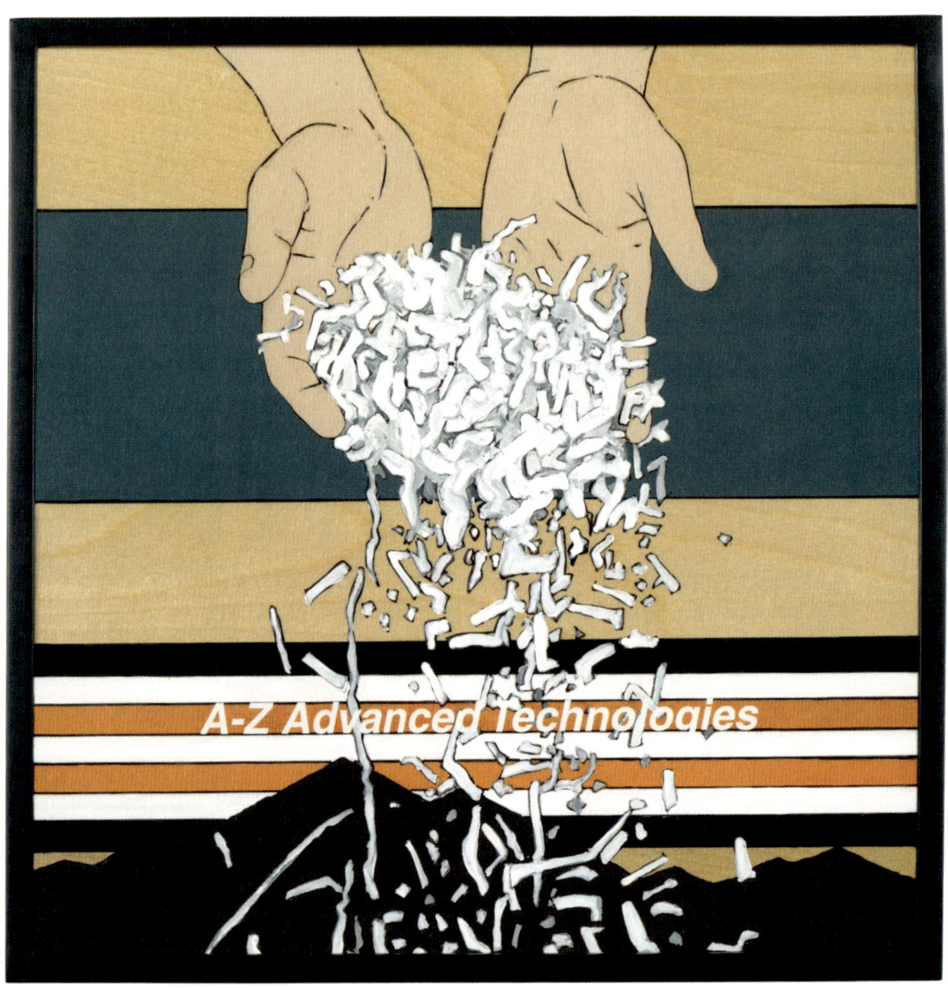
A-Z Advanced Technologies

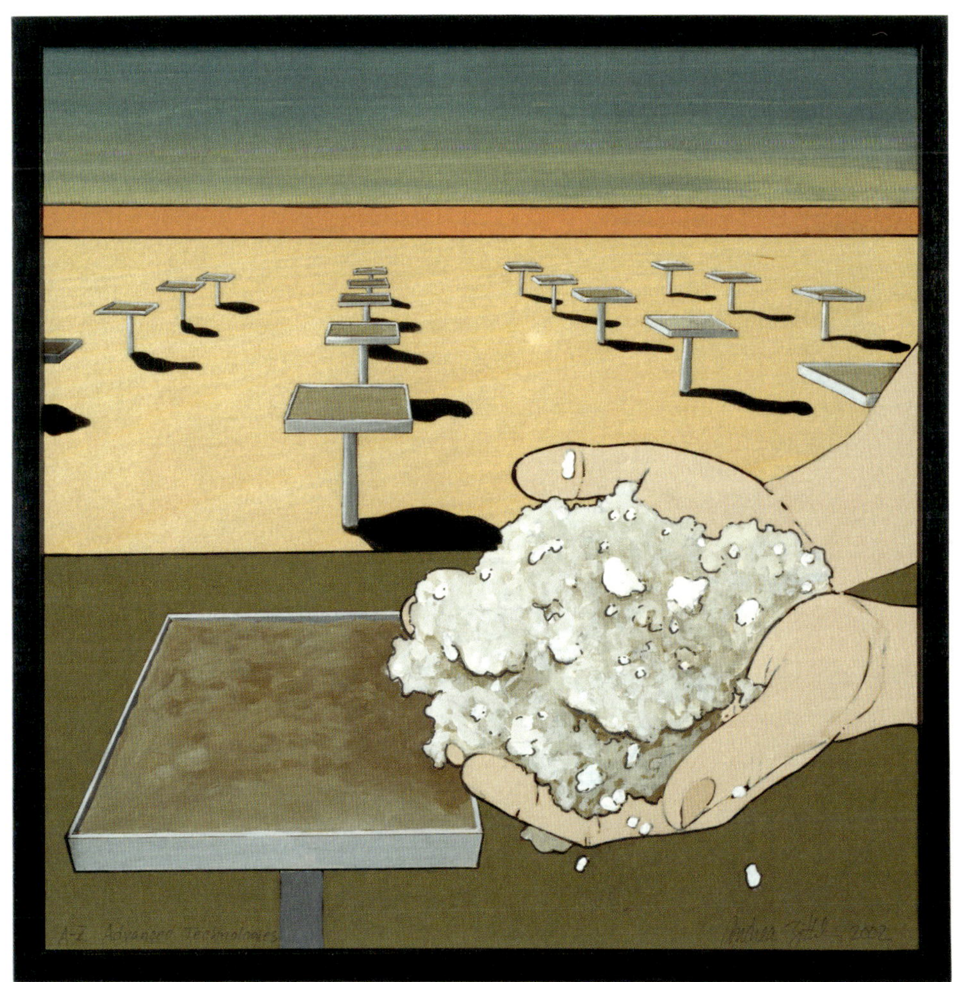
A-Z Advanced Technologies
2002

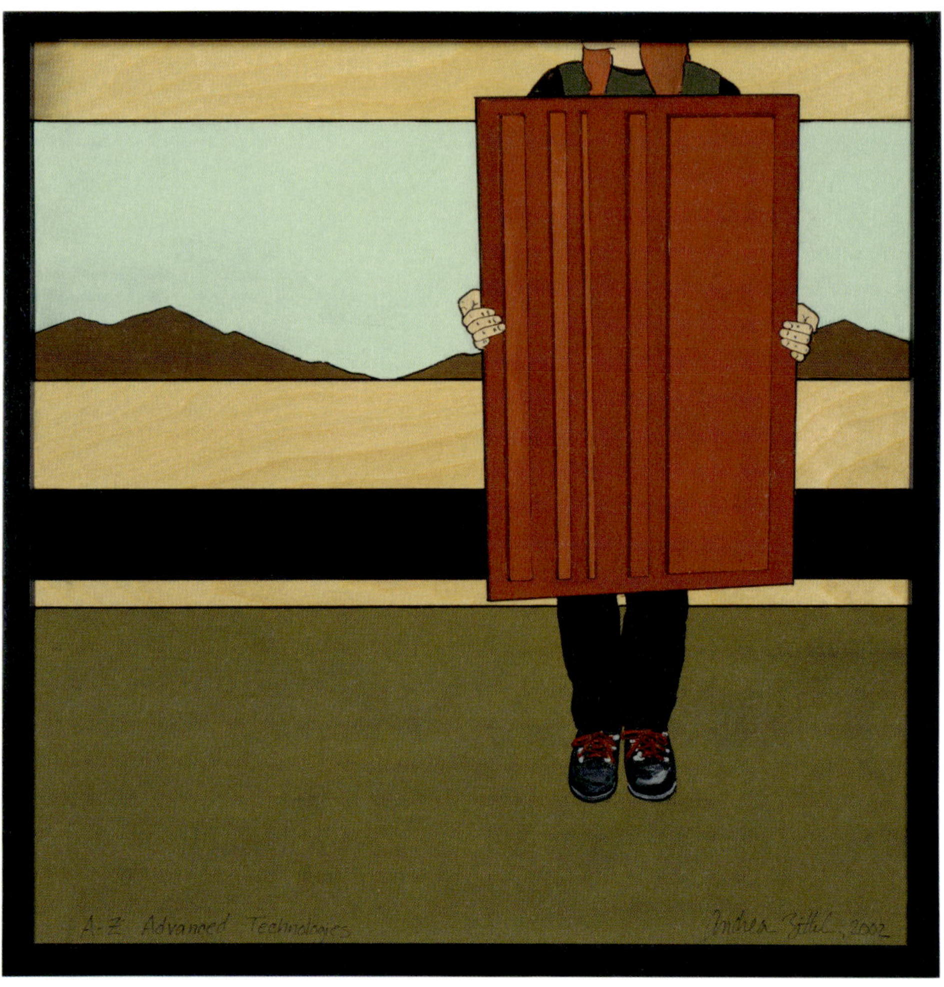
A–Z Advanced Technologies
Andrea Zittel, 2002

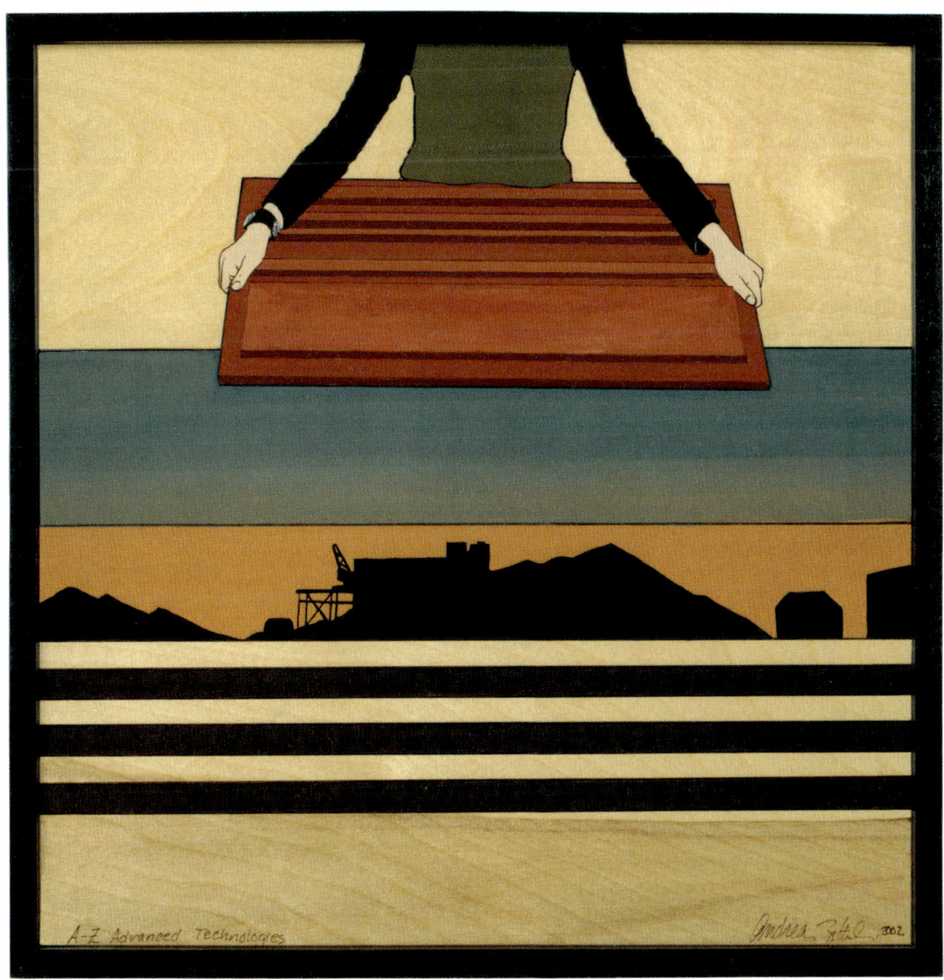
A-Z Advanced Technologies
Andrea Ventura 2002

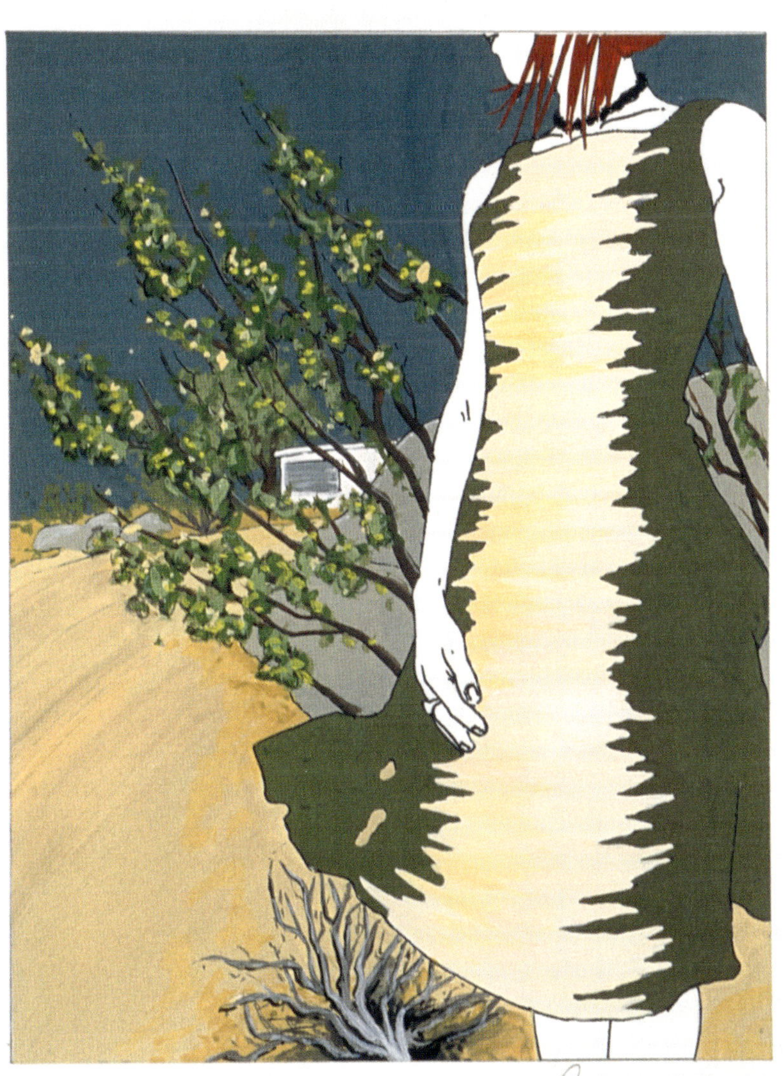

"A-Z Advanced Technologies" Andrea Zittel, 2002

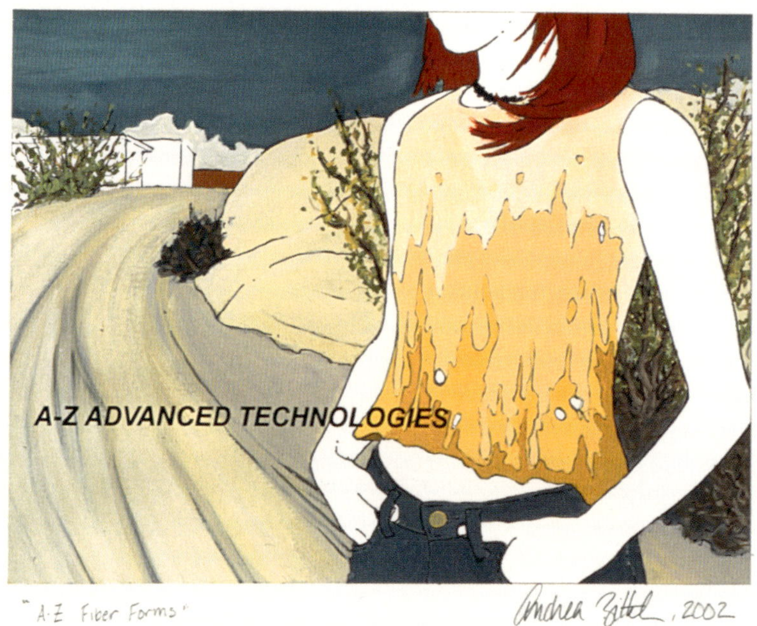

"A-Z Fiber Forms" Andrea Zittel, 2002

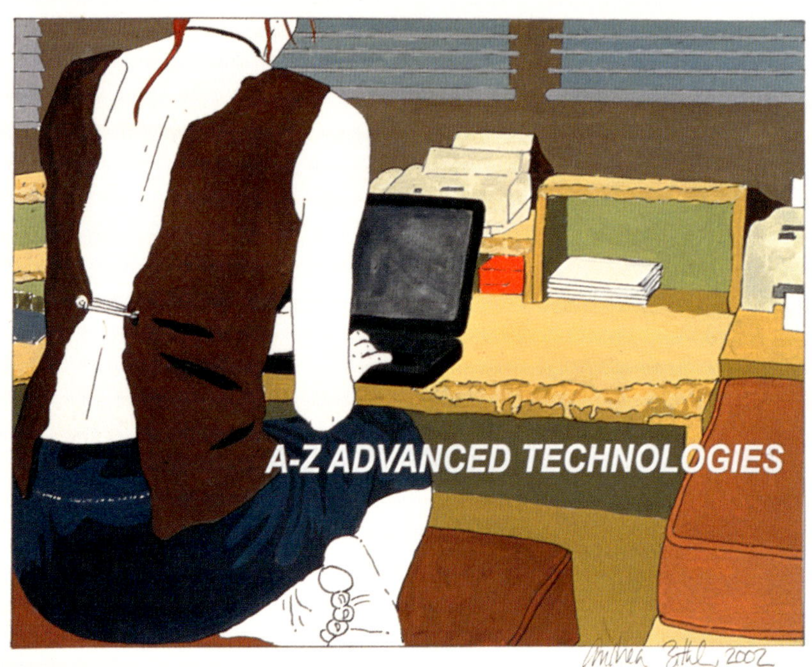

Andrea Zittel, 2002

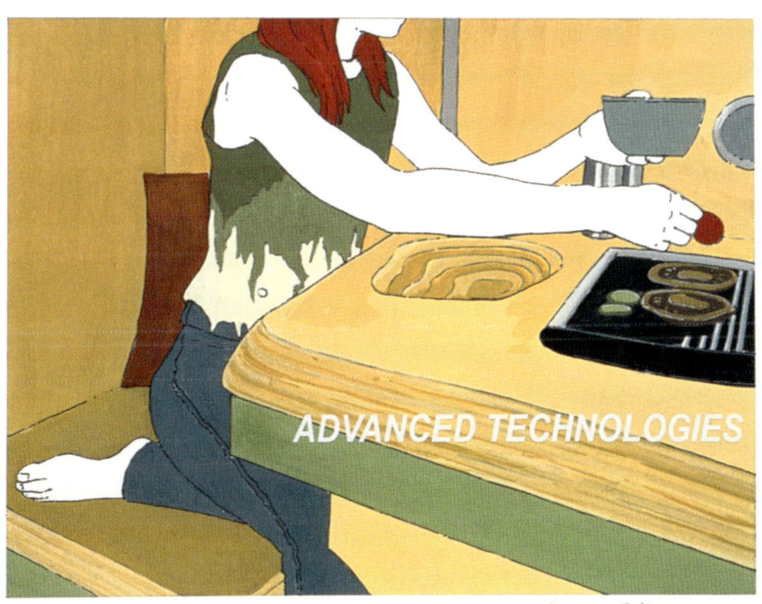

Andrea Zittel, 2002

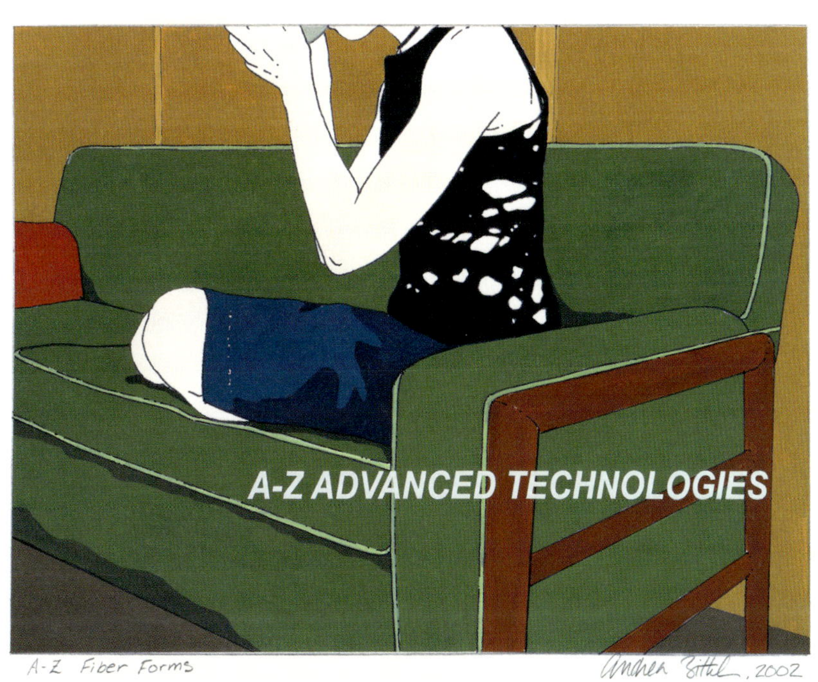

A-Z Fiber Forms

Andrea Zittel, 2002

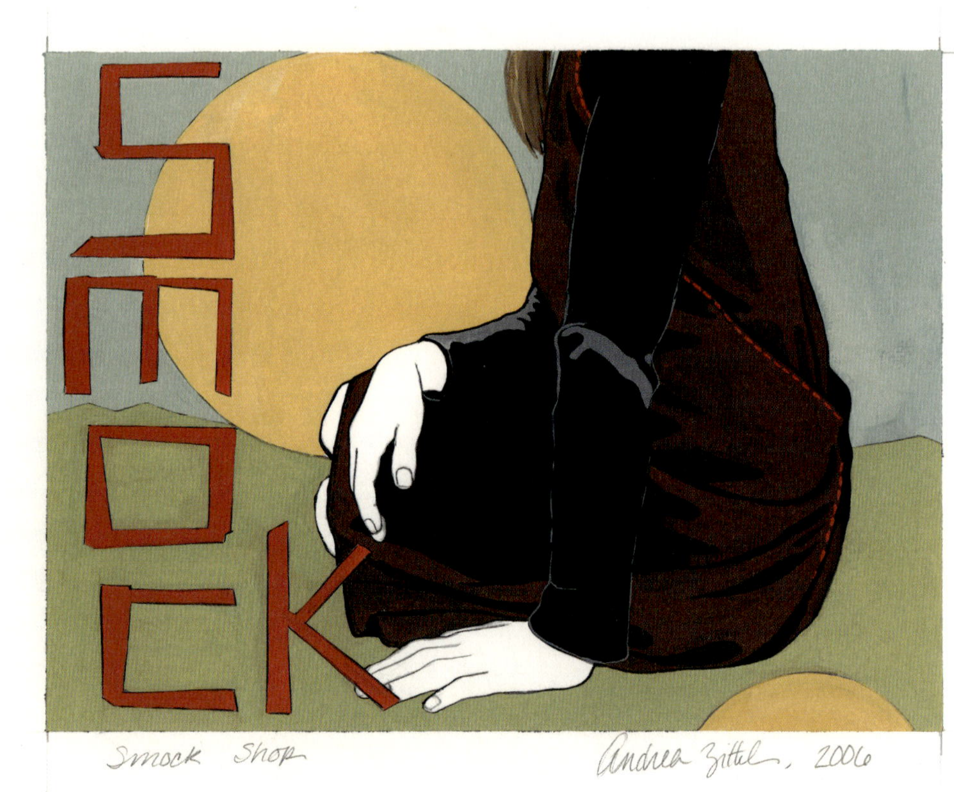

Smock Shop   Andrea Zittel, 2006

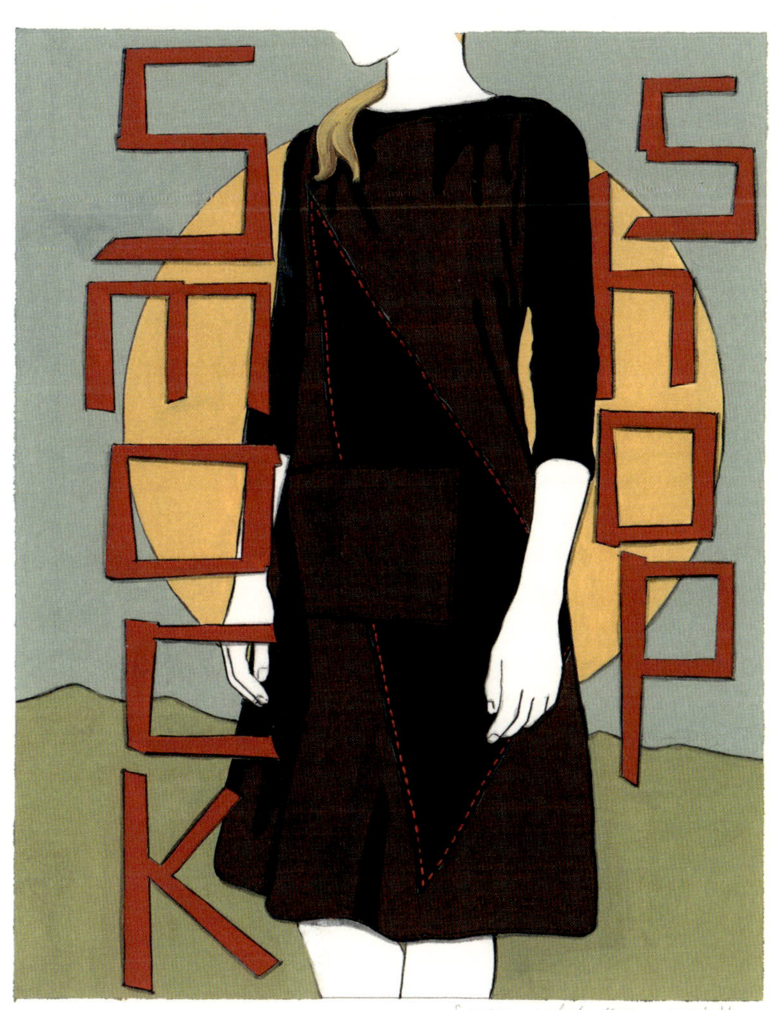

"wear what you work."
Andrea Zittel, 2006

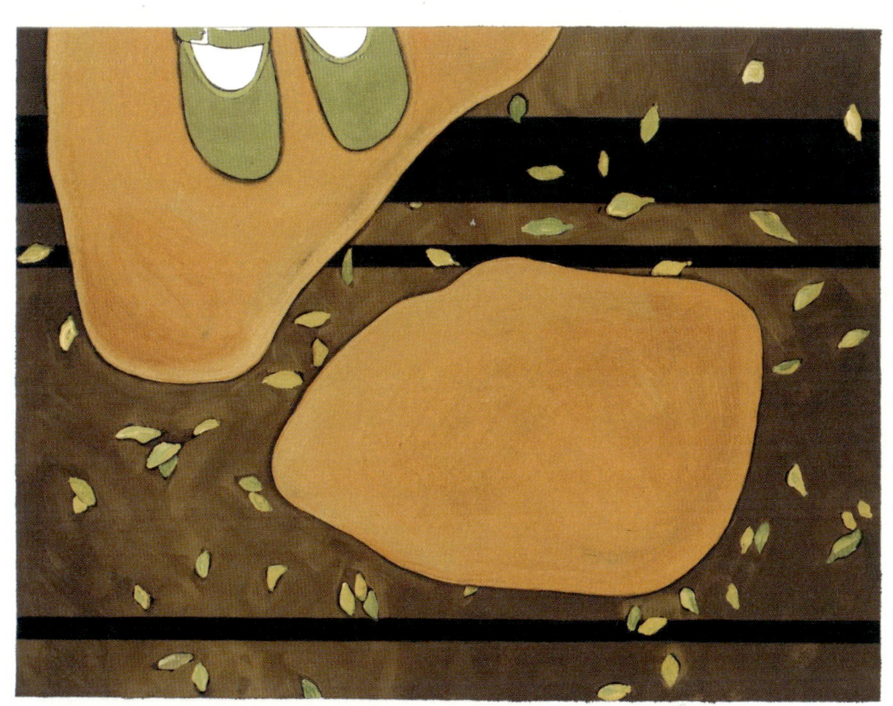

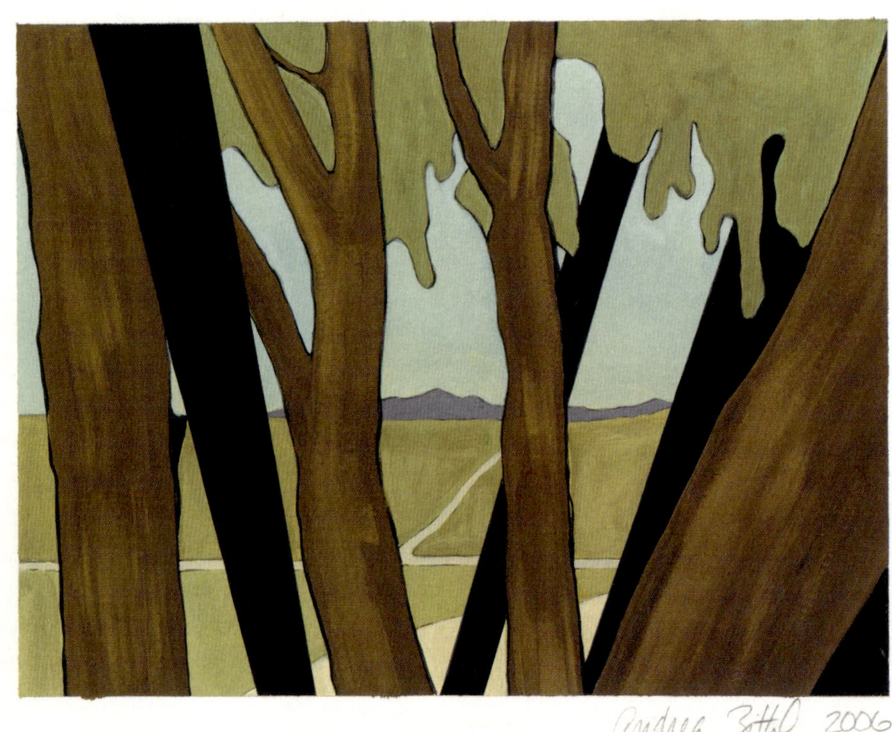

Andrea Zittel, 2006

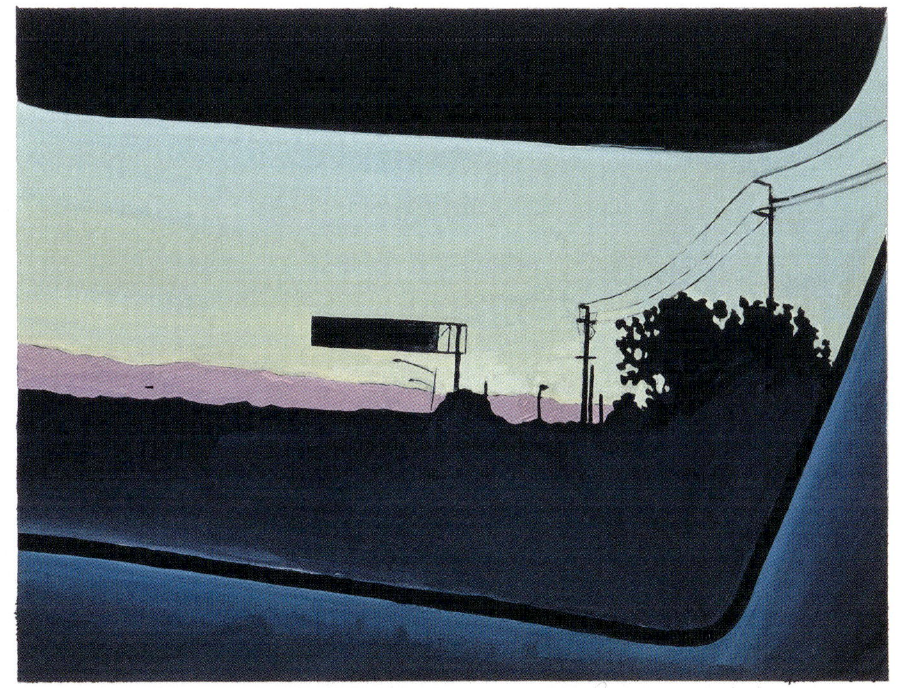

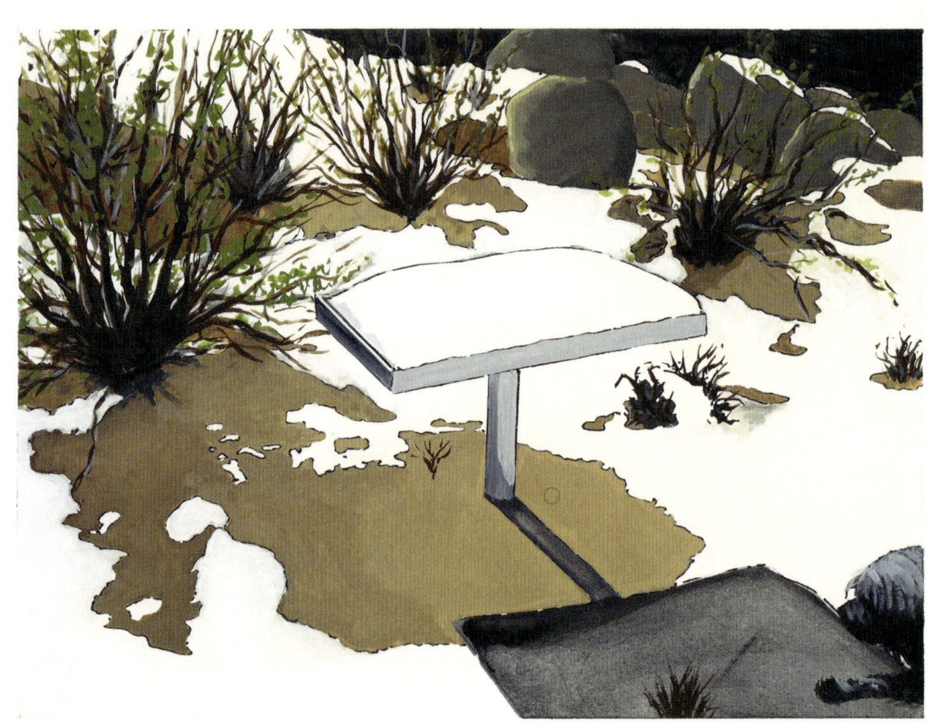

Snow on Regenerating Field, A-Z West - November 2004

Andrea Zittel

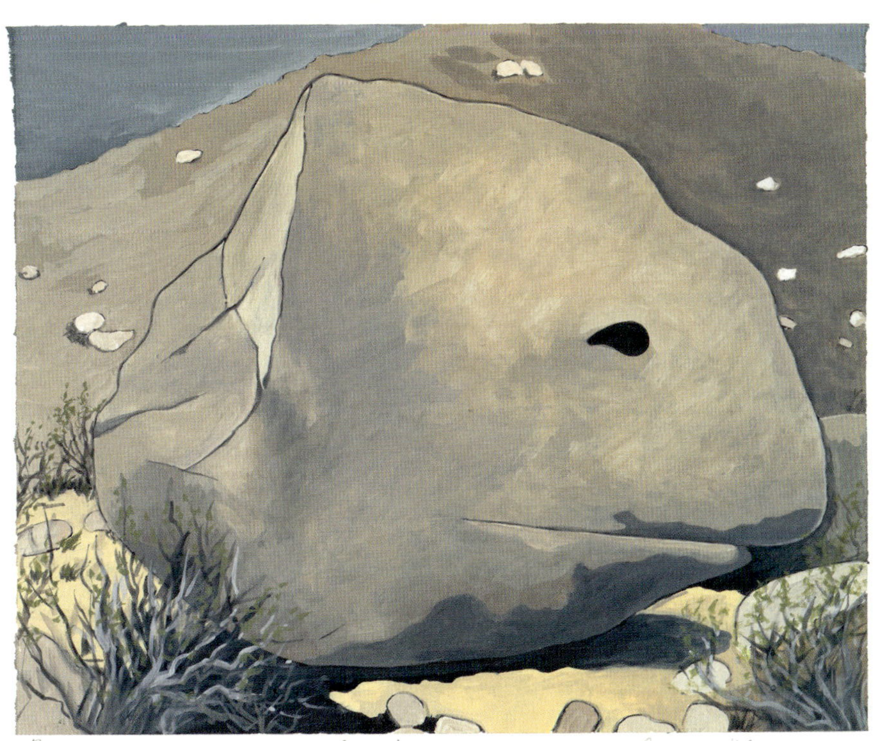

Rock in wash behind A-Z West   Andrea Zittel, 2004

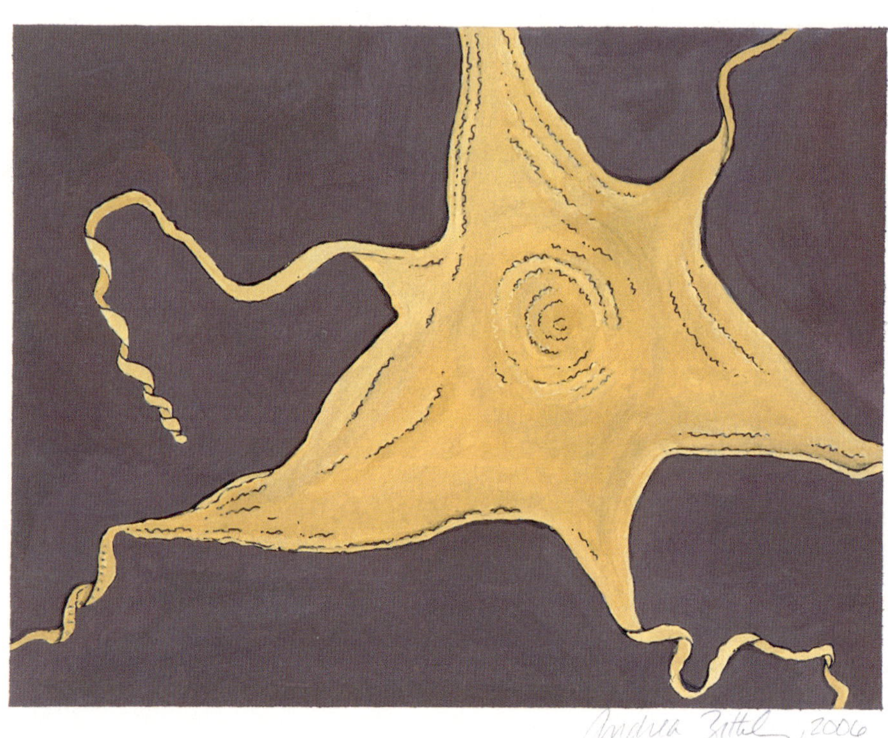

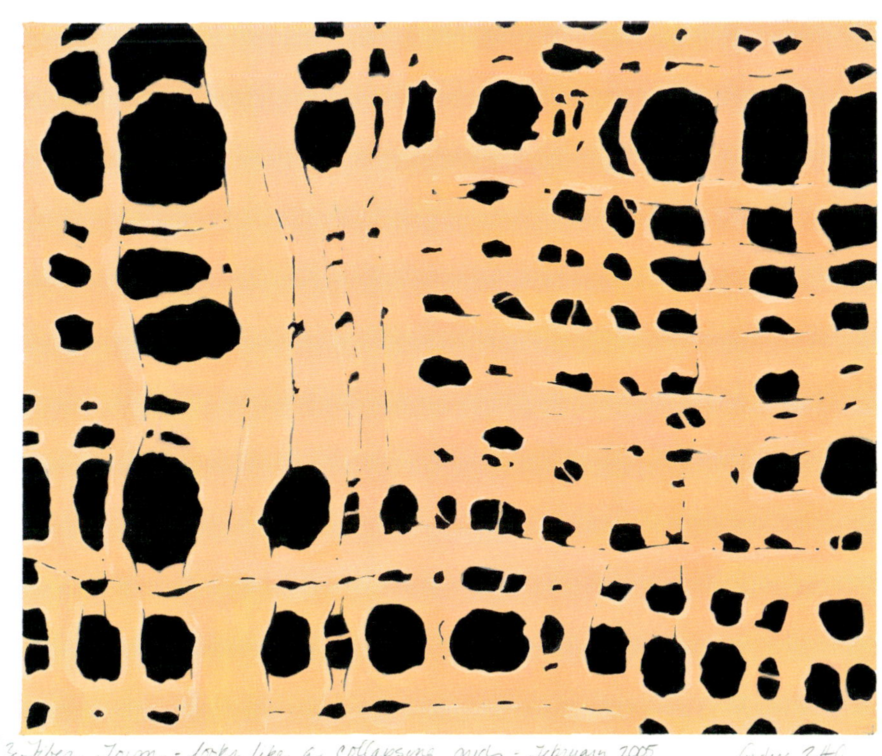

63 Fiber Form - looks like a collapsing grid - February 2005   Andrea Zittel

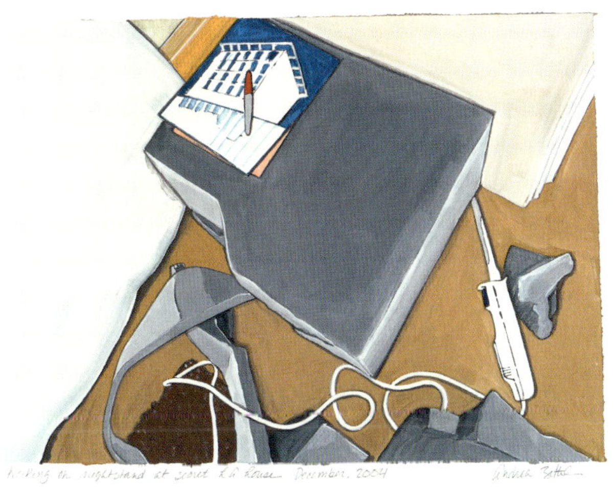

Working on nightstand at secret LA house   December, 2004

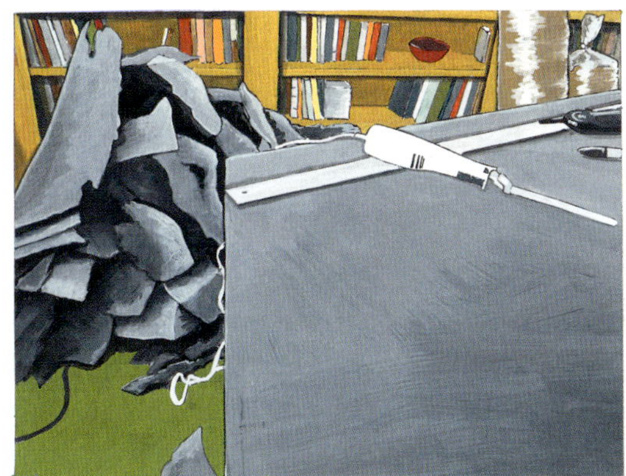

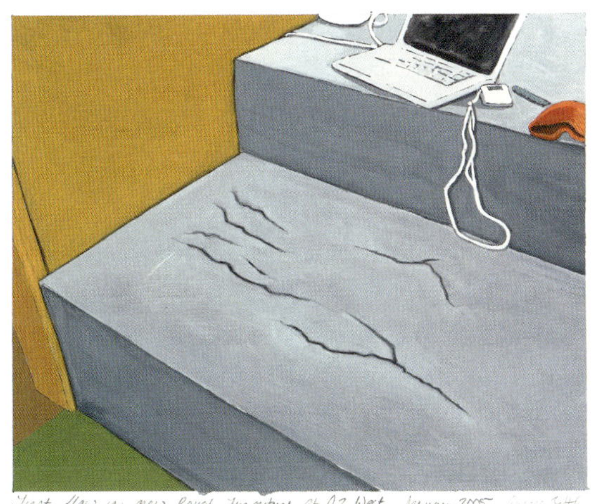

First flow in new Rough Furniture at A-Z West   January 2005

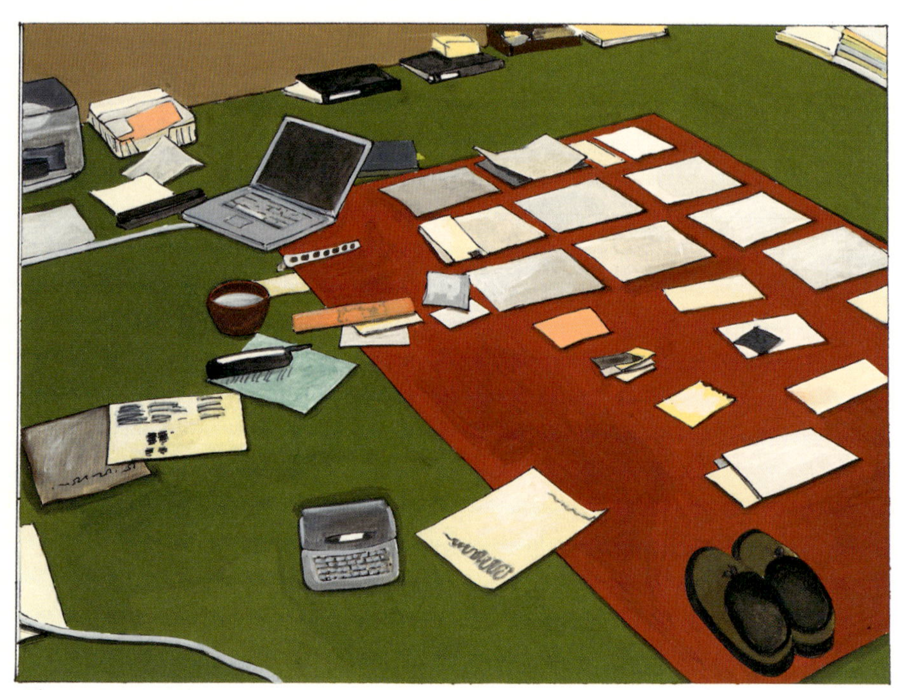

Filing system – Joshua Tree, March 2004   Andrea Zittel

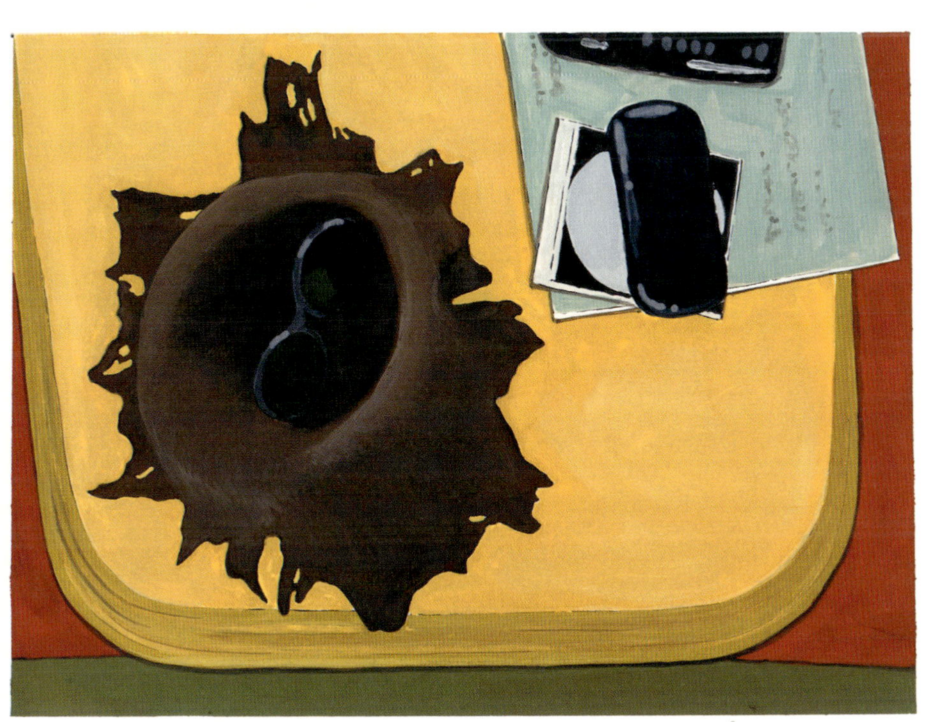

Favorite felted bowl (what I want to keep) 2004   Andrea Zittel

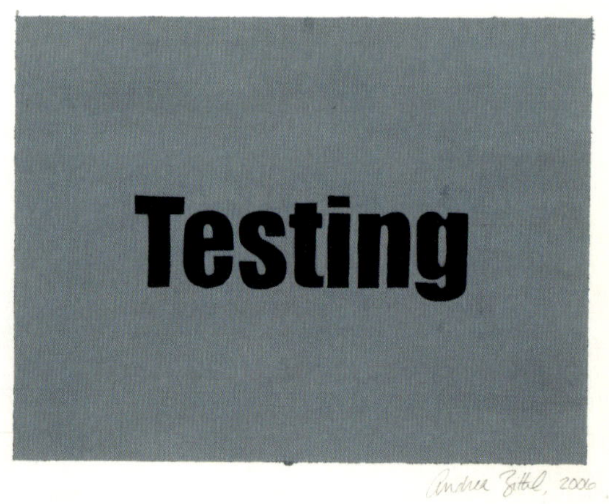

Andrea Zittel, 2006

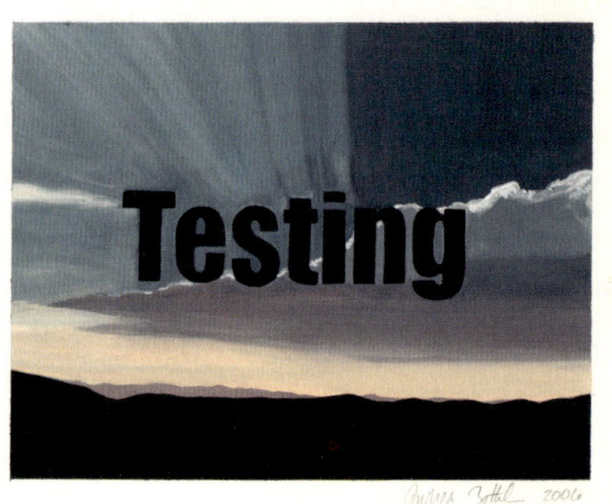

Andrea Zittel, 2006

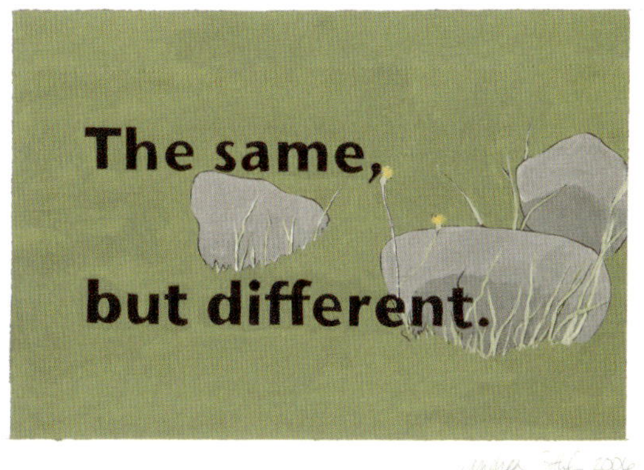
The same,
but different.

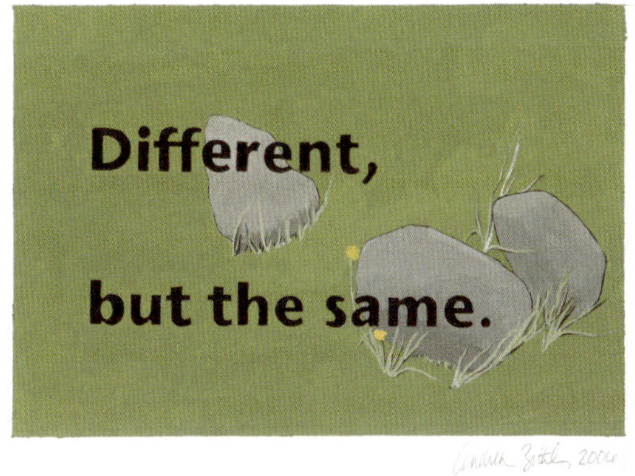
Different,
but the same.

About ten years ago, frustrated that after years of reading, writing, and thinking I still felt as if I knew nothing, I decided to make a list of the few things that (I thought) I knew for sure. These small realities slowly coalesced into an evolving cluster of truths, which are both profound and trivial.

Ich weiss alles und ich weiss nichts

Frustriert von dem Gefühl, nach Jahren des Lesens, Schreibens und Nachdenkens immer noch nichts zu wissen, beschloss ich vor etwa zehn Jahren, eine Liste der wenigen Dinge zu machen, die ich – so meinte ich – sicher wusste. Diese kleinen Wirklichkeiten wuchsen allmählich zu einer sich weiter entwickelnden Gruppe von Wahrheiten zusammen, die ebenso tiefgründig und gleichzeitig trivial sind.

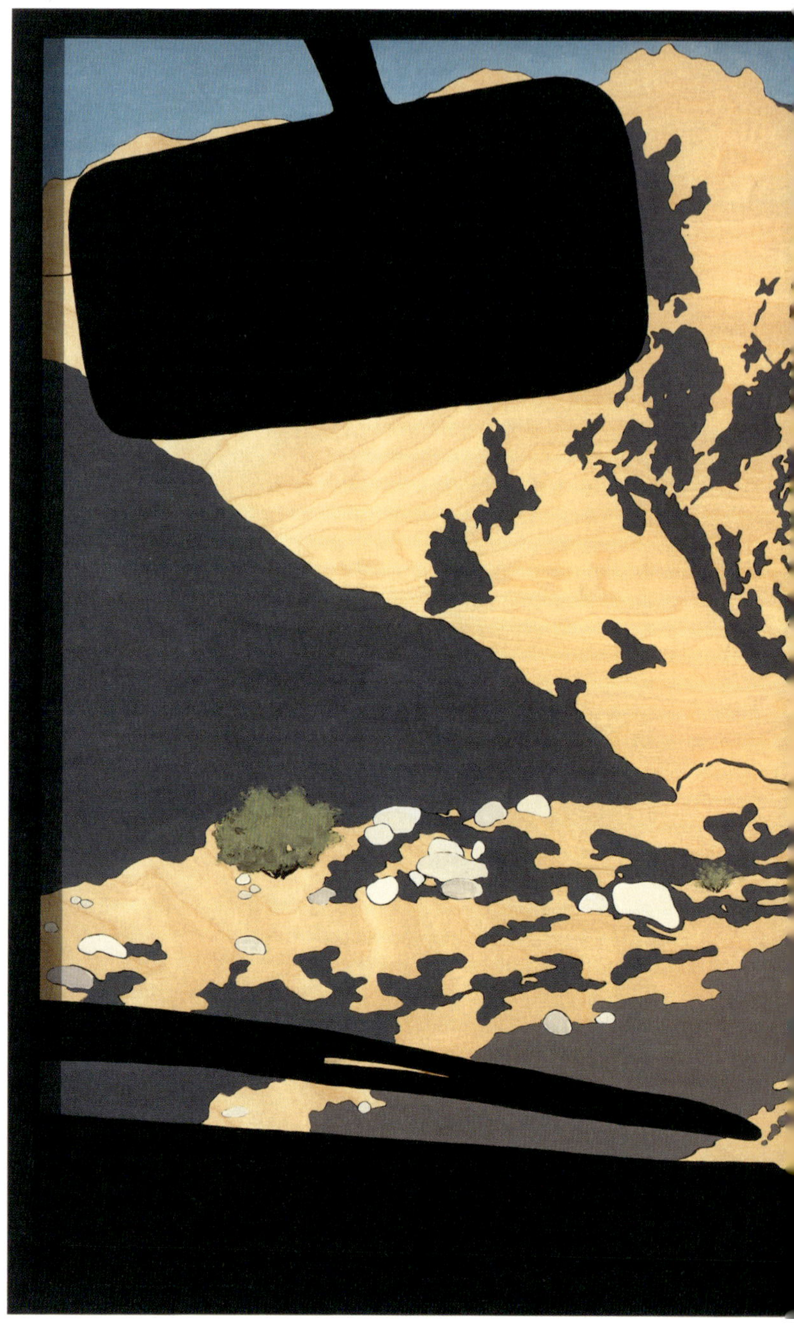

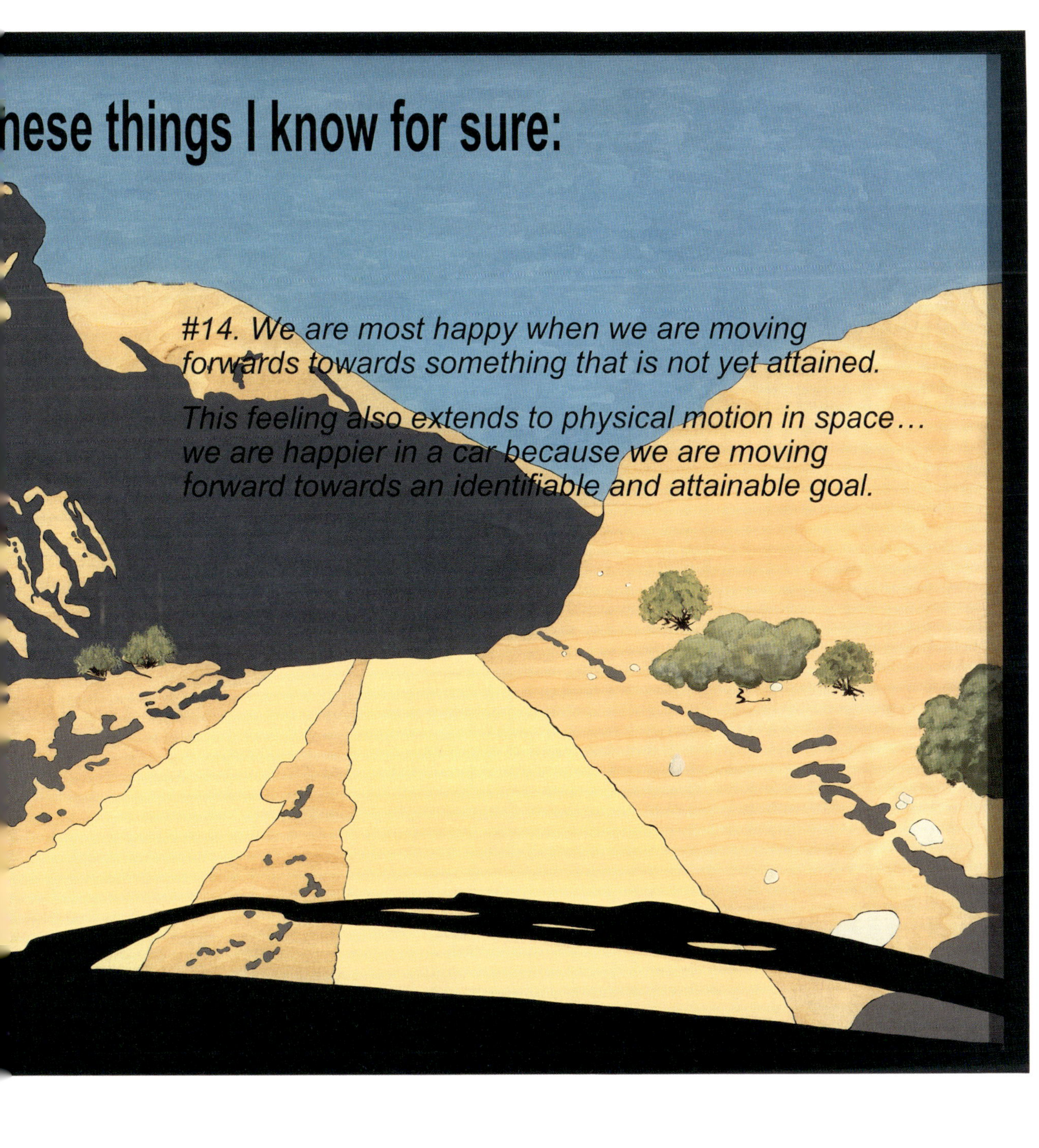
hese things I know for sure:

#14. We are most happy when we are moving forwards towards something that is not yet attained.

This feeling also extends to physical motion in space… we are happier in a car because we are moving forward towards an identifiable and attainable goal.

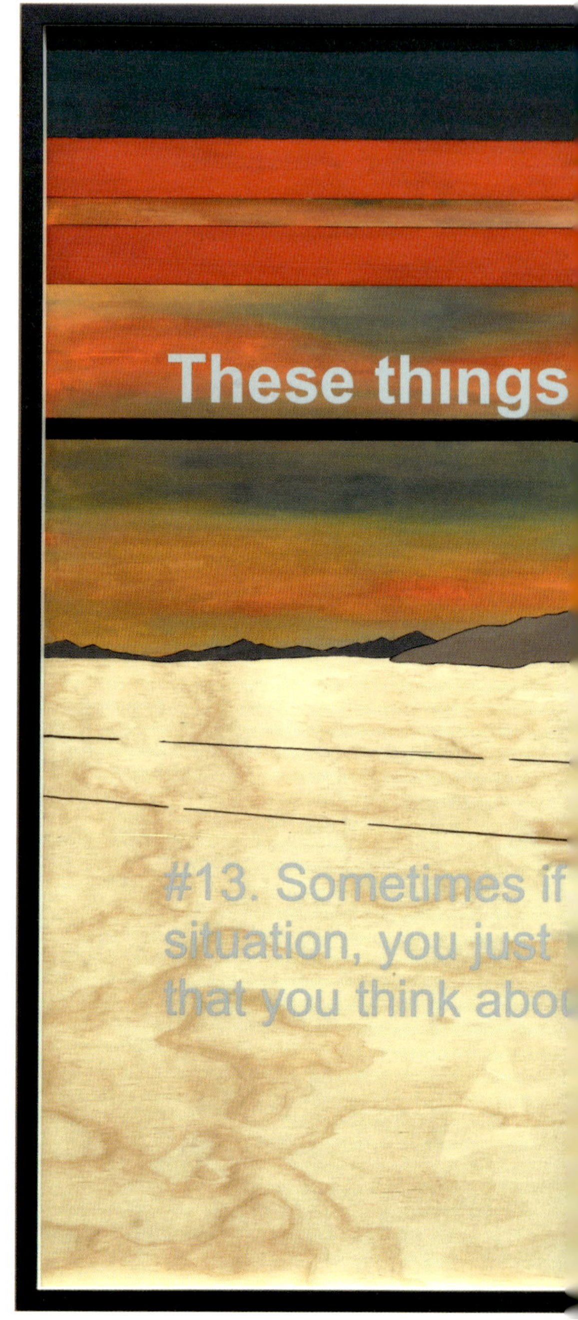
These things
#13. Sometimes if
situation, you just
that you think abou

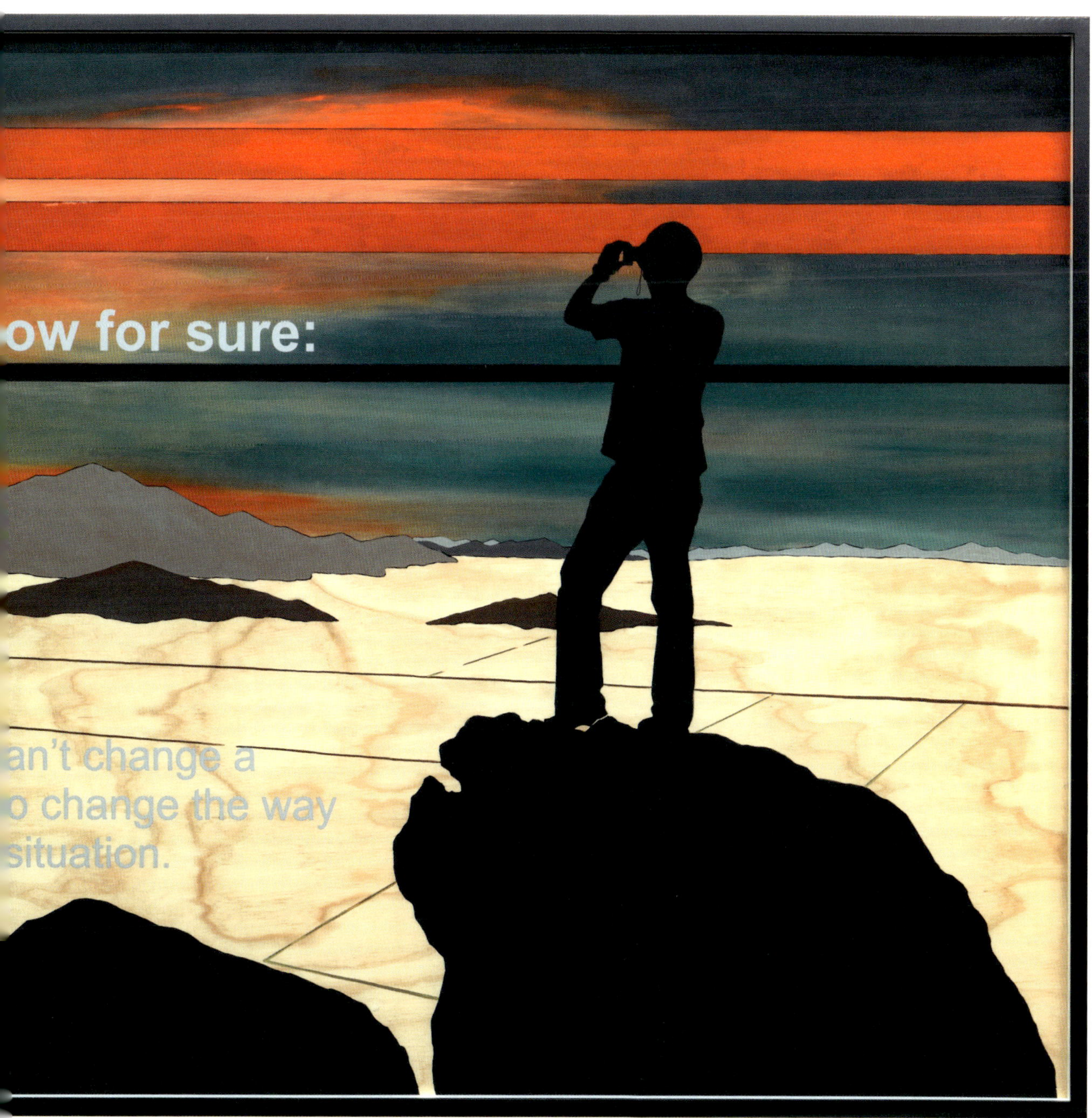
ow for sure:
an't change a
o change the way
situation.

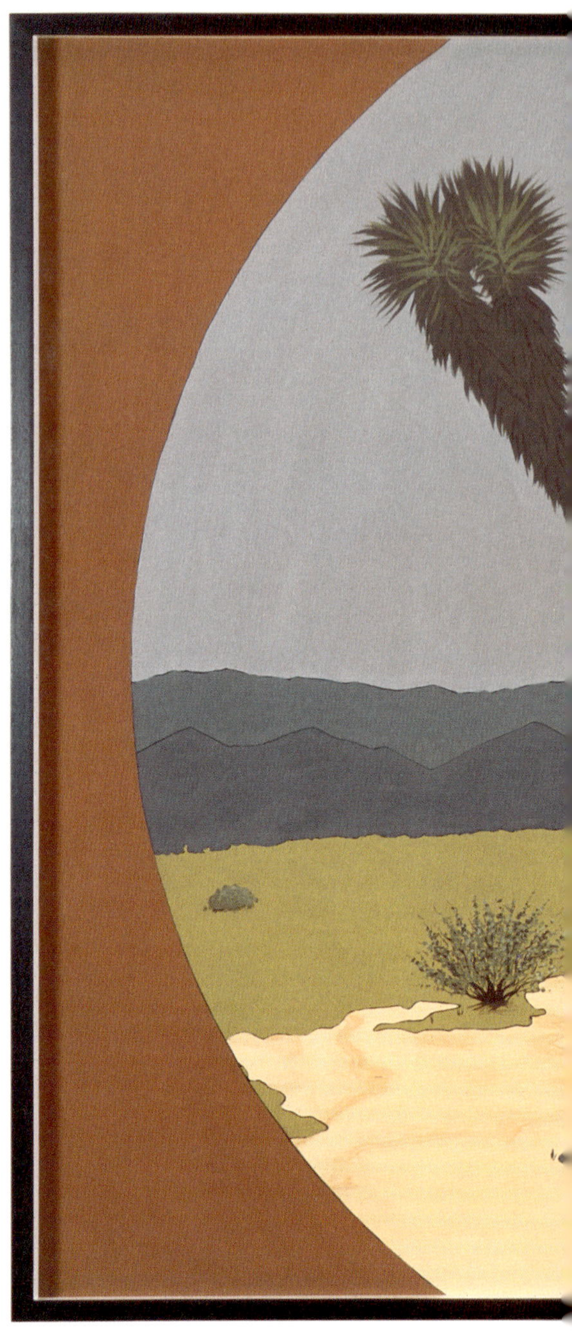

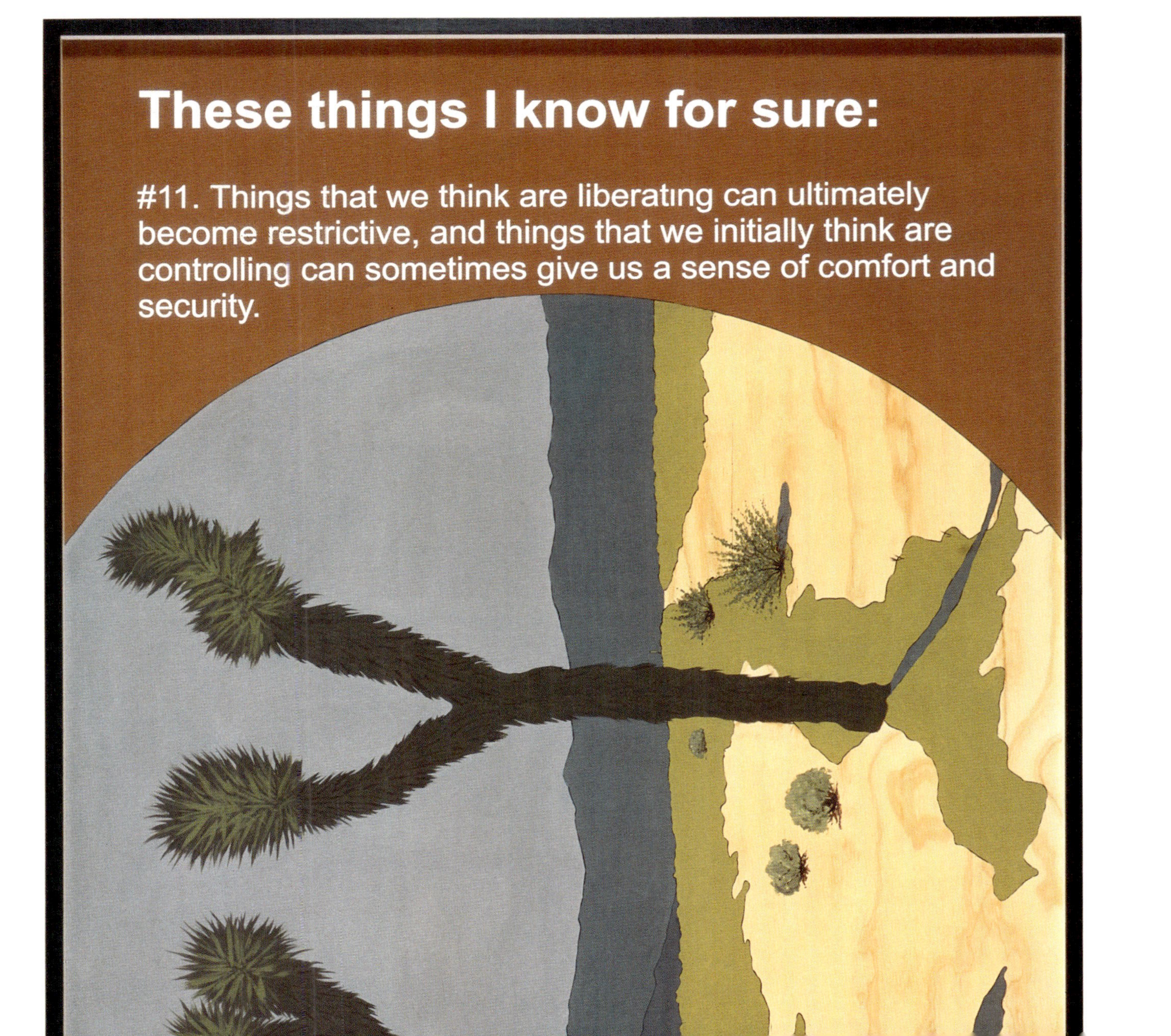

These things I know for sure:
#11. Things that we think are liberating can ultimately become restrictive, and things that we initially think are controlling can sometimes give us a sense of comfort and security.

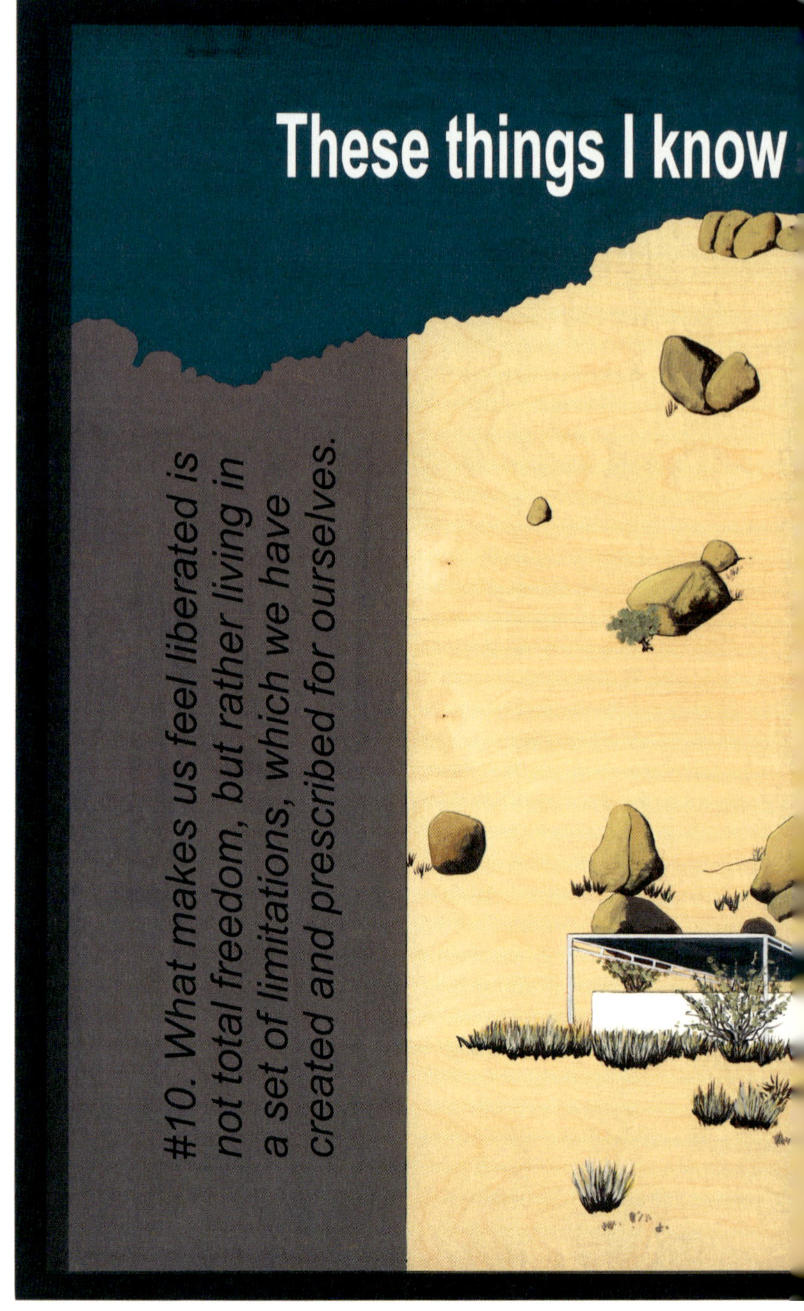
These things I know

#10. What makes us feel liberated is not total freedom, but rather living in a set of limitations, which we have created and prescribed for ourselves.

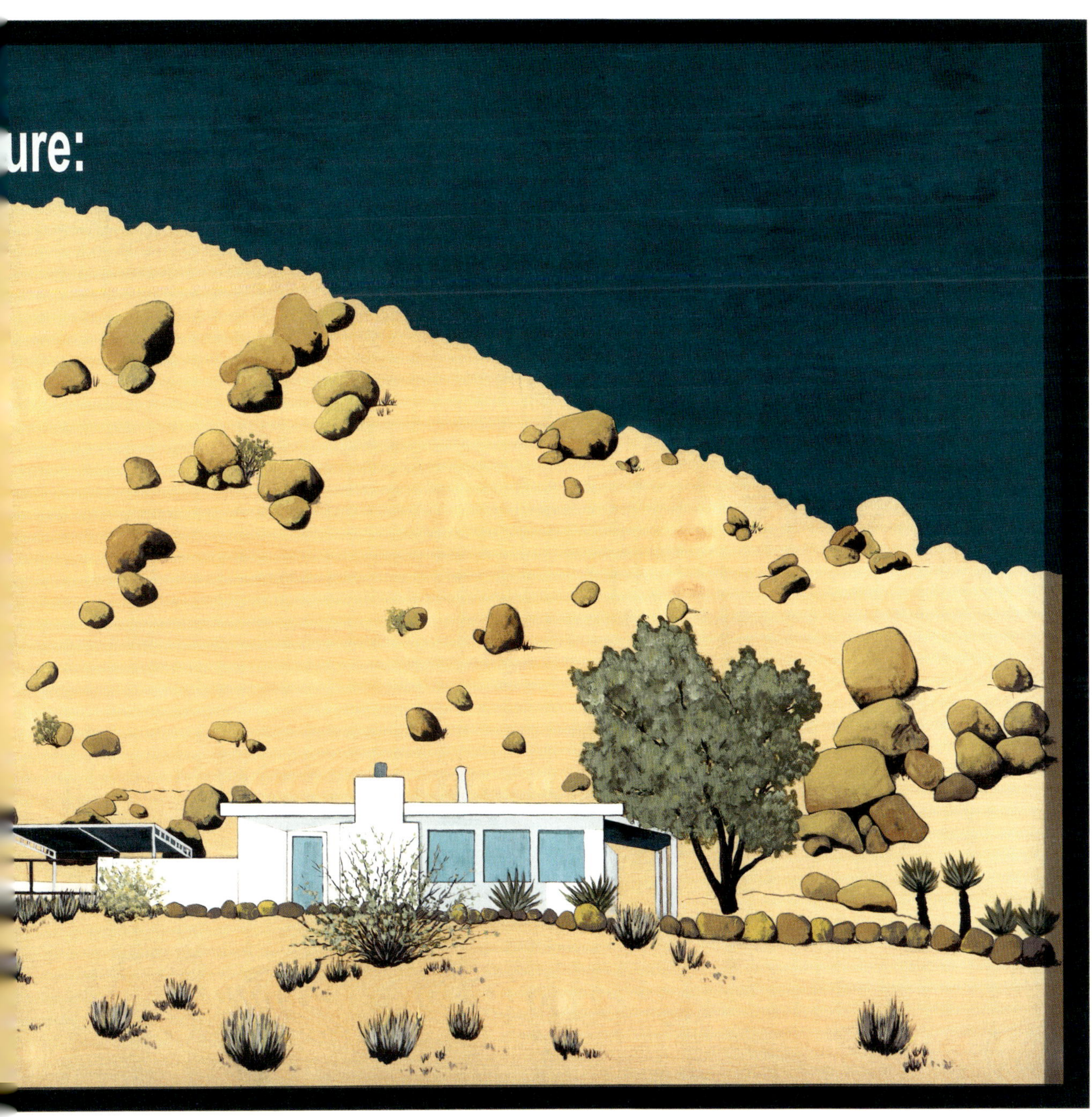
ure:

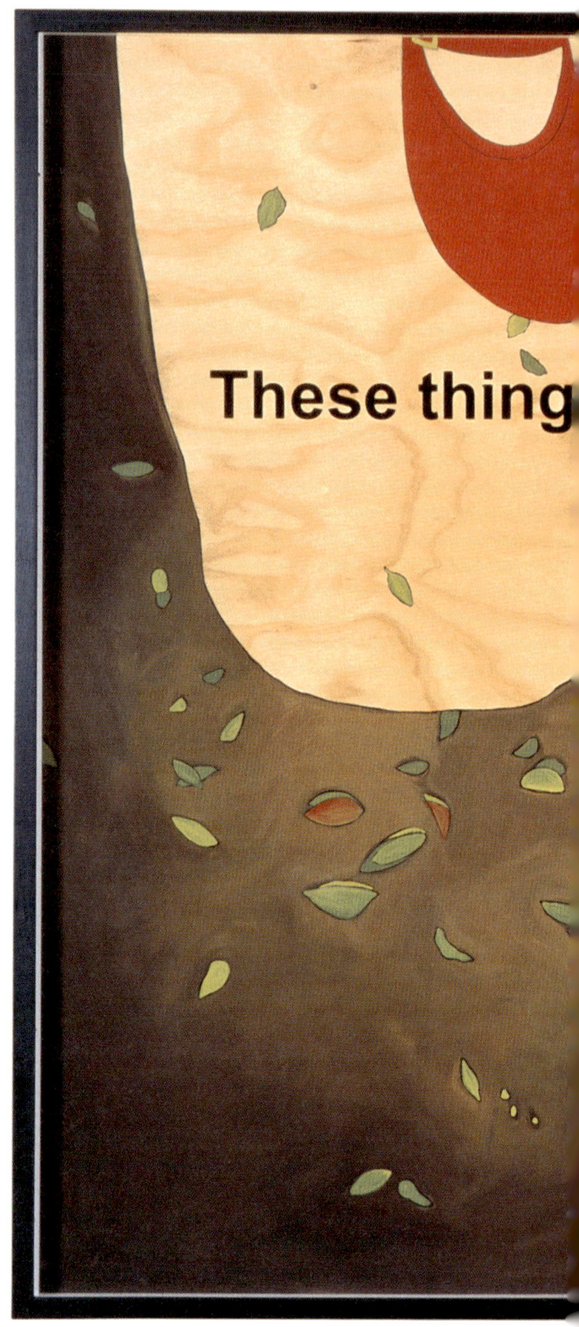
These thing

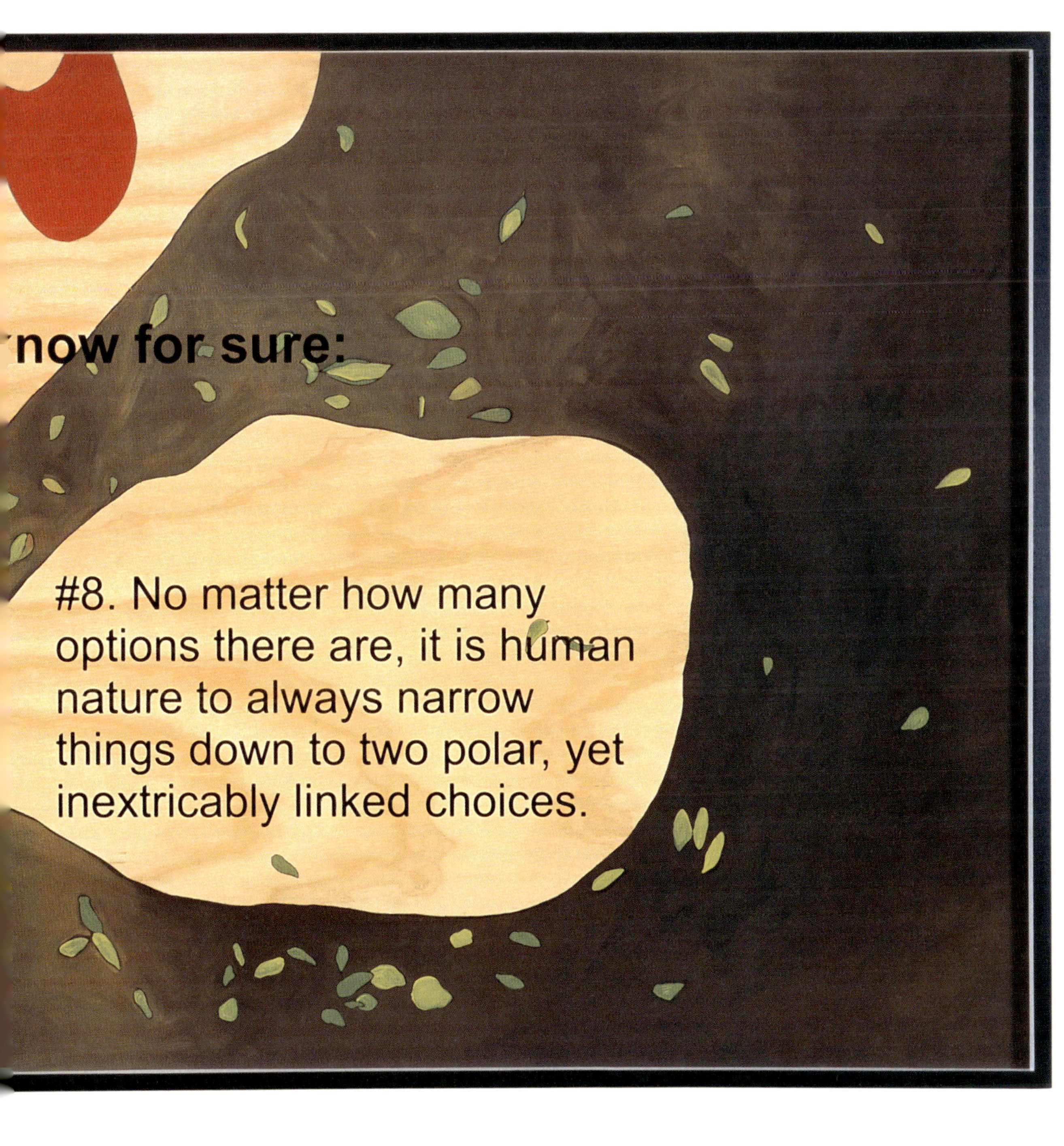
now for sure:

#8. No matter how many
options there are, it is human
nature to always narrow
things down to two polar, yet
inextricably linked choices.

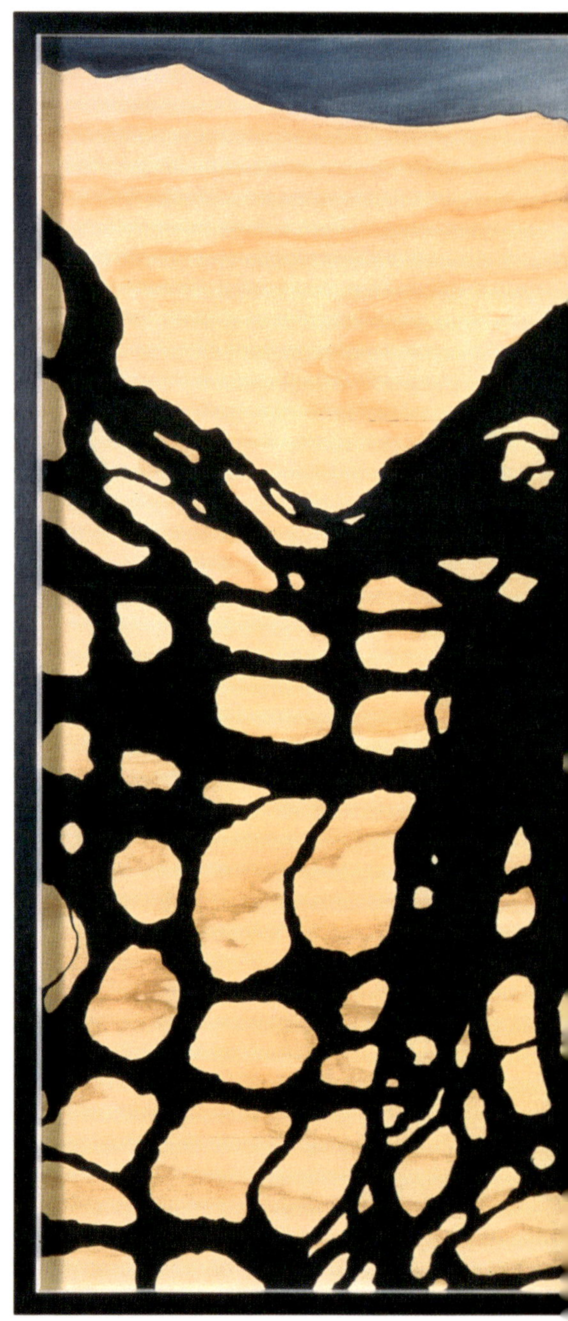

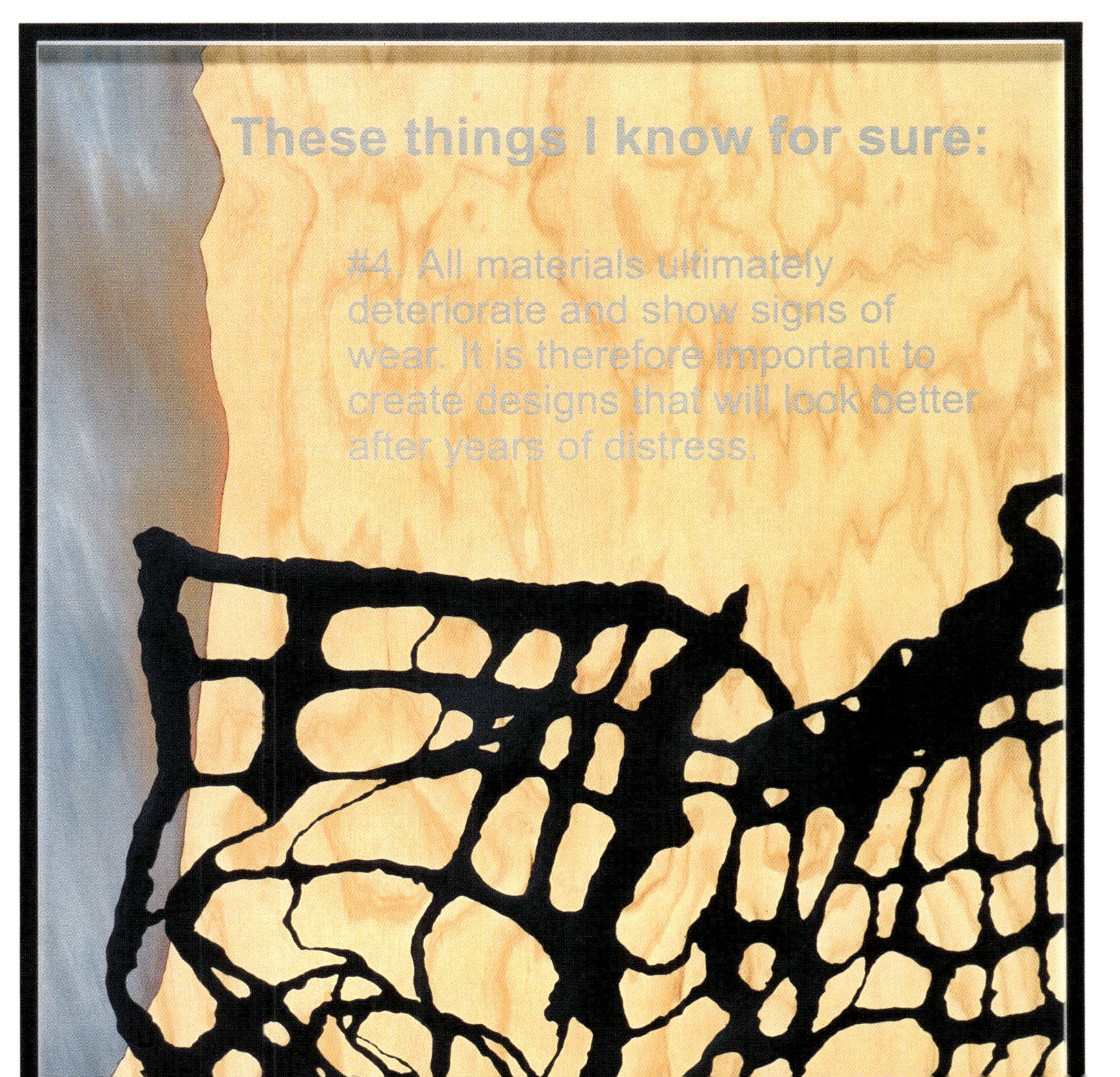

These things I know for sure:

#4. All materials ultimately deteriorate and show signs of wear. It is therefore important to create designs that will look better after years of distress.

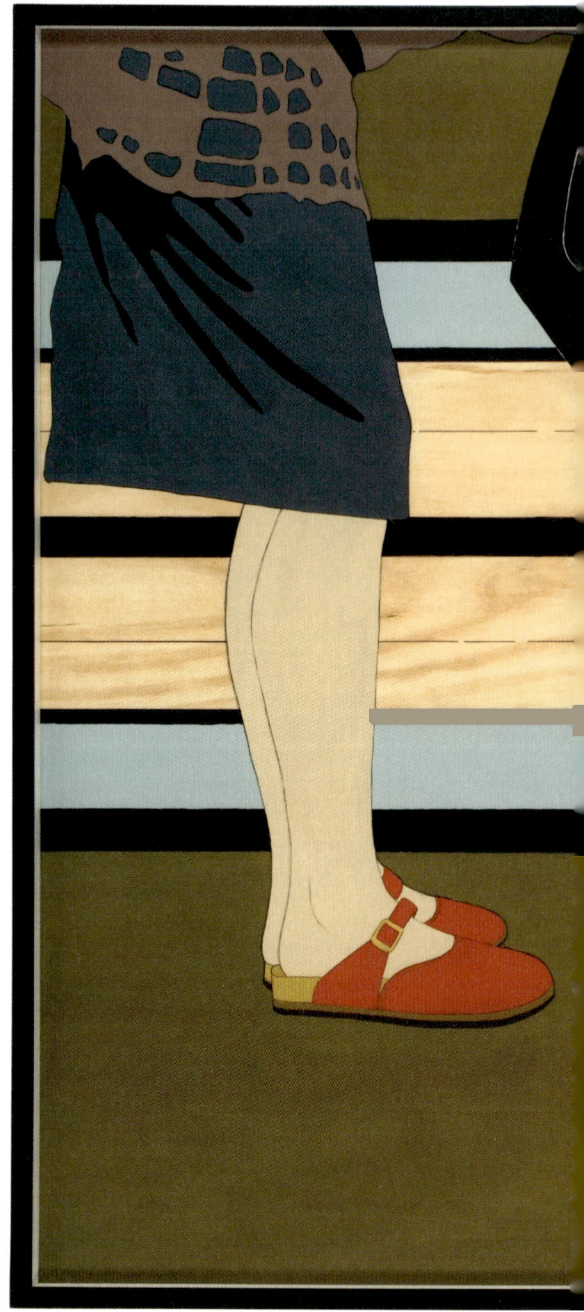

These things I know for sure:

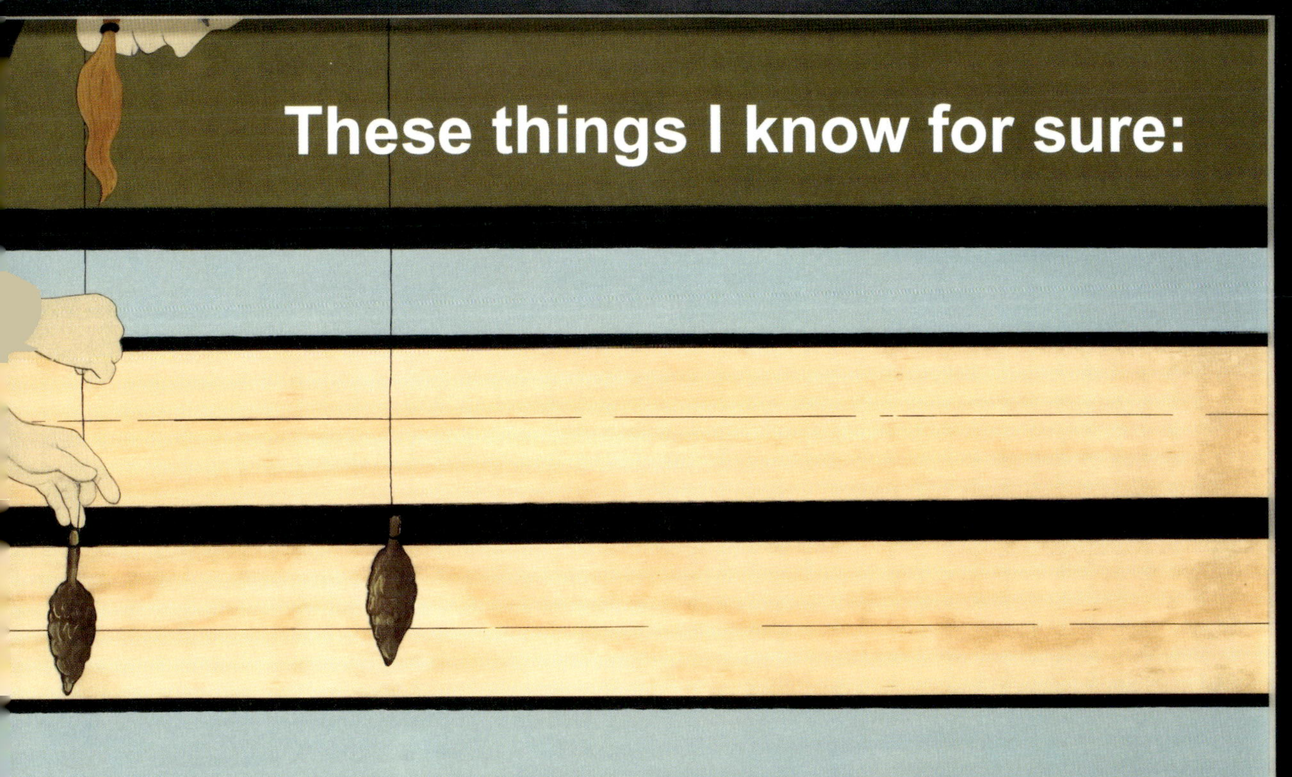

9. The creation of rules is more creative than the
destruction of them. Creation demands a higher
level of reasoning and draws connections
between cause and effect The best rules are
never stable or permanent, but evolve naturally
according to context or need.

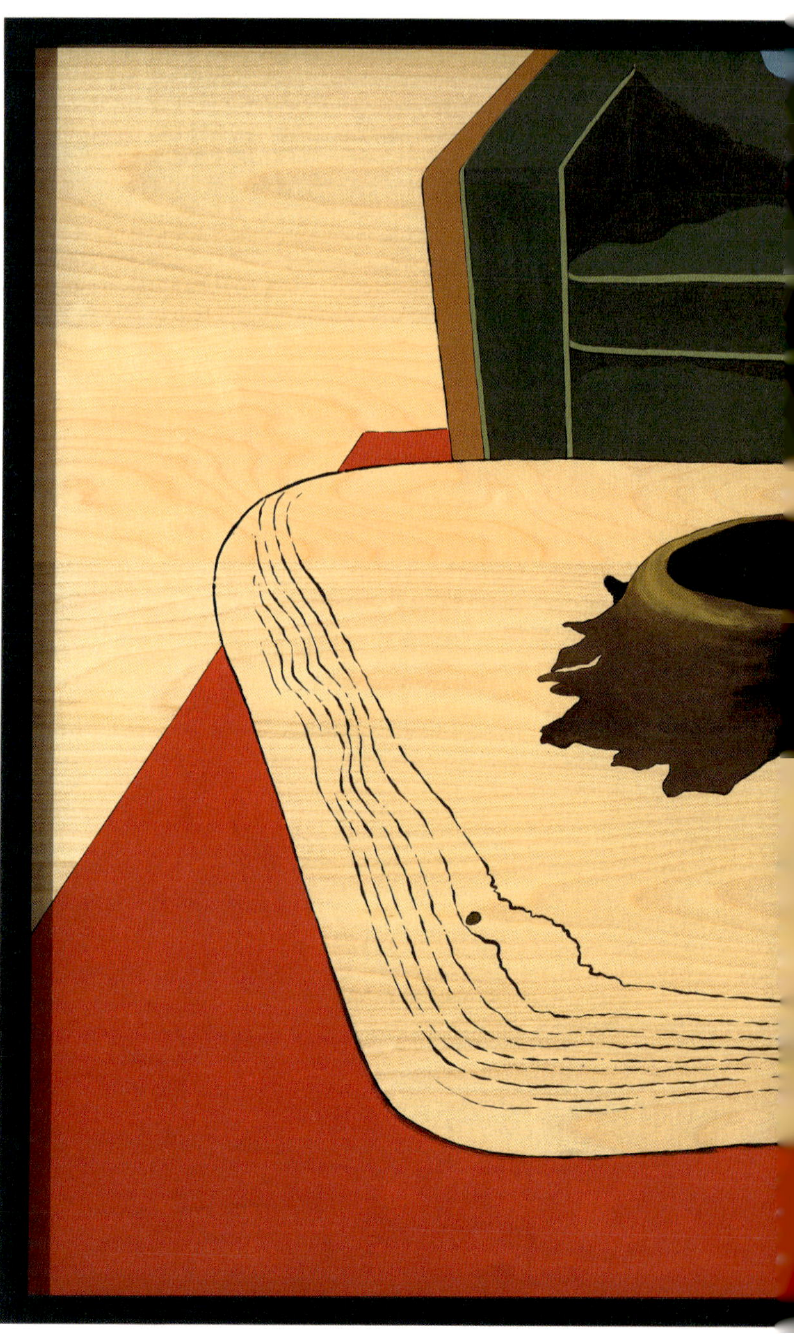

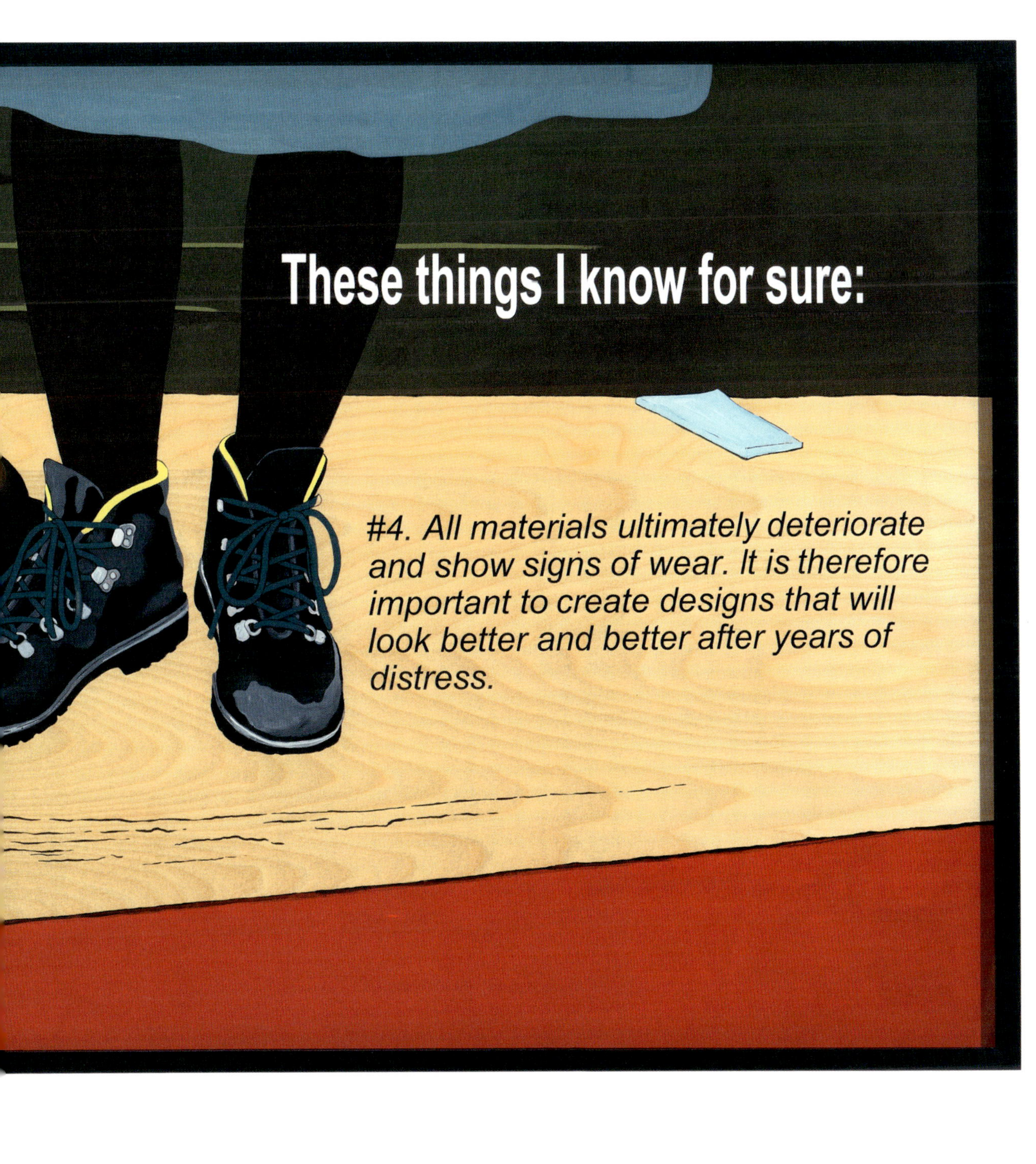
These things I know for sure:

#4. All materials ultimately deteriorate and show signs of wear. It is therefore important to create designs that will look better and better after years of distress.

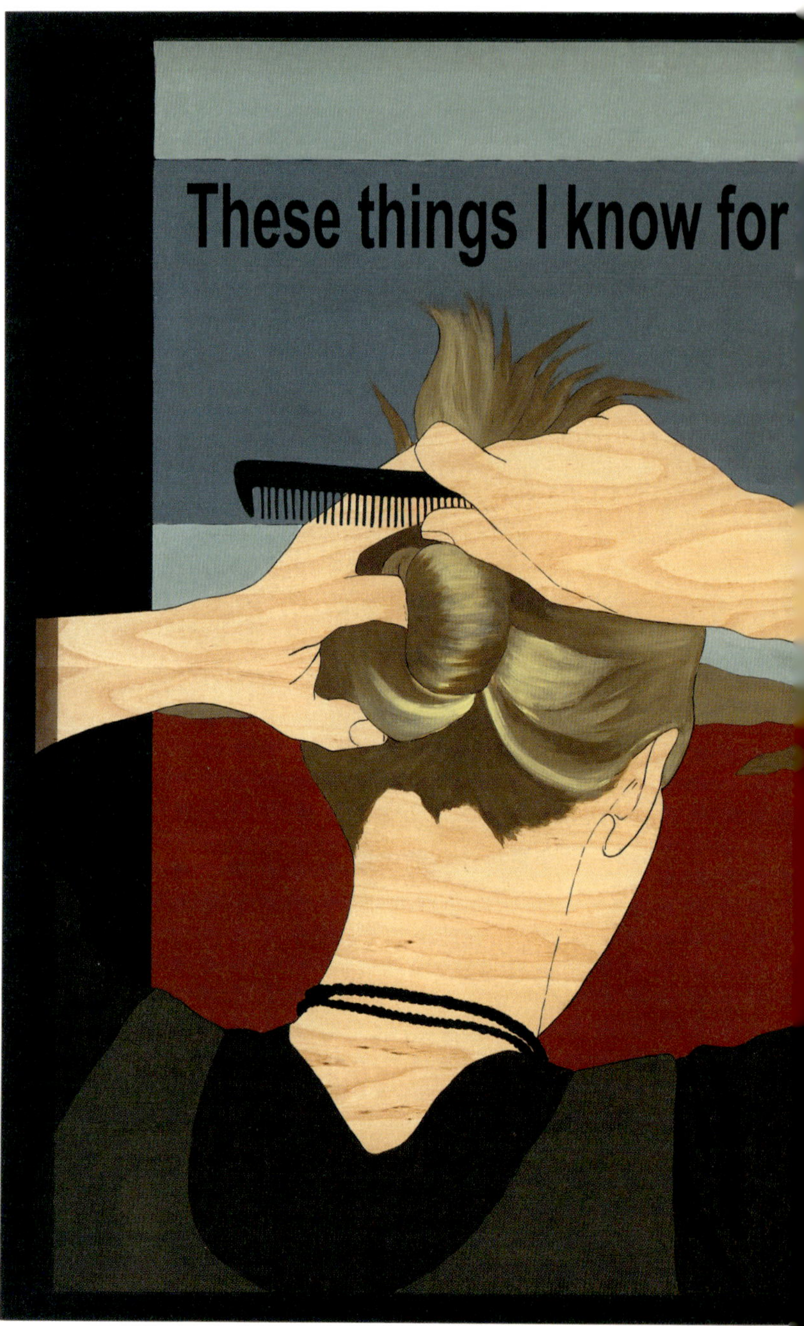
These things I know for

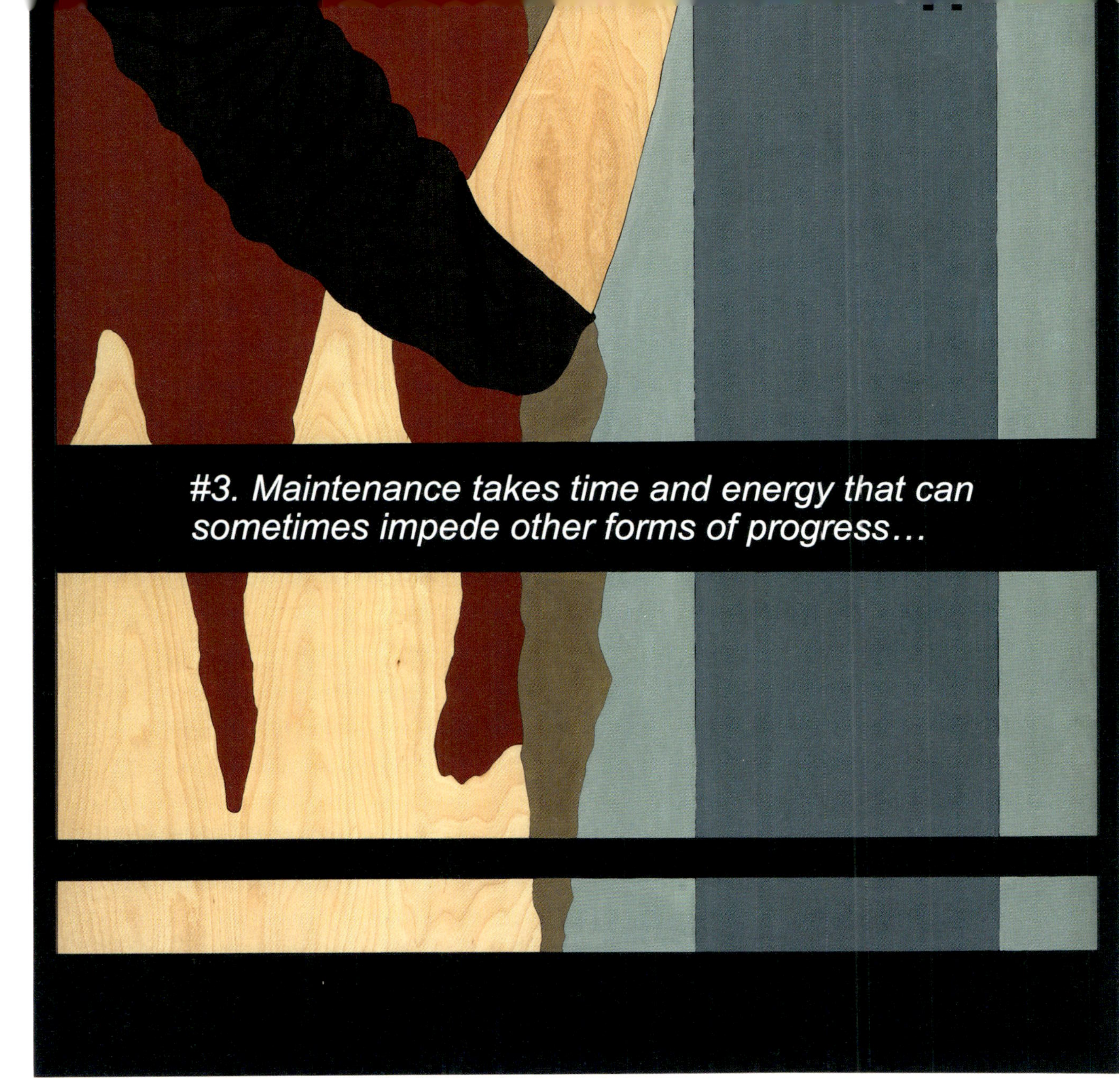
#3. Maintenance takes time and energy that can sometimes impede other forms of progress…

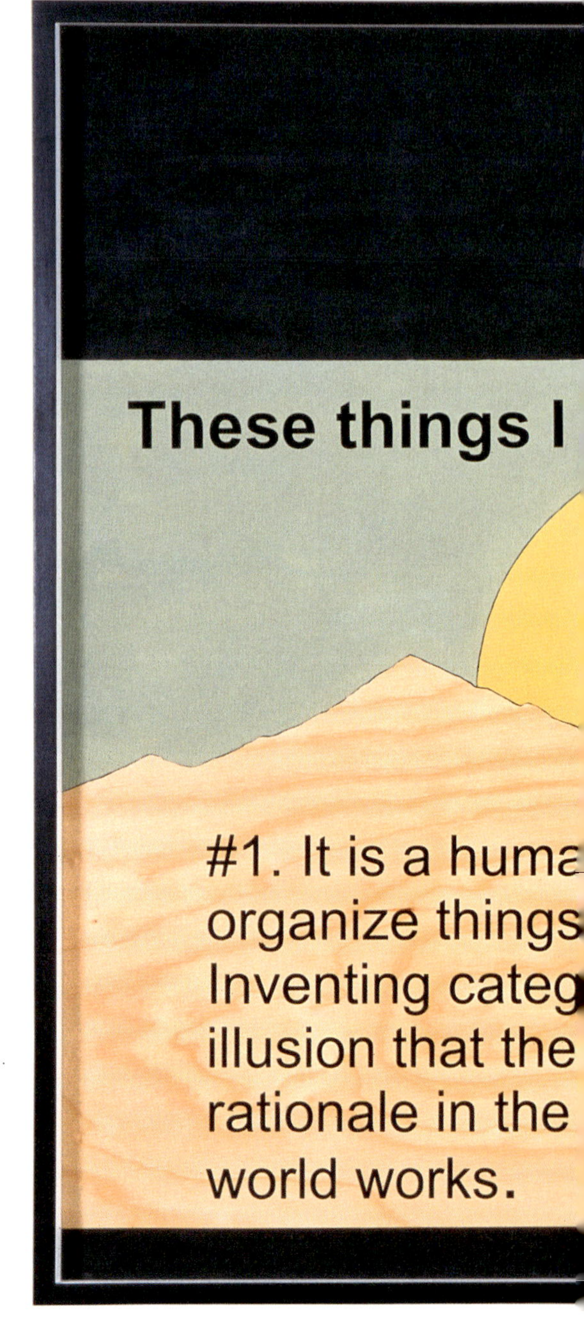
These things I

#1. It is a huma
organize things
Inventing categ
illusion that the
rationale in the
world works.

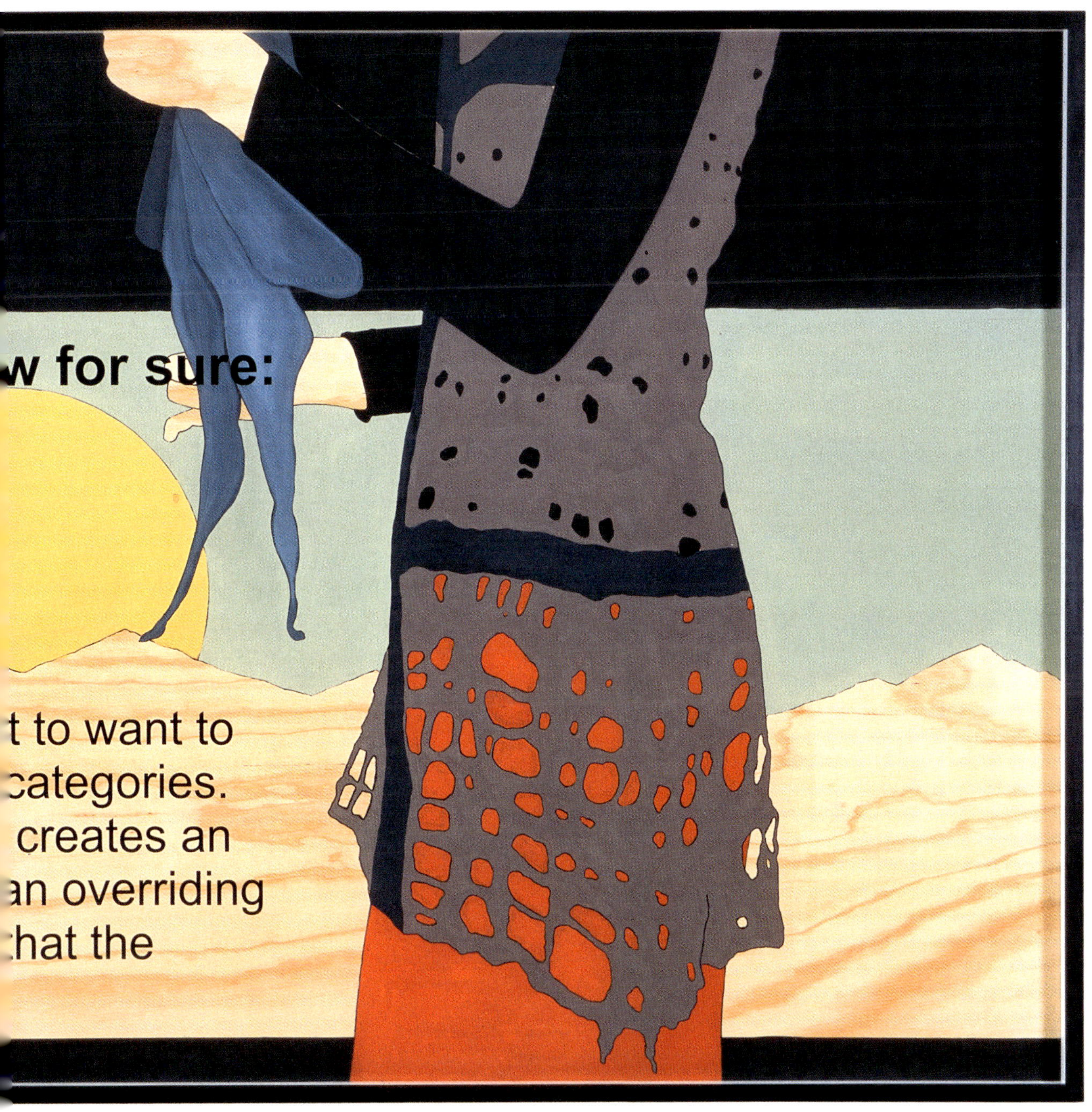
w for sure:
t to want to
categories.
creates an
an overriding
hat the

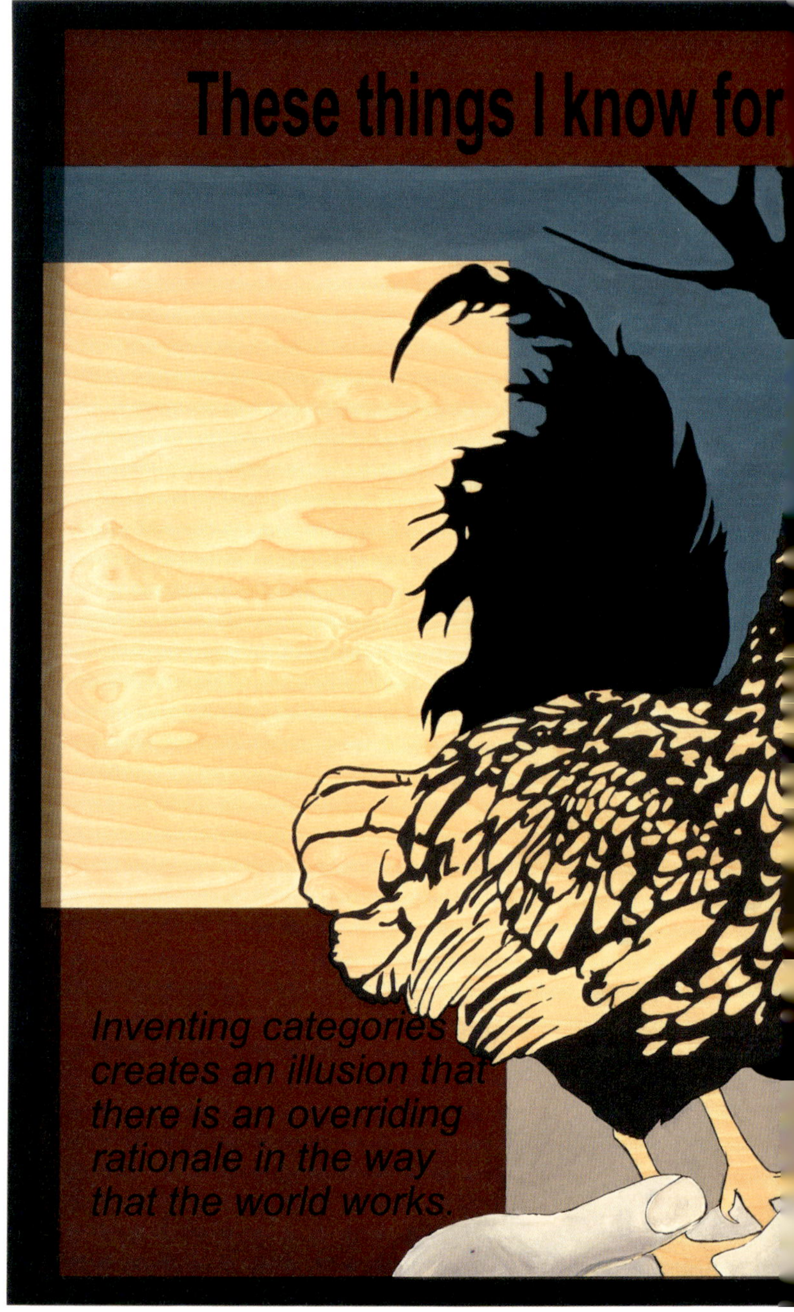
These things I know for
Inventing categories
creates an illusion that
there is an overriding
rationale in the way
that the world works.

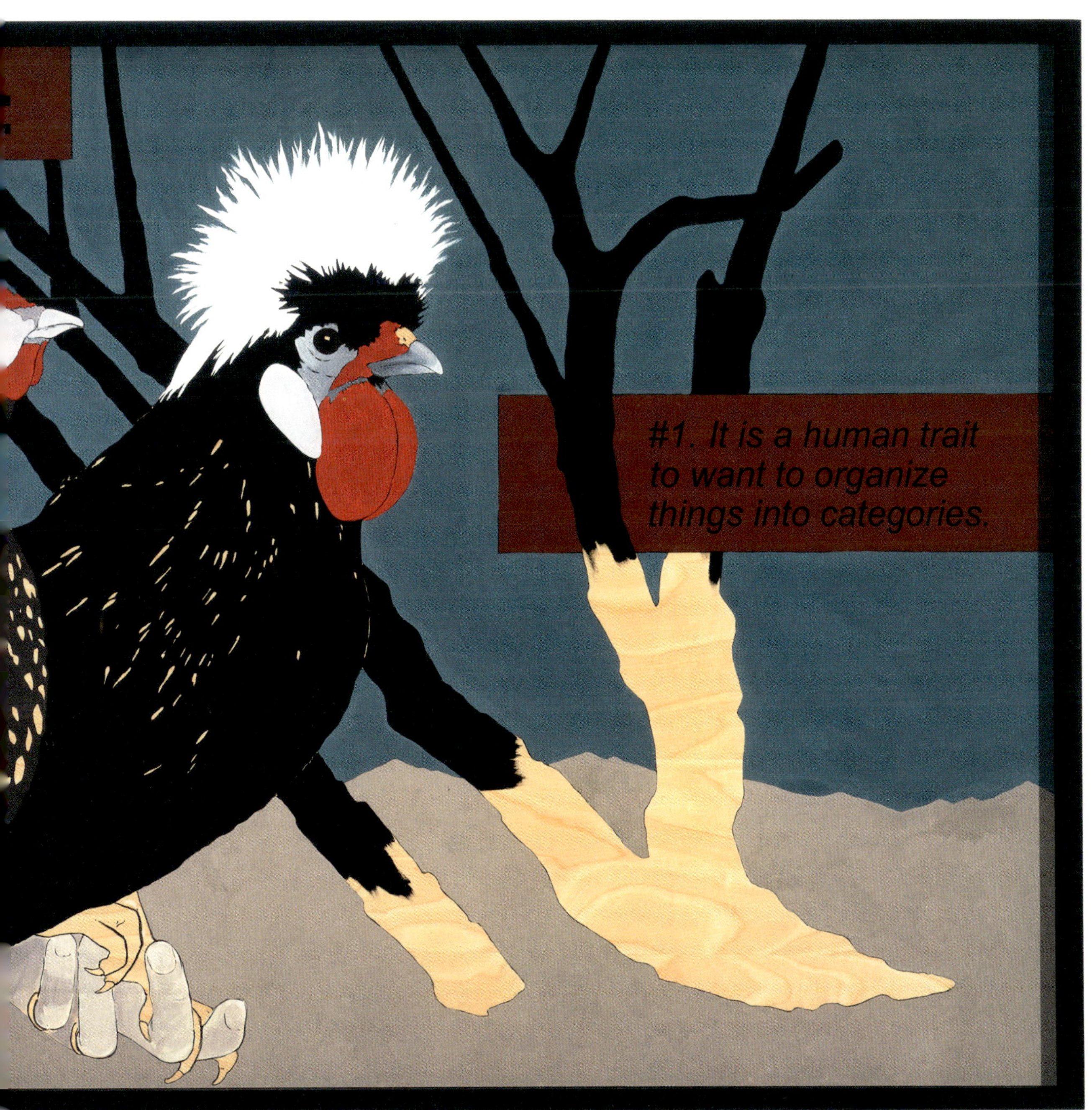
#1. It is a human trait to want to organize things into categories.

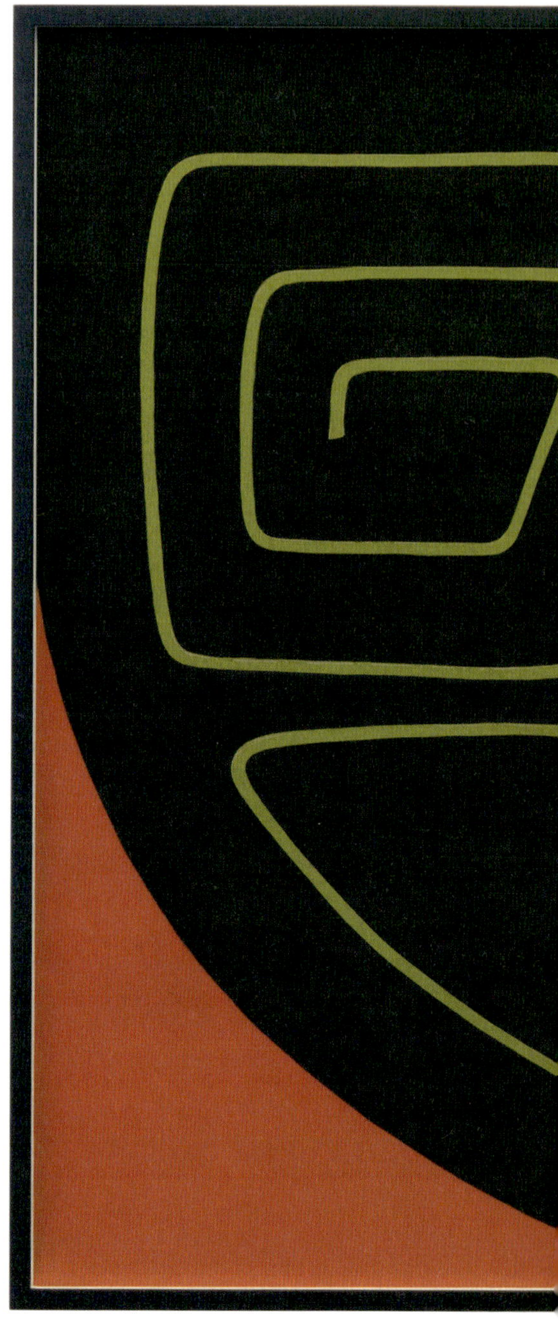

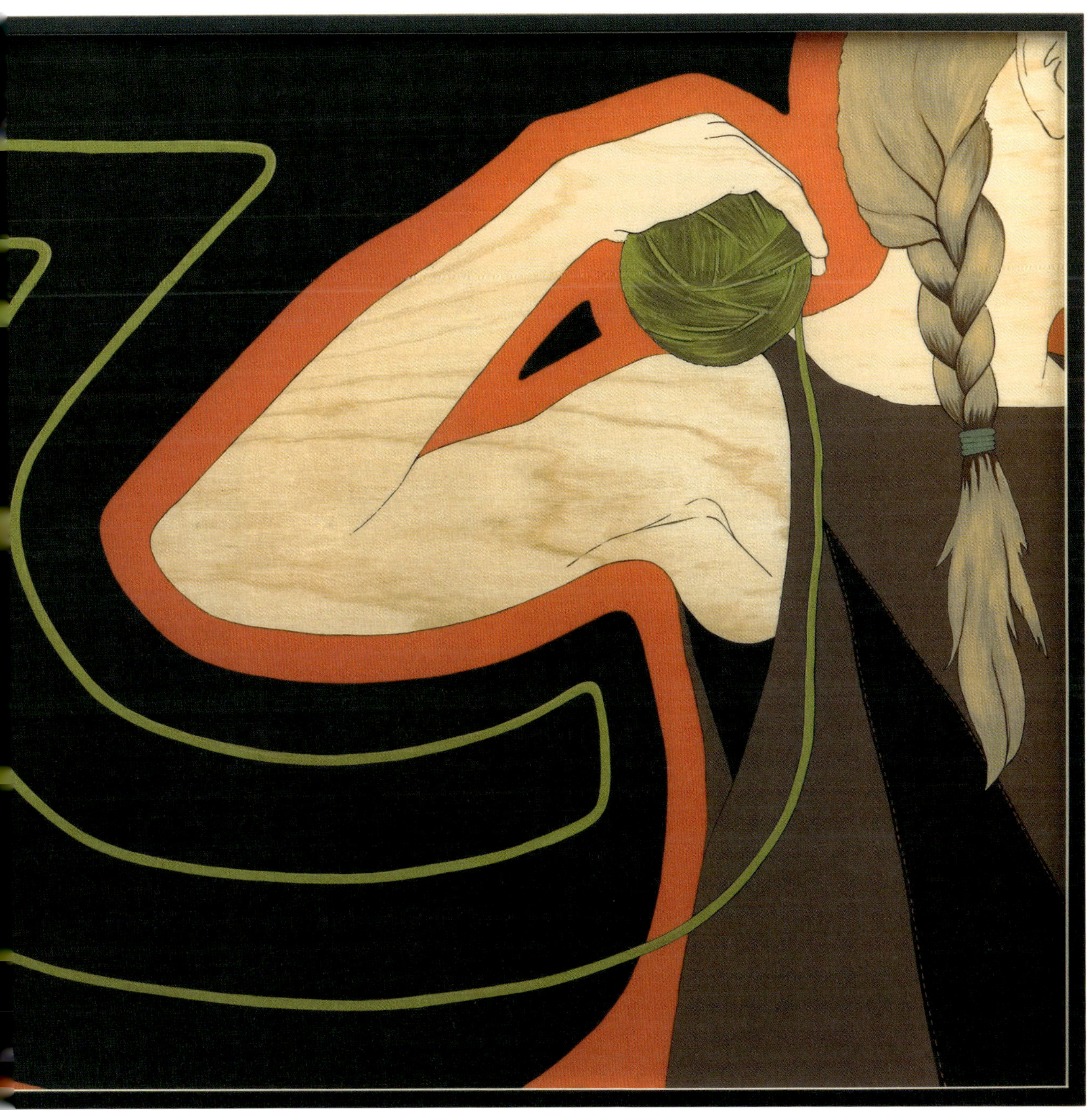

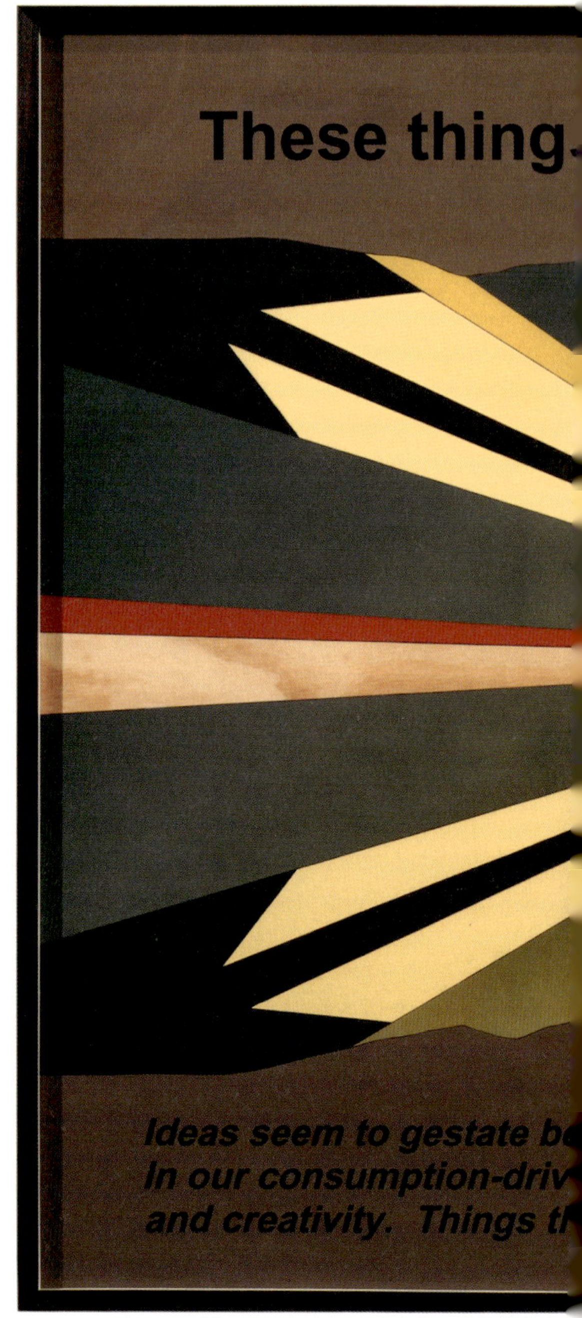
These thing...
Ideas seem to gestate be
In our consumption-driv
and creativity. Things th

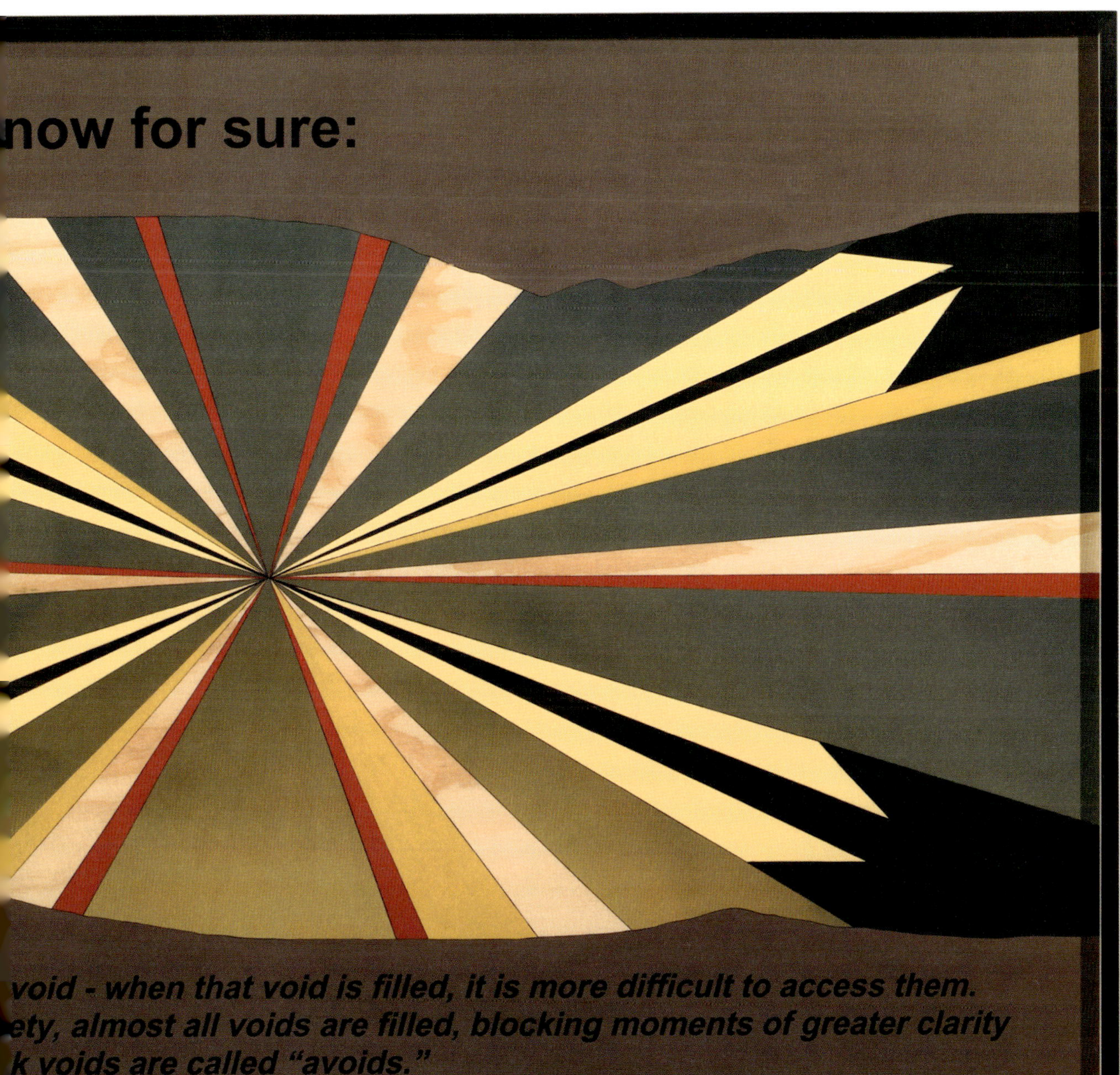

void - when that void is filled, it is more difficult to access them.
ety, almost all voids are filled, blocking moments of greater clarity
k voids are called "avoids."

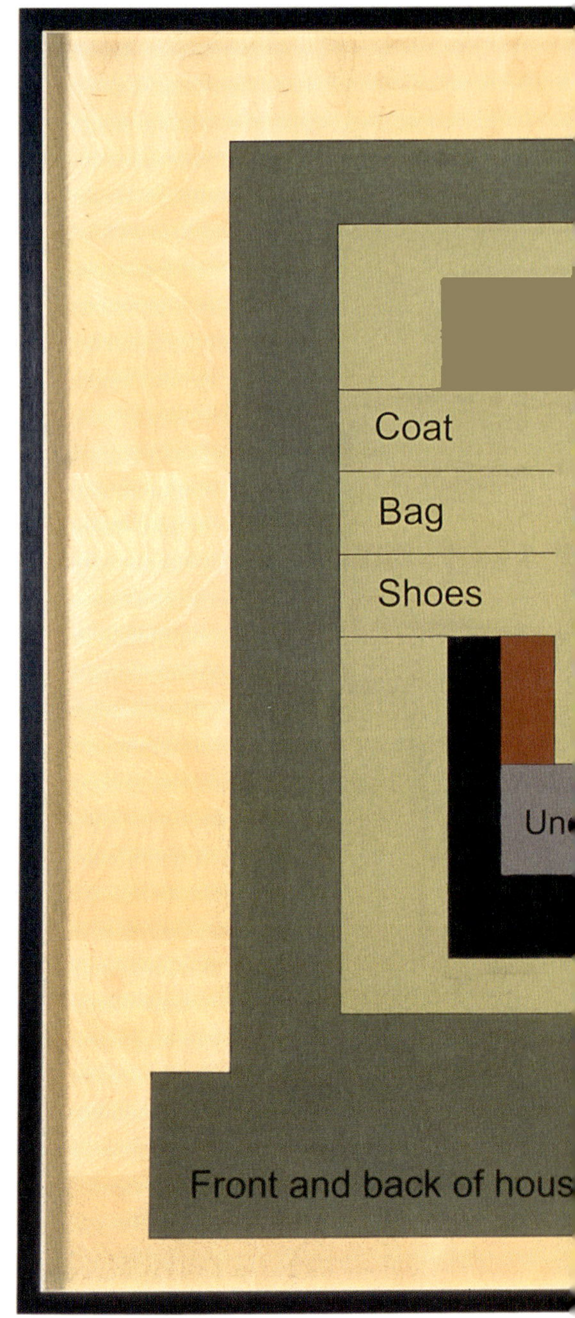
Coat
Bag
Shoes
Un
Front and back of hous

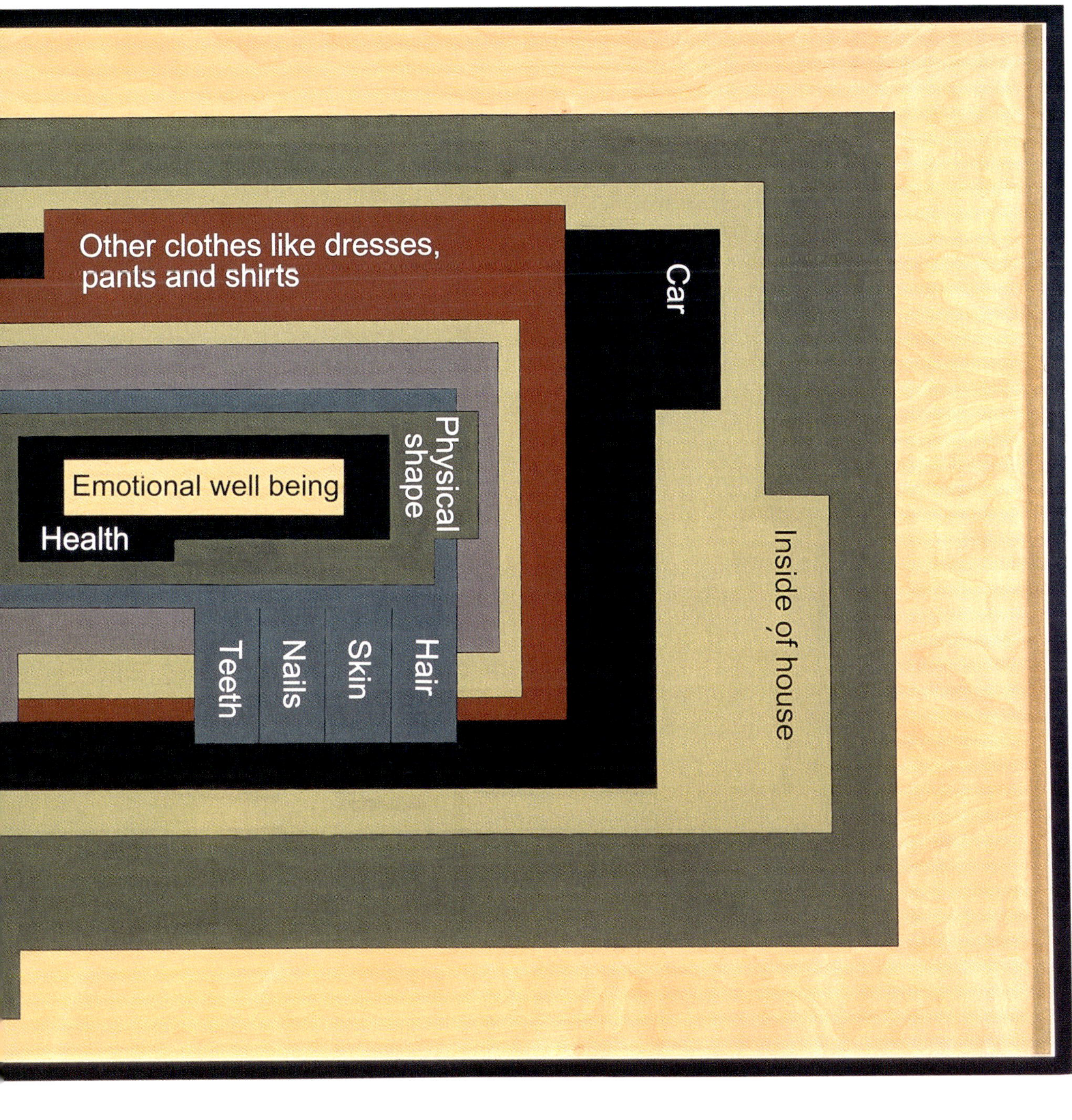

Other clothes like dresses, pants and shirts
Car
Physical shape
Emotional well being
Health
Inside of house
Teeth
Nails
Skin
Hair

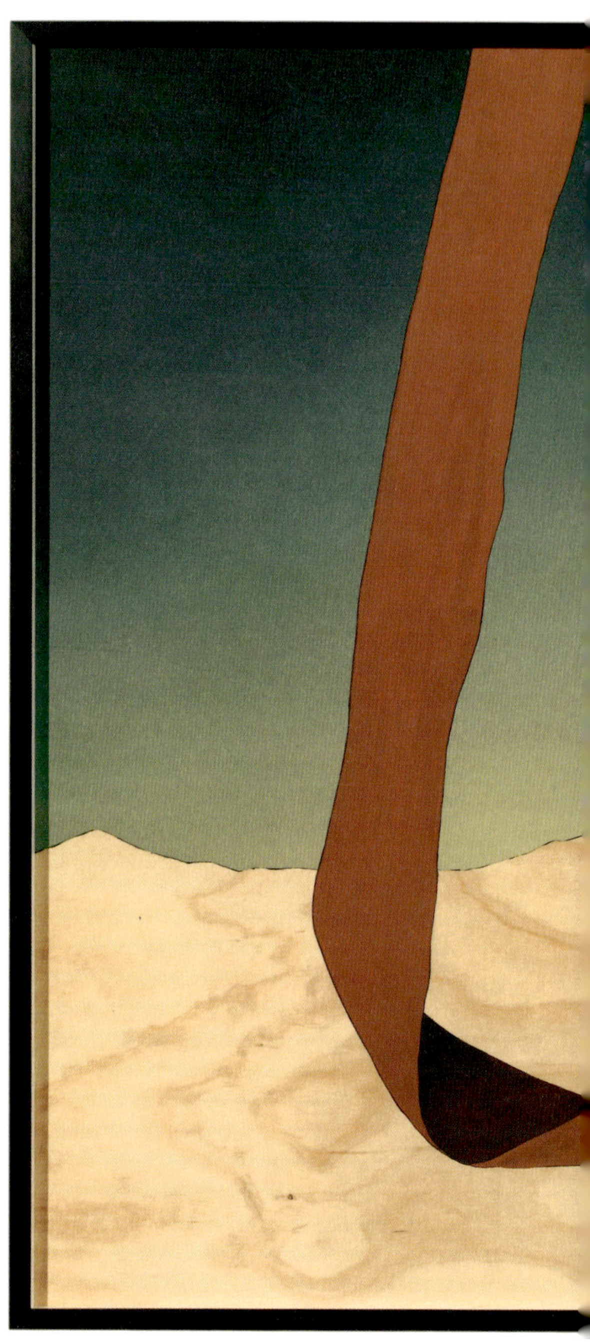

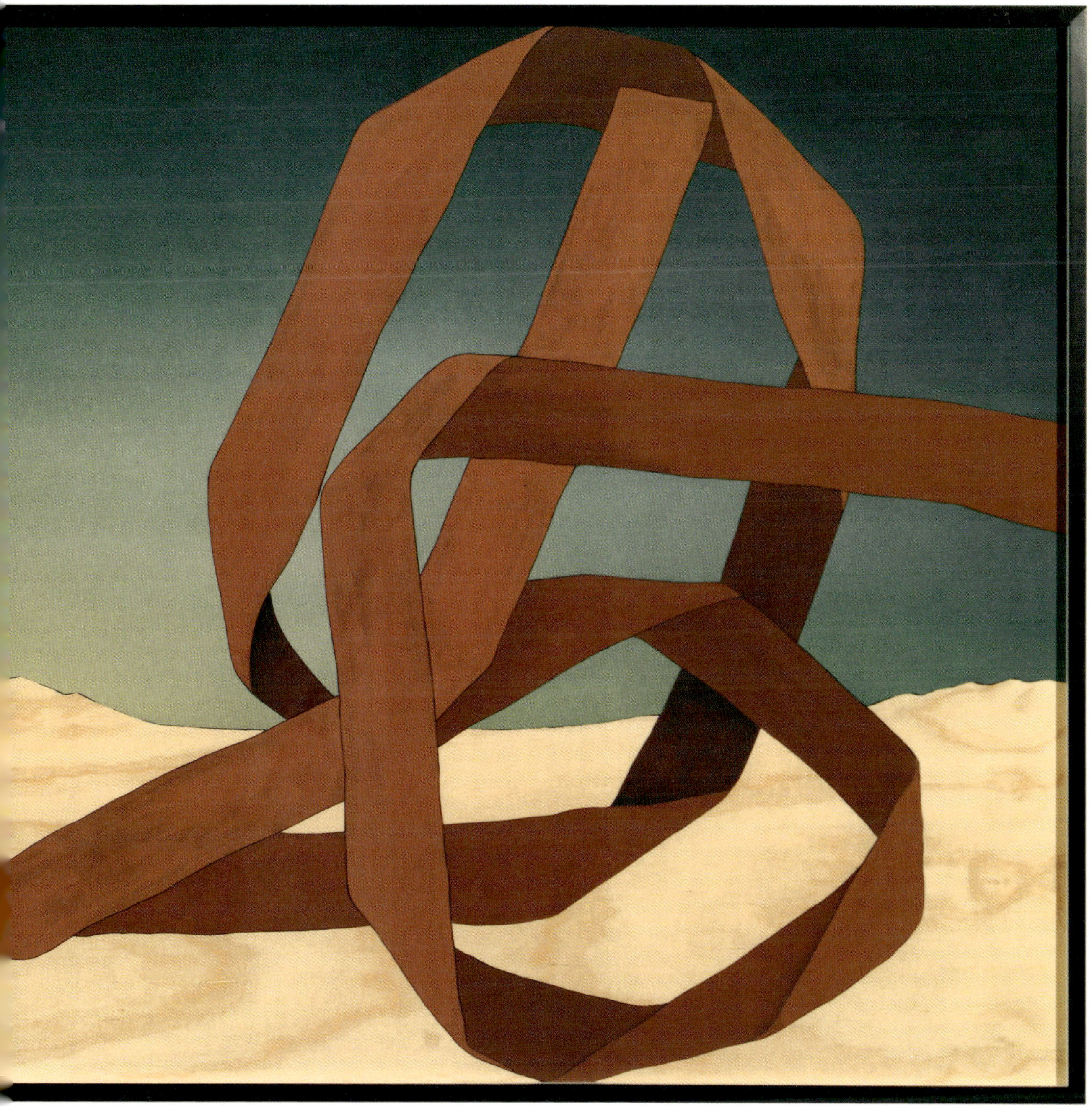

zusammengestellt von / compiled by Bettina Friedli

S. 6 A–Z Time Trials, Note #8 2000; Polyurethanlack, latex- und ölbasierte Farbe, Gouache und Filzstift auf Birkensperrholz; 94 x 63,7 cm; Sammlung Goetz

S. 21 Study for A–Z Carpet Furniture 1992; Gouache und Bleistift auf Papier; 28 x 35.6 cm

S. 22 Study for A–Z Carpet Furniture 1992; Gouache und Bleistift auf Papier; 38 x 50.8 cm

S. 23 Study for A–Z Carpet Furniture 1992; Gouache und Bleistift auf Papier; 38 x 50.8 cm; Privatsammlung, Paris

S. 24 Study for A–Z Carpet Furniture 1992; Gouache und Bleistift auf Papier; 28 x 35.6 cm; Privatsammlung, New York

S. 25 Study for A–Z Carpet Furniture 1992; Gouache und Bleistift auf Papier; 28 x 35.6 cm; Privatsammlung, Stuttgart

S. 26 Study for A–Z Carpet Furniture 1992; Gouache und Bleistift auf Papier; 28 x 35.6 cm

S. 27 Study for A–Z Carpet Furniture 1992; Gouache und Bleistift auf Papier; 28 x 35.6 cm; Privatsammlung, New York

S. 28 Study for A–Z Carpet Furniture 1992; Gouache und Bleistift auf Papier; 28 x 35.6 cm; Privatsammlung, San Francisco

S. 29 Study for A–Z Carpet Furniture 1992; Gouache und Bleistift auf Papier; 28 x 35.6 cm; Privatsammlung, New York

S. 30 Study for A–Z Carpet Furniture 1992; Gouache und Bleistift auf Papier; 38 x 50.8 cm

S. 31 Study for A–Z Carpet Furniture 1992; Gouache und Bleistift auf Papier; 38 x 50.8 cm

S. 32 Study for A–Z Carpet Furniture 1993; Gouache und Bleistift auf Papier; 38 x 50.8 cm

S. 33 Study for A–Z Carpet Furniture 1993; Gouache und Bleistift auf Papier; 38 x 50.8 cm; Privatsammlung, New York

S. 34 Study for A–Z Carpet Furniture 1993; Gouache und Bleistift auf Papier; 38 x 50.8 cm; Besitzer unbekannt

p. 6 A–Z *Time Trials, Note #8* 2000; Polyurethane, latex paint, oil based paint, gouache and pen on birch plywood; 37 x 25"; Goetz Collection

p. 21 *Study for A–Z Carpet Furniture* 1992; gouache and pencil on paper; 11 x 14"

p. 22 *Study for A–Z Carpet Furniture* 1992; gouache and pencil on paper; 15 x 20"

p. 23 *Study for A–Z Carpet Furniture* 1992; gouache and pencil on paper; 15 x 20"; Private Collection, Paris

p. 24 *Study for A–Z Carpet Furniture* 1992; gouache and pencil on paper; 11 x 14"; Private Collection, New York

p. 25 *Study for A–Z Carpet Furniture* 1992; gouache and pencil on paper; 11 x 14"; Private Collection, Stuttgart

p. 26 *Study for A–Z Carpet Furniture* 1992; gouache and pencil on paper; 11 x 14"

p. 27 *Study for A–Z Carpet Furniture* 1992; gouache and pencil on paper; 11 x 14"; Private Collection, New York

p. 28 *Study for A–Z Carpet Furniture* 1992; gouache and pencil on paper; 11 x 14"; Private Collection, San Francisco

p. 29 *Study for A–Z Carpet Furniture* 1992; gouache and pencil on paper; 11 x 14"; Private Collection, New York

p. 30 *Study for A–Z Carpet Furniture* 1992; gouache and pencil on paper; 15 x 20"

p. 31 *Study for A–Z Carpet Furniture* 1992; gouache and pencil on paper; 15 x 20"

p. 32 *Study for A–Z Carpet Furniture* 1993; gouache and pencil on paper; 15 x 20"

p. 33 *Study for A–Z Carpet Furniture* 1993; gouache and pencil on paper; 15 x 20"; Private Collection, New York

p. 34 *Study for A–Z Carpet Furniture* 1993; gouache and pencil on paper; 15 x 20"; owner unknown

S. 35 Study for A–Z Carpet Furniture 1993; 4 Teile; Gouache und Bleistift auf Papier; je 38 x 50.8 cm; Privatsammlung, New York

S. 36 Study for A–Z Carpet Furniture 1993 (Detail); 4 Teile; Gouache und Bleistift auf Papier; je 28 x 35.6 cm

S. 37 Study for A–Z Carpet Furniture 1993; Gouache und Bleistift auf Papier; 38 x 50.8 cm

S. 38 Study for A–Z Carpet Furniture 1993; Gouache und Bleistift auf Papier; 38 x 50.8 cm; Privatsammlung, Paris

S. 39 Study for A–Z Carpet Furniture 1993; Gouache und Bleistift auf Papier; 28 x 38 cm

S. 40o Study for A–Z Ottoman Furniture 1994; Gouache und Bleistift auf Papier; 38 x 50.6 cm; Sammlung Goetz

S. 40u Study for A–Z Ottoman Furniture 1994; Gouache und Bleistift auf Papier; 23 x 30.5 cm; The Museum of Modern Art, New York, Geschenk von Patricia und Morris Orden

S. 41 Study for A–Z Ottoman Furniture 1994; Gouache und Bleistift auf Papier; 23 x 30.5 cm; Privatsammlung, Paris

S. 42 Study for A–Z Ottoman Furniture 1994; Gouache und Bleistift auf Papier; 23 x 30.5 cm; Privatsammlung, New York

S. 43 Study for A–Z Ottoman Furniture 1994; Gouache und Bleistift auf Papier; 28 x 38 cm

S. 44 Study for A–Z Ottoman Furniture 1994; Gouache und Bleistift auf Papier; 38 x 50.8 cm

S. 45 Study for A–Z Ottoman Furniture 1994; Gouache und Bleistift auf Papier; 38 x 50.8 cm

S. 46-47 My Linoleum Floor 1995-1998; 2 Teile; Gouache und Bleistift auf Papier; je 28 x 38 cm

S. 48o Study for A–Z Personal Panels 1994; Gouache auf Papier; 30.5 x 23 cm

S. 48u Study for A–Z Personal Panels 1994; Gouache auf Papier; 30.5 x 23 cm

S. 49 Study for A–Z Personal Panels 1994; Gouache auf Papier; 38 x 50.8 cm; Privatsammlung, Boston

S. 50-51 Eight A–Z Personal Panels 1998; 8 Teile; Gouache auf Papier; je 30.5 x 23 cm; Sammlung Goetz

S. 52 The Making of the RAUGH Skirt 1998; Gouache auf Papier; 38 x 50.8 cm; Privatsammlung, London

p. 35 *Study for A–Z Carpet Furniture* 1993; 4 parts; gouache and pencil on paper; each 15 x 20"; Private Collection, New York

p. 36 *Study for A–Z Carpet Furniture* 1993 (Detail); 4 parts; gouache and pencil on paper; each 11 x 14"

p. 37 *Study for A–Z Carpet Furniture* 1993; gouache and pencil on paper; 15 x 20"

p. 38 *Study for A–Z Carpet Furniture* 1993; gouache and pencil on paper; 15 x 20"; Private Collection, Paris

p. 39 *Study for A–Z Carpet Furniture* 1993; gouache and pencil on paper; 11 x 15"

p. 40t *Study for A–Z Ottoman Furniture* 1994; gouache and pencil on paper; 15 x 20"; Goetz Collection

p. 40b *Study for A–Z Ottoman Furniture* 1994; gouache and pencil on paper; 9 x 12"; The Museum of Modern Art, New York. Gift of Patricia and Morris Orden

p. 41 *Study for A–Z Ottoman Furniture* 1994; gouache and pencil on paper; 9 x 12"; Private Collection, Paris

p. 42 *Study for A–Z Ottoman Furniture* 1994; gouache and pencil on paper; 9 x 12"; Private Collection, New York

p. 43 *Study for A–Z Ottoman Furniture* 1994; gouache and pencil on paper; 11 x 15"

p. 44 *Study for A–Z Ottoman Furniture* 1994; gouache and pencil on paper; 15 x 20"

p. 45 *Study for A–Z Ottoman Furniture* 1994; gouache and pencil on paper; 15 x 20"

p. 46-47 *My Linoleum Floor* 1995-1998; 2 parts; gouache and pencil on paper; each 11 x 15"

p. 48t *Study for A–Z Personal Panels* 1994; gouache on paper; 12 x 9"

p. 48b *Study for A–Z Personal Panels* 1994; gouache on paper; 12 x 9"

p. 49 *Study for A–Z Personal Panels* 1994; gouache on paper; 15 x 20"; Private Collection, Boston

p. 50-51 *Eight A–Z Personal Panels* 1998; 8 parts; gouache on paper; each 12 x 9"; Goetz Collection

p. 52 *The Making of the RAUGH Skirt* 1998; gouache on paper; 15 x 20"; Private Collection, London

S. 53 My Fastest, Most Complete Dress Plan 1998;
Gouache auf Papier; 50.8 x 38 cm; Privatsammlung,
New York

S. 57 The A–Z Escape Vehicle... 1996; Gouache auf
Papier; 42 x 56 cm; Privatsammlung, New York

S. 58 A–Z Escape Vehicle: „Interior World Model"
1996; Gouache auf Papier; 28 x 38 cm; The Museum
of Modern Art, New York, Geschenk von Patricia und
Morris Orden

S. 59 A–Z Escape Vehicle: „Exterior World Model"
1996; Gouache auf Papier; 28 x 38 cm

S. 60 A–Z Logo Study 1996; Gouache auf Papier;
28 x 38 cm; The Museum of Modern Art, New York,
Geschenk von Patricia und Morris Orden

S. 61 A–Z Emblem 1999; Gouache auf Papier; 38 x 28 cm

S. 62 Point of Interest: An A–Z Land Brand 1999;
Gouache auf Papier; 33 x 50.8 cm

S. 63 Point of Interest: An A–Z Land Brand 1999;
Gouache auf Papier; 38 x 50.8 cm; The Museum of
Modern Art, New York, Geschenk von Patricia und
Morris Orden

S. 65 Models for Eating Terrains 2001; Gouache und
Bleistift auf Papier; 30.5 x 23 cm

S. 69 Me in a RAUGH Dress on a Field Trip 1998; Gouache
auf Papier; 50.8 x 38 cm; Privatsammlung, Jersey

S. 70o Attractive Fasteners: Front 1998; Gouache auf
Papier; 25.3 x 38 cm; Privatsammlung

S. 70m Attractive Fasteners: Back 1998; Gouache auf
Papier; 25.3 x 38 cm; Privatsammlung, Frankfurt
am Main

S. 70u The RAUGH Skirt 1998; Gouache auf Papier;
38 x 50.8 cm; Privatsammlung, London

S. 71 Drawstring Skirts 1998; Gouache auf Papier;
38 x 25.3 cm; Privatsammlung, New York

S. 72 Orange A–Z Personal Panel on Our Kitchen Towel
Rack 1998; Gouache auf Papier; 38 x 25.3 cm;
Privatsammlung, Italien

S. 73o Pink A–Z Personal Panel on Table in My
Bedroom 1998; Gouache auf Papier; 25.3 x 38 cm;
Sammlung Goetz

S. 73o Grey A–Z Personal Panel on My Bedroom Floor
1998; Gouache auf Papier; 25.3 x 38 cm

p. 53 *My Fastest, Most Complete Dress Plan* 1998;
gouache on paper; 20 x 15"; Private Collection,
New York

p. 57 *The A–Z Escape Vehicle...* 1996; gouache on
paper; 16 1/2 x 22"; Private Collection, New York

p. 58 *A–Z Escape Vehicle: "Interior World Model"* 1996;
gouache on paper; 11 x 15"; The Museum
of Modern Art, New York. Gift of Patricia and
Morris Orden

p. 59 *A–Z Escape Vehicle: "Exterior World Model"* 1996;
gouache on paper; 11 x 15"

p. 60 *A–Z Logo Study* 1996; gouache on paper; 11 x 15";
The Museum of Modern Art, New York. Gift of Patricia
and Morris Orden

p. 61 *A–Z Emblem* 1999; gouache on paper; 15 x 11"

p. 62 *Point of Interest: An A–Z Land Brand* 1999;
gouache on paper; 13 x 20"

p. 63 *Point of Interest: An A–Z Land Brand* 1999;
gouache on paper; 15 x 20"; The Museum of
Modern Art, New York. Gift of Patricia and
Morris Orden

p. 65 *Models for Eating Terrains* 2001; gouache and
pencil on paper; 12 x 9"

p. 69 *Me in a RAUGH Dress on a Field Trip* 1998; gouache on paper; 20 x 15"; Private Collection, Jersey

p. 70t *Attractive Fasteners: Front* 1998; gouache on
paper; 10 x 15"; Private Collection

p. 70m *Attractive Fasteners: Back* 1998; gouache on
paper; 10 x 15"; Private Collection, Frankfurt
am Main

p. 70b *The RAUGH Skirt* 1998; gouache on paper;
15 x 20"; Private Collection, London

p. 71 *Drawstring Skirts* 1998; gouache on paper;
15 x 10"; Private Collection, New York

p. 72 *Orange A–Z Personal Panel on Our Kitchen Towel
Rack* 1998; gouache on paper; 15 x 10"; Private
Collection, Italy

p. 73t *Pink A–Z Personal Panel on Table in My Bedroom*
1998; gouache on paper; 10 x 15";
Goetz Collection

p. 73b *Grey A–Z Personal Panel on My Bedroom Floor*
1998; gouache on paper; 10 x 15"

S. 74 Sebastian Using Some Traditional Panels 1998; Gouache auf Papier; 38 x 50.8 cm

S. 75 Paper Towels Are Panels Too 1998; Gouache auf Papier; 38 x 50.8 cm; Privatsammlung

S. 76 Me in A–Z Personal Panel in Front of the A–Z 1998; Gouache auf Papier; 50.8 x 38 cm; Sammlung Goetz

S. 77l Me in A–Z Personal Panel with Poppy 1998; Gouache auf Papier; 50.8 x 38 cm; Privatsammlung, Frankfurt

S. 77r Me in A–Z Personal Panel Cleaning A–Z Yard Yacht 1998; Gouache auf Papier; 50.8 x 38 cm; Privatsammlung, Athen

S. 78l A–Z Personal Panel, Brooklyn, NY, 1994 1999; Gouache und Bleistift auf Papier; 76.2 x 56 cm; Privatsammlung, London

S. 78r Me in A–Z Personal Panel in Our Kitchen in Altadena 1998; Gouache auf Papier; 50.8 x 38 cm; Privatsammlung, Jersey

S. 79 A–Z Personal Panel, Altadena, CA, 1998 1999; Gouache und Bleistift auf Papier; 76.2 x 56 cm; Privatsammlung, Frankfurt

S. 82 A–Z Chamber Pot 1999; Gouache auf Papier; 62 x 87.4 cm; Privatsammlung, Berlin

S. 83 Rules of RAUGH 1999; Gouache auf Papier; 72.4 x 101.6 cm

S. 84l The A–Z Body Processing Unit 1999; Gouache auf Papier; 101.6 x 72.4 cm

S. 84r Don't Do Your Dishes 2001; Gouache auf Papier; 76.2 x 56 cm

S. 85 Find New Ways to Position Yourself in the World 2001; Gouache auf Papier; 76.2 x 56 cm

S. 86 Pit Bed vs. Platform Bed 1999; 2 Teile; Gouache auf Papier; je 62 x 87.4 cm; Privatsammlung, New York

S. 87 My Neighbor Charles with His Carpet Furniture 1999; Gouache auf Papier; 72.4 x 101.6 cm; Privatsammlung, Madrid

S. 89 A–Z Food Group for You 2001; Gouache auf Papier; 76.2 x 56 cm

S. 90 A–Z Everlasting and Complete 2001; Gouache auf Papier; 56 x 76.2 cm; Privatsammlung, Mailand

S. 91l A–Z Food Group: The Compounds of Life 2001; Gouache auf Papier; 76.2 x 56 cm; Sammlung Goetz

p. 74 *Sebastian Using Some Traditional Panels* 1998; gouache on paper; 15 x 20"

p. 75 *Paper Towels Are Panels Too* 1998; gouache on paper; 15 x 20"; Private Collection

p. 76 *Me in A–Z Personal Panel in Front of the A–Z* 1998; gouache on paper; 20 x 15"; Goetz Collection

p. 77l *Me in A–Z Personal Panel with Poppy* 1998; gouache on paper; 20 x 15"; Private Collection, Frankfurt

p. 77r *Me in A–Z Personal Panel Cleaning A–Z Yard Yacht* 1998; gouache on paper; 20 x 15"; Private Collection, Athens

p. 78l *A–Z Personal Panel, Brooklyn, NY, 1994* 1999; gouache and pencil on paper; 30 x 22"; Private Collection, London

p. 77r *Me in A–Z Personal Panel in Our Kitchen in Altadena* 1998; gouache on paper; 20 x 15"; Private Collection, Jersey

p. 79 *A–Z Personal Panel, Altadena, CA, 1998* 1999; gouache and pencil on paper; 30 x 22"; Private Collection, Frankfurt

p. 82 *A–Z Chamber Pot* 1999; gouache on paper; 24 x 34"; Private Collection, Berlin

p. 83 *Rules of RAUGH* 1999; gouache on paper; 28 1/2 x 40"

p. 84l *The A–Z Body Processing Unit* 1999; gouache on paper; 40 x 28 1/2"

p. 84r *Don't Do Your Dishes* 2001; gouache on paper; 30 x 22"

p. 85 *Find New Ways to Position Yourself in the World* 2001; gouache on paper; 30 x 22"

p. 86 *Pit Bed vs. Platform Bed* 1999; 2 parts; gouache on paper; each 24 x 34"; Private Collection, New York

p. 87 *My Neighbor Charles with His Carpet Furniture* 1999; gouache on paper; 28 1/2 x 40"; Private Collection, Madrid

p. 89 *A–Z Food Group for You* 2001; gouache on paper; 30 x 22"

p. 90 *A–Z Everlasting and Complete* 2001; gouache on paper; 22 x 30"; Private Collection, Milan

p. 91l *A–Z Food Group: The Compounds of Life* 2001; gouache on paper; 30 x 22"; Goetz Collection

S. 91r Me Making Squash in My A–Z Food Processing Unit 2001; Gouache auf Papier; 76.2 x 56 cm

S. 94-97 Free Running Rhythms and Patterns: Version II 2000; 28 Teile; Walnussfurnier, auf Latex- und Öl basierte Farbe, Vinylbeschriftung, schwarz-weiss Fotografien; je 201 x 80 x 5 cm; Privatsammlung, Essen

S. 98 Study for A–Z Cellular Compartment Units #8 2002; Gouache und Tusche auf Papier; 20.3 x 40.6 cm; Privatsammlung, New York

S. 99 Study for A–Z Cellular Compartment Units #7 2002; Gouache und Tusche auf Papier; 40.6 x 40.6 cm; Privatsammlung, Athen

S. 101 Study for A–Z Cellular Compartment Units #2 2002; Gouache und Tusche auf Papier; 20.3 x 56 cm; Deka Bank, Frankfurt am Main

S. 102 Sprawl #2 2001; 1 Gouache auf Papier und 15 Inkjetprints auf Papier; insgesamt 99 x 78.7 cm; Privatsammlung, USA

S. 103 Sprawl #3 2001; 1 Gouache auf Papier und 15 Inkjetprints auf Papier; insgesamt 101.6 x 78.7 cm; Privatsammlung, Dallas

S. 104 Sprawl #1 2001; 1 Gouache auf Papier und 15 Inkjetprints auf Papier; insgesamt 101.6 x 71 cm

S. 105 A–Z Suburban Islands I 2001; 1 Gouache auf Papier und 19 Inkjetprints auf Papier; insgesamt 96.8 x 99.4 cm

S. 106 A–Z Suburban Islands IV 2001; 1 Gouache auf Papier und 15 Inkjetprints auf Papier; insgesamt 78.7 x 78.7 cm

S. 107 Sprawl #4 2001; 1 Gouache auf Papier und 15 Inkjetprints auf Papier; insgesamt 91 x 83 cm; Emanuel Hoffmann-Stiftung, Depositum in der Öffentlichen Kunstsammlung Basel

S. 111 A–Z Homestead Units #2 2001; Acryl, Gouache und Filzstift auf Papier; 46 x 58.6 cm; Sammlung Deutsche Bank

S. 112 A–Z Homestead Units #6 2001; Acryl, Gouache und Filzstift auf Papier; 46 x 58.6 cm; Sammlung Deutsche Bank

S. 113 A–Z Homestead Units #4 (orange) 2001; Acryl, Gouache und Filzstift auf Papier; 26.7 x 33.5 cm; Privatsammlung, London

S. 114 A–Z Advanced Technologies: Study for Billboard (at A–Z West) #1 2002; Flashe und Filzstift auf Birkensperrholz; 40.6 x 40.6 cm; Privatsammlung, Schweiz

p. 91r *Me Making Squash in My A–Z Food Processing Unit* 2001; gouache on paper; 30 x 22"

p. 94-97 *Free Running Rhythms and Patterns: Version II* 2000; 28 parts; walnut veneer, latex and oil-based paint, vinyl lettering, black-and-white photos; each 79 1/8 x 31 1/2 x 2"; Private Collection, Essen

p. 98 *Study for A–Z Cellular Compartment Units #8* 2002; gouache and ink on paper; 8 x 16"; Private Collection, New York

p. 99 *Study for A–Z Cellular Compartment Units #7* 2002; gouache and ink on paper; 16 x 16"; Private Collection, Athens

p. 101 *Study for A–Z Cellular Compartment Units #2* 2002; gouache and ink on paper; 8 x 22"; Deka Bank, Frankfurt am Main

p. 102 *Sprawl #2* 2001; 1 unique gouache on paper and 15 inkjet prints; overall 39 x 31"; Private Collection, USA

p. 103 *Sprawl #3* 2001; 1 unique gouache on paper and 15 inkjet prints; overall 40 x 31"; Private Collection, Dallas

p. 104 *Sprawl #1* 2001; 1 unique gouache on paper and 15 inkjet prints; overall 40 x 28"

p. 105 *A–Z Suburban Islands I* 2001; 1 unique gouache on paper and 19 inkjet prints; overall 38 1/8 x 39 1/8"

p. 106 *A–Z Suburban Islands IV* 2001; 1 unique gouache on paper and 15 inkjet prints; overall 31 x 31"

p. 107 *Sprawl #4* 2001; 1 unique gouache on paper and 15 inkjet prints; overall 35 4/5 x 32 3/5"; Emanuel Hoffmann Foundation, on permanent loan to the Öffentliche Kunstsammlung Basel

p. 111 *A–Z Homestead Units #2* 2001; acrylic, gouache and pen on paper; 18 x 23"; Collection Deutsche Bank

p. 112 *A–Z Homestead Units #6* 2001; acrylic, gouache and pen on paper; 18 x 23"; Collection Deutsche Bank

p. 113 *A–Z Homestead Units #4 (orange)* 2001; acrylic, gouache and pen on paper; 10 x 13"; Private Collection, London

p. 114 *A–Z Advanced Technologies: Study for Billboard (at A–Z West) #1* 2002; Flashe and pen on birch plywood; 16 x 16"; Private Collection, Switzerland

S. 115 A–Z Advanced Technologies: Study for Billboard (at A–Z West) #2 2002; Flashe und Filzstift auf Birkensperrholz; 40.6 x 40.6 cm; Privatsammlung, Schweiz

S. 116 A–Z Advanced Technologies: Study for Billboard (at A–Z West) #3 2002; Flashe und Filzstift auf Birkensperrholz; 40.6 x 40.6 cm; Privatsammlung, Schweiz

S. 117 A–Z Advanced Technologies: Study for Billboard (at A–Z West) #4 2002; Flashe und Filzstift auf Birkensperrholz; 40.6 x 40.6 cm; Privatsammlung, Schweiz

S. 119 A–Z Advanced Technologies: Me in a Green Fiber Form in Front of A–Z West 2002; Gouache und Filzstift auf Papier; 23 x 30.5 cm; Emanuel Hoffmann-Stiftung, Depositum in der Öffentlichen Kunstsammlung Basel

S. 120o A–Z Advanced Technologies: Me Wearing a Flame Fiber Form in Front of A–Z West #1 2002; Gouache und Filzstift auf Papier; 23 x 30.5 cm; Emanuel Hoffmann-Stiftung, Depositum in der Öffentlichen Kunstsammlung Basel

S. 120u A–Z Advanced Technologies: Me Wearing a Brown Fiber Form While Working at RAUGH Desk 2002; Gouache und Filzstift auf Papier; 23 x 30.5 cm; Emanuel Hoffmann-Stiftung, Depositum in der Öffentlichen Kunstsammlung Basel

S. 121o A–Z Advanced Technologies: Me Wearing a Green Fiber Form & Cooking at „Food Prep Station" #1 2002; Gouache und Filzstift auf Papier; 23 x 30.5 cm; Emanuel Hoffmann-Stiftung, Depositum in der Öffentlichen Kunstsammlung Basel

S. 121u A–Z Advanced Technologies: Me Wearing a Black Fiber Form and Sitting on the Sofa at A–Z West #3 2002; Gouache und Filzstift auf Papier; 23 x 30.5 cm

S. 122 Smock Shop 2006; Gouache auf Papier; 23 x 30.5 cm; Museum of Art, Rhode Island School of Design: Paula and Leonard Granoff Fund, 2008.10.2

S. 123 Wear What You Work 2006; Gouache auf Papier; 30.5 x 23 cm

S. 125 Study for Billboard: Feet on Stepping Stones 2006; Gouache und Bleistift auf Papier; 23 x 30.5 cm

S. 126 Tamarisks at A–Z West 2006; Gouache und Bleistift auf Papier; 23 x 30.5 cm

S. 127 Forward Motion: Highway 62 to Joshua Tree 2006; Gouache und Bleistift auf Papier; 23 x 30.5 cm

S. 128 Snow on Regenerating Field, A–Z West, November 2004 2004; Gouache und Bleistift auf Papier; 23 x 30.5 cm; Privatsammlung, Los Angeles

p. 115 *A–Z Advanced Technologies: Study for Billboard (at A–Z West) #2* 2002; Flashe and pen on birch plywood; 16 x 16"; Private Collection, Switzerland

p. 116 *A–Z Advanced Technologies: Study for Billboard (at A–Z West) #3* 2002; Flashe and pen on birch plywood; 16 x 16"; Private Collection, Switzerland

p. 117 *A–Z Advanced Technologies: Study for Billboard (at A–Z West) #4* 2002; Flashe and pen on birch plywood; 16 x 16"; Private Collection, Switzerland

p. 119 *A–Z Advanced Technologies: Me in a Green Fiber Form in Front of A–Z West* 2002; gouache and pen on paper; 9 x 12"; Emanuel Hoffmann Foundation, on permanent loan to the Öffentliche Kunstsammlung Basel

p. 120t *A–Z Advanced Technologies: Me Wearing a Flame Fiber Form in Front of A–Z West #1* 2002; gouache and pen on paper; 9 x 12"; Emanuel Hoffmann Foundation, on permanent loan to the Öffentliche Kunstsammlung Basel

p. 120b *A–Z Advanced Technologies: Me Wearing a Brown Fiber Form While Working at RAUGH Desk* 2002; gouache and pen on paper; 9 x 12"; Emanuel Hoffmann Foundation, on permanent loan to the Öffentliche Kunstsammlung Basel

p. 121t *A–Z Advanced Technologies: Me Wearing a Green Fiber Form & Cooking at "Food Prep Station" #1* 2002; gouache and pen on paper; 9 x 12"; Emanuel Hoffmann Foundation, on permanent loan to the Öffentliche Kunstsammlung Basel

p. 121b *A–Z Advanced Technologies: Me Wearing a Black Fiber Form and Sitting on the Sofa at A–Z West #3* 2002; gouache and pen on paper; 9 x 12"

p. 122 *Smock Shop* 2006; gouache on paper; 9 x 12"; Museum of Art, Rhode Island School of Design: Paula and Leonard Granoff Fund, 2008.10.2

p. 123 *Wear What You Work* 2006; gouache on paper; 12 x 9"

p. 125 *Study for Billboard: Feet on Stepping Stones* 2006; gouache and pencil on paper; 9 x 12"

p. 126 *Tamarisks at A–Z West* 2006; gouache and pencil on paper; 9 x 12

p. 127 *Forward Motion: Highway 62 to Joshua Tree* 2006; gouache and pencil on paper; 9 x 12"

p. 128 *Snow on Regenerating Field, A–Z West, November 2004* 2004; gouache and pencil on paper; 9 x 12"; Private Collection, Los Angeles

S. 129 Rock in Wash Behind A–Z West 2004; Gouache und Bleistift auf Papier; 23 x 30.5 cm

p. 129 *Rock in Wash Behind A–Z West* 2004; gouache and pencil on paper; 9 x 12"

S. 130 Gold Star Crochet Piece 2006; Gouache und Bleistift auf Papier; 23 x 30.5 cm; Privatsammlung, Athen

p. 130 *Gold Star Crochet Piece* 2006; gouache and pencil on paper; 9 x 12"; Private Collection, Athens

S. 131 A–Z Fiber Form, Looks like a Collapsing Grid, February 2005 2005; Gouache und Bleistift auf Papier; 23 x 30.5 cm; Privatsammlung, New York

p. 131 *A–Z Fiber Form, Looks like a Collapsing Grid, February 2005* 2005; gouache and pencil on paper; 9 x 12"; Private Collection, New York

S. 133o Working on Nightstand at Secret L.A. House, December 2004 2004; Gouache und Bleistift auf Papier; 23 x 30.5 cm

p. 133t *Working on Nightstand at Secret L.A. House, December 2004* 2004; gouache and pencil on paper; 9 x 12"

S. 133m Carving New RAUGH Furniture, A–Z West, October 2004 2004; Gouache und Bleistift auf Papier; 23 x 30.5 cm

p. 133m *Carving New RAUGH Furniture, A–Z West, October 2004* 2004; gouache and pencil on paper; 9 x 12"

S. 133u First Flaw in New RAUGH Furniture at A–Z West, January 2005 2005; Gouache und Bleistift auf Papier; 23 x 30.5 cm

p. 133b *First Flaw in New RAUGH Furniture at A–Z West, January 2005* 2005; gouache and pencil on paper; 9 x 12"

S. 134 Filing System, Joshua Tree, March 2004 2004; Gouache und Bleistift auf Papier; 23 x 30.5 cm; Privatsammlung, Deutschland

p. 134 *Filing System, Joshua Tree, March 2004* 2004; gouache and pencil on paper; 9 x 12"; Private Collection, Germany

S. 135 Favorite Felted Bowl (that I want to keep) 2004; Gouache und Bleistift auf Papier; 23 x 30.5 cm

p. 135 *Favorite Felted Bowl (that I want to keep)* 2004; gouache and pencil on paper; 9 x 12"

S. 136 Testing/Testing 2006; 2 Teile; Gouache auf Papier; je 23 x 30.5 cm

p. 136 *Testing/Testing* 2006; 2 parts; gouache on paper; each 9 x 12"

S. 137 The Same but Different 2006; 2 Teile; Gouache auf Papier; je 23 x 30.5 cm; Privatsammlung, Zürich

p. 137 *The Same but Different* 2006; 2 parts; gouache on paper; each 9 x 12"; Private Collection, Zurich

S. 141 Prototype for Billboard at A–Z West: These Things I Know for Sure #14 2005; Flashe-Vinylfarbe, Vinylbeschriftung und Polyurethanlack auf Birkensperrholz; 104 x 181 cm; Privatsammlung, New York

p. 141 *Prototype for Billboard at A–Z West: These Things I Know for Sure #14* 2005; Flashe, vinyl lettering and polyurethane on birch plywood; 41 x 71 1/4"; Private Collection, New York

S. 143 Prototype for Billboard at A–Z West: These Things I Know for Sure #13 2006; Flashe-Vinylfarbe, Vinylbeschriftung und Polyurethanlack auf Fichtensperrholz; 120 x 186 cm; Privatsammlung, Mailand

p. 143 *Prototype for Billboard at A–Z West: These Things I Know for Sure #13* 2006; Flashe, vinyl lettering and polyurethane on fir plywood; 47 1/4 x 73 1/4"; Private Collection, Milan

S. 145 Prototype for Billboard at A–Z West: These Things I Know for Sure #11 2006; Flashe-Vinylfarbe, Vinylbeschriftung und Polyurethanlack auf Fichtensperrholz; 120 x 186 cm

p. 145 *Prototype for Billboard at A–Z West: These Things I Know for Sure #11* 2006; Flashe, vinyl lettering and polyurethane on fir plywood; 47 1/4 x 73 1/4"

S. 147 Prototype for Billboard at A–Z West: These Things I Know for Sure #10 2005; Flashe-Vinylfarbe, Vinylbeschriftung und Polyurethanlack auf Birkensperrholz; 104 x 181 cm; Emanuel Hoffmann-Stiftung, Depositum in der Öffentlichen Kunstsammlung Basel

p. 147 *Prototype for Billboard at A–Z West: These Things I Know for Sure #10* 2005; Flashe, vinyl lettering and polyurethane on birch plywood; 41 x 71 1/4"; Emanuel Hoffmann Foundation, on permanent loan to the Öffentliche Kunstsammlung Basel

S. 149 Prototype for Billboard at A–Z West: These Things I Know for Sure #8 2006; Flashe-Vinylfarbe, Vinylbeschriftung und Polyurethanlack auf Fichtensperrholz; 120 x 186 cm; Privatsammlung, Meilen

p. 149 *Prototype for Billboard at A–Z West: These Things I Know for Sure #8* 2006; Flashe, vinyl lettering and polyurethane on fir plywood; 47 1/4 x 73 1/4"; Private Collection, Meilen

S. 151 Prototype for Billboard at A–Z West: These Things I Know for Sure #4 2006; Flashe-Vinylfarbe, Vinylbeschriftung und Polyurethanlack auf Fichtensperrholz; 120 x 186 cm

S. 153 Prototype for Billboard at A–Z West: These Things I Know for Sure #9 2006; Flashe-Vinylfarbe, Vinylbeschriftung und Polyurethanlack auf Fichtensperrholz; 120 x 186 cm; Privatsammlung, Los Angeles

S. 155 Prototype for Billboard at A–Z West: These Things I Know for Sure #4 2005; Flashe-Vinylfarbe, Vinylbeschriftung und Polyurethanlack auf Birken sperrholz; 104 x 181 cm; Goya Contemporary, Baltimore

S. 157 Prototype for Billboard at A–Z West: These Things I Know for Sure #3 2005; Flashe-Vinylfarbe, Vinylbeschriftung und Polyurethanlack auf Birken- sperrholz; 104 x 181 cm; Privatsammlung, Madrid

S. 159 Prototype for Billboard at A–Z West: These Things I Know for Sure #1 (AZ in fiber form holding scarf) 2006; Flashe-Vinylfarbe, Vinylbeschriftung und Polyurethanlack auf Fichtensperrholz; 120 x 186 cm

S. 161 Prototype for Billboard at A–Z West: These Things I Know for Sure #1 2005; Flashe-Vinylfarbe, Vinylbeschriftung und Polyurethanlack auf Birken- sperrholz; 104 x 181 cm; Privatsammlung, New York

S. 163 Prototype for Billboard at A–Z West: Single Strand 2006; Flashe-Vinylfarbe und Polyurethanlack auf Fichten- sperrholz; 120 x 186 cm; Privatsammlung, Italien

S. 165 Prototype for Billboard at A–Z West: Voids and Avoids 2007; Flashe-Vinylfarbe, Vinylbeschriftung und Polyurethanlack auf Fichtensperrholz; 120 x 186 cm; Privatsammlung, Los Angeles

S. 167 Prototype for Billboard at A–Z West: Radiating Arenas of Enhancement #1 2006; Flashe-Vinylfarbe, Vinylbeschriftung und Polyurethanlack auf Birken- sperrholz; 120 x 186 cm

S. 169 Prototype for Billboard at A–Z West: Ribbon 2007; Flashe-Vinylfarbe und Polyurethanlack auf Fichtensperrholz; 120 x 186 cm

Sofern nicht anders angegeben, sind alle Werke Courtesy die Künstlerin, Andrea Rosen Gallery, New York; ausser S. 105, 106: Courtesy die Künstlerin, Regen Projects, Los Angeles; S. 127, 145, 151, 159, 167: Courtesy die Künstlerin, Sadie Coles HQ, London; S. 126, 136: Courtesy die Künstlerin, Galleria Massimo de Carlo, Mailand; S. 48o, 48u, 73u: Courtesy die Künstlerin, Monika Sprüth Philomene Magers Köln München.

p. 151 *Prototype for Billboard at A–Z West: These Things I Know for Sure #4* 2006; Flashe, vinyl lettering and polyurethane on fir plywood; 47 1/4 x 73 1/4"

p. 153 *Prototype for Billboard at A–Z West: These Things I Know for Sure #9* 2006; Flashe, vinyl lettering and polyurethane on fir plywood; 47 1/4 x 73 1/4"; Private Collection, Los Angeles

p. 155 *Prototype for Billboard at A–Z West: These Things I Know for Sure #4* 2005; Flashe, vinyl lettering and polyurethane birch plywood; 41 x 71 1/4"; Goya Contemporary, Baltimore

p. 157 *Prototype for Billboard at A–Z West: These Things I Know for Sure #3* 2005; Flashe, vinyl lettering and polyurethane on birch plywood; 41 x 71 1/4"; Private Collection, Madrid

p. 159 *Prototype for Billboard at A–Z West: These Things I Know for Sure #1 (AZ in fiber form holding scarf)* 2006; Flashe, vinyl lettering and polyurethane on fir plywood; 47 1/4 x 73 1/4"

p. 161 *Prototype for Billboard at A–Z West: These Things I Know for Sure #1* 2005; Flashe, vinyl lettering and polyurethane on birch plywood; 41 x 71 1/4"; Private Collection, New York

p. 163 *Prototype for Billboard at A–Z West: Single Strand* 2006; Flashe and polyurethane on fir plywood; 47 1/4 x 73 1/4"; Private Collection, Italy

p. 165 *Prototype for Billboard at A–Z West: Voids and Avoids* 2007; Flashe, vinyl lettering and polyurethane on fir plywood; 47 1/4 x 73 1/4"; Private Collection, Los Angeles

p. 167 *Prototype for Billboard at A–Z West: Radiating Arenas of Enhancement #1* 2006; Flashe, vinyl lettering and polyurethane on birch plywood; 47 1/4 x 73 1/4"

p. 169 *Prototype for Billboard at A–Z West: Ribbon* 2007; Flashe and polyurethane on fir plywood; 47 1/4 x 73 1/4"

All works are Courtesy the artist, Andrea Rosen Gallery, New York; except pp. 105, 106: Courtesy the artist, Regen Projects, Los Angeles; pp. 127, 145, 151, 159, 167: Courtesy the artist, Sadie Coles HQ, London; pp. 126, 136: Courtesy the artist, Galleria Massimo de Carlo, Milan; pp. 48t, 48b, 73b: Courtesy the artist, Monika Sprüth Philomene Magers Cologne Munich.

Ausstellung im Schaulager   Exhibition at Schaulager

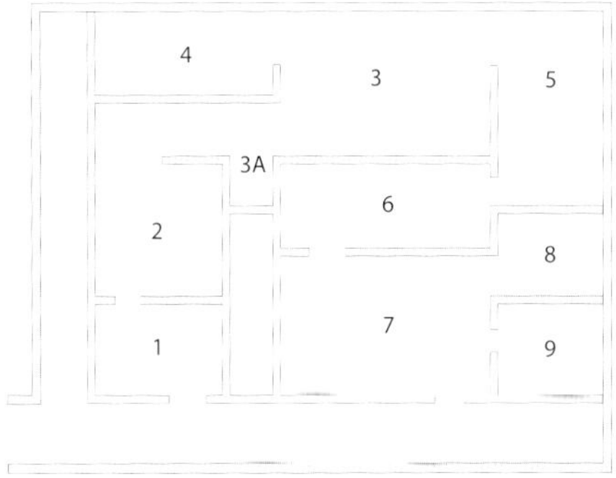

Die vorliegende Publikation entstand aus Anlass der Ausstellung „Andrea Zittel, Monika Sosnowska. 1:1". Parallel dazu erschien die Publikation „Fotografien und Skizzen" von Monika Sosnowska.

Die Werke von Andrea Zittel waren im Erdgeschoss des Schaulagers eingerichtet. Wie der Grundriss zeigt, war die Ausstellungsfläche in neun Räume aufgeteilt.

Im Folgenden werden die Exponate nach Räumen aufgeführt. Innerhalb der Räume sind in jeweils chronologischer Reihenfolge zuerst die Zeichnungen, Gouachen und Holztafeln, zweitens die Objekte und Skulpturen, und drittens die „Uniforms" aufgeführt. Allfällige, von der Liste abweichende Änderungen haben sich während der Einrichtung der Ausstellung nach Redaktionsschluss der Publikation ergeben.

Die „Uniforms" sind ohne Massangaben aufgelistet. Die meisten von ihnen wurden von der Künstlerin selbst getragen und entsprechen ihrer Kleidergrösse. Eine Ausnahme dazu bilden die „A–Z Personal Panel Uniforms", die von der Form einer rechteckigen Stoffbahn abgeleitet sind, und die „A–Z Fiber Forms: White Felted Dresses", die Zittel anders als die übrigen „Uniforms" als Skulpturen versteht. Diese beiden Gruppen sind mit Massangaben versehen.

The present publication accompanies the exhibition *Andrea Zittel, Monika Sosnowska. 1:1*. A companion volume on Monika Sosnowska's photographs and sketches was published in parallel with it.

Andrea Zittel's works were installed on Schaulager's ground floor. As the floor plan shows, the exhibition architecture consisted of nine spaces.

In the list that follows, the exhibits are arranged according to room. Within each room they are listed in chronological order with the drawings, gouaches, and wooden panels first, the objects and sculptures second, and the *Uniforms* third. Any deviations from the list are the result of changes to the exhibition after the catalog went to press.

No dimensions are indicated for the *Uniforms*. Most of them were worn by the artist herself and hence were in sizes to fit her. Exceptions to this include the *A–Z Personal Panel Uniforms*, which were derived from the form of a rectangular length of cloth, and the *A–Z Fiber Forms: White Felted Dresses*, which Zittel sees as sculptures, unlike the other *Uniforms*. Dimensions are indicated for both these groups.

1

Repair Work 1991
consisting of 8 parts: *Bowl*:
porcelain and glue, 3 x 10"; *Cup*:
porcelain and glue; 2 1/2 x 5";
Cup Inscribed Mother: porcelain and
glue; 3 x 6"; *Elephant*: plaster and
glue; 18 x 24 x 9"; *Hub Cap*: steel;
16 1/2 diameter; *Dish*: porcelain
and glue; 3/4 x 9 1/2"; *Table*:
wood, glue, nails; 22 x 18 x 13";
Wise Man: papier-mâché and paint;
approx. 7 x 3"
Howard and Barbara Morse

2

A–Z Wallens 2002
screen-printed cast aluminum,
tempered-glass port lights and
hardware in silk-screened wooden
crate; lights: 14" diameter, crate:
22 x 39 x 10"
Edition 12
Courtesy the artist and Editions
Fawbush, New York

Room 1

3

Study for A–Z Carpet Furniture
1992
gouache and pencil on paper;
11 x 14"
Collection of Jack Hanley

4

Study A–Z Carpet Furniture 1992
gouache and pencil on paper;
11 x 14"
Private Collection, New York

5

Study for A–Z Carpet Furniture
1992
gouache and pencil on paper;
11 x 14"
Collection of Jack Hanley

6

Study for A–Z Carpet Furniture
1992

gouache and pencil on paper;
11 x 14"
Courtesy the artist and Andrea
Rosen Gallery, New York

7 ill. p. 29
Study for A–Z Carpet Furniture
1992
gouache and pencil on paper;
11 x 14"
Private Collection, New York

8 ill. p. 21
Study for A–Z Carpet Furniture
1992
gouache and pencil on paper;
11 x 14"
Courtesy the artist and Andrea
Rosen Gallery, New York

9

Study for A–Z Carpet Furniture
1992
gouache and pencil on paper;
11 x 14"
Courtesy the artist and Andrea
Rosen Gallery, New York

10 ill. p. 28
Study for A–Z Carpet Furniture
1992
gouache and pencil on paper;
11 x 14"
Collection of Themistocles and Dare
Michos, San Francisco

11 ill. p. 24
Study for A–Z Carpet Furniture
1992
gouache and pencil on paper;
11 x 14"
Collection of Andrea Rosen,
New York

12

Study for A–Z Carpet Furniture
1992
gouache and pencil on paper;
11 x 14"
Collection of Jack Hanley

13

Study for A–Z Carpet Furniture
1992

gouache and pencil on paper;
11 x 14"
Courtesy the artist and Andrea
Rosen Gallery, New York

14 ill. p. 26
Study for A–Z Carpet Furniture
1992
gouache and pencil on paper;
11 x 14"
Courtesy the artist and Andrea
Rosen Gallery, New York

15 ill. p. 27
Study for A–Z Carpet Furniture
1992
gouache and pencil on paper;
11 x 14"
Hort Family Collection

16

Study for A–Z Carpet Furniture
1992
gouache and pencil on paper;
11 x 14"
Private Collection, Jersey

17 ill. p. 25
Study for A–Z Carpet Furniture
1992
gouache and pencil on paper;
11 x 14"
Collection Landesbank Baden-
Württemberg

18 ill. p. 31
Study for A–Z Carpet Furniture
1992
gouache and pencil on paper;
15 x 20"
Courtesy the artist and Andrea
Rosen Gallery, New York

19 ill. p. 23
Study for A–Z Carpet Furniture
1992
gouache and pencil on paper;
15 x 20"
Collection Jennifer Flay, Paris

20 ill. p. 22
Study for A–Z Carpet Furniture
1992
gouache and pencil on paper;

Eingang

1

Repair Work 1991
bestehend aus 8 Teilen: Bowl:
Porzellan und Klebstoff, 7.6 x
25.3 cm, Cup: Porzellan und Klebstoff; 6.4 x 12.8 cm; Cup Inscribed
Mother: Porzellan und Klebstoff;
7.6 x 15.2 cm; Elefant: Gips und
Klebstoff; 46 x 62 x 23 cm; Hub
Cap: Stahl, 42 cm Durchmesser;
Dish: Porzellan und Klebstoff;
2 x 24 cm; Table: Holz, Klebstoff
und Nägel; 56 x 46 x 33 cm;
Wise Man: Papiermaché und Farbe;
ca. 12.7 cm
Howard und Barbara Morse

2

A–Z Wallens 2002
Aluminium, mit Serigraphie
bedruckt, Hartglas, Befestigung in
Holzkiste mit Serigraphie bedruckt;
Bullauge: 35.6 cm Durchmesser;
Kiste: 56 x 99 x 25.3 cm
Edition 12
Courtesy die Künstlerin und Editions
Fawbush, New York

Raum 1

3

Study for A–Z Carpet Furniture 1992
Gouache und Bleistift auf Papier;
28 x 35.6 cm
Sammlung Jack Hanley

4

Study A–Z Carpet Furniture 1992
Gouache und Bleistift auf Papier;
28 x 35.6 cm
Privatsammlung, New York

5

Study for A–Z Carpet Furniture 1992
Gouache und Bleistift auf Papier;
28 x 35.6 cm
Sammlung Jack Hanley

6

Study for A–Z Carpet Furniture 1992
Gouache und Bleistift auf Papier;
28 x 35.6 cm
Courtesy die Künstlerin und Andrea
Rosen Gallery, New York

7 Abb. S. 29
Study for A–Z Carpet Furniture 1992
Gouache und Bleistift auf Papier;
28 x 35.6 cm
Privatsammlung, New York

8 Abb. S. 21
Study for A–Z Carpet Furniture 1992
Gouache und Bleistift auf Papier;
28 x 35.6 cm
Courtesy die Künstlerin und Andrea
Rosen Gallery, New York

9

Study for A–Z Carpet Furniture 1992
Gouache und Bleistift auf Papier;
28 x 35.6 cm
Courtesy die Künstlerin und Andrea
Rosen Gallery, New York

10 Abb. S. 28
Study for A–Z Carpet Furniture 1992
Gouache und Bleistift auf Papier;
28 x 35.6 cm
Sammlung Themistocles und Dare
Michos, San Francisco

11 Abb. S. 24
Study for A–Z Carpet Furniture 1992
Gouache und Bleistift auf Papier;
28 x 35.6 cm
Sammlung Andrea Rosen,
New York

12

Study for A–Z Carpet Furniture 1992
Gouache und Bleistift auf Papier;
28 x 35.6 cm
Sammlung Jack Hanley

13

Study for A–Z Carpet Furniture 1992
Gouache und Bleistift auf Papier;
28 x 35.6 cm
Courtesy die Künstlerin und Andrea
Rosen Gallery, New York

14 Abb. S. 26
Study for A–Z Carpet Furniture 1992
Gouache und Bleistift auf Papier;
28 x 35.6 cm

Courtesy die Künstlerin und Andrea
Rosen Gallery, New York

15 Abb. S. 27
Study for A–Z Carpet Furniture 1992
Gouache und Bleistift auf Papier;
28 x 35.6 cm
Hort Family Collection

16

Study for A–Z Carpet Furniture 1992
Gouache und Bleistift auf Papier;
28 x 35.6 cm
Privatsammlung, Jersey

17 Abb. S. 25
Study for A–Z Carpet Furniture 1992
Gouache und Bleistift auf Papier;
28 x 35.6 cm
Sammlung Landesbank Baden-
Württemberg

18 Abb. S. 31
Study for A–Z Carpet Furniture 1992
Gouache und Bleistift auf Papier;
38 x 50.8 cm
Courtesy die Künstlerin und Andrea
Rosen Gallery, New York

19 Abb. S. 23
Study for A–Z Carpet Furniture 1992
Gouache und Bleistift auf Papier;
38 x 50.8 cm
Sammlung Jennifer Flay, Paris

20 Abb. S. 22
Study for A–Z Carpet Furniture 1992
Gouache und Bleistift auf Papier;
38 x 50.8 cm
Courtesy die Künstlerin und Andrea
Rosen Gallery, New York

21 Abb. S. 30
Study for A–Z Carpet Furniture 1992
Gouache und Bleistift auf Papier;
38 x 50.8 cm
Courtesy die Künstlerin und Andrea
Rosen Gallery, New York

22

Study for A–Z Carpet Furniture 1992
Gouache und Bleistift auf Papier;
38 x 50.6 cm
Sammlung Goetz

15 x 20"
Courtesy the artist and Andrea
Rosen Gallery, New York

21 ill. p. 30
Study for A–Z Carpet Furniture
1992
gouache and pencil on paper;
15 x 20"
Courtesy the artist and Andrea
Rosen Gallery, New York

22
Study for A–Z Carpet Furniture
1992
gouache and pencil on paper;
15 x 20"
Goetz Collection

23
Study for A–Z Carpet Furniture
1993
gouache and pencil on paper;
11 x 14"
Courtesy the artist and Andrea
Rosen Gallery, New York

24
Study for A–Z Carpet Furniture
1993
gouache and pencil on paper;
11 x 14"
Collection Landesbank Baden-
Württemberg

25 ill. p. 35
Study for A–Z Carpet Furniture
1993
4 parts; gouache and pencil on
paper; each 15 x 20"
Collection of Nancy Stillpass,
New York

26 ill. p. 36
Study for A–Z Carpet Furniture
1993
4 parts; gouache and pencil on
paper; each 11 x 14"
Courtesy the artist and Andrea
Rosen Gallery, New York

27
Study for A–Z Carpet Furniture
1993

2 parts; gouache and pencil on
paper; each 11 x 14"
Private Collection, Belgium

28 ill. p. 39
Study for A–Z Carpet Furniture
1993
gouache on paper; 11 x 15"
Courtesy the artist and Andrea
Rosen Gallery, New York

29
Study for A–Z Carpet Furniture
1993
gouache and pencil on paper;
15 x 20"
Goetz Collection

30 ill. p. 32
Study for A–Z Carpet Furniture
1993
gouache and pencil on paper;
15 x 20"
Courtesy the artist and Andrea
Rosen Gallery, New York

31 ill. p. 33
Study for A–Z Carpet Furniture
1993
gouache and pencil on paper;
15 x 20"
Martina Yamin Collection

32 ill. p. 38
Study for A–Z Carpet Furniture
1993
gouache and pencil on paper;
15 x 20"
Collection Florence and Philippe
Segalot, Paris

33 ill. p. 37
Study for A–Z Carpet Furniture
1993
gouache and pencil on paper;
15 x 20"
Courtesy the artist and Andrea
Rosen Gallery, New York

34 ill. p. 41
Study for A–Z Ottoman Furniture
1994
gouache and pencil on paper;
9 x 12"

Collection Florence and Philippe
Segalot, Paris

35
Study for A–Z Ottoman Furniture
1994
gouache and pencil on paper;
11 x 15"
Courtesy Tanya Bonakdar Gallery,
New York

36 ill. p. 40b
Study for A–Z Ottoman Furniture
1994
gouache and pencil on paper;
9 x 12"
The Museum of Modern Art, New
York. Gift of Patricia and Morris
Orden

37 ill. p. 43
Study for A–Z Ottoman Furniture
1994
gouache and pencil on paper;
11 x 15"
Courtesy the artist and Andrea
Rosen Gallery, New York

38 ill. p. 44
Study for A–Z Ottoman Furniture
1994
gouache and pencil on paper;
15 x 20"
Courtesy the artist and Andrea
Rosen Gallery, New York

39 ill. p. 45
Study for A–Z Ottoman Furniture
1994
gouache and pencil on paper;
15 x 20"
Courtesy the artist and Andrea
Rosen Gallery, New York

40 ill. p. 40t
Study for A–Z Ottoman Furniture
1994
gouache and pencil on paper;
15 x 20"
Goetz Collection

41 ill. p. 46-47
My Linoleum Floor 1995-98
2 parts; gouache and pencil on

23
Study for A–Z Carpet Furniture 1993
Gouache und Bleistift auf Papier;
28 x 35.6 cm
Courtesy die Künstlerin und Andrea
Rosen Gallery, New York

24
Study for A–Z Carpet Furniture 1993
Gouache und Bleistift auf Papier;
28 x 35.6 cm
Sammlung Landesbank Baden-
Württemberg

25 Abb. S. 35
Study for A–Z Carpet Furniture 1993
4 Teile; Gouache und Bleistift auf
Papier; je 38 x 50.8 cm
Sammlung Nancy Stillpass,
New York

26 Abb. S. 36
Study for A–Z Carpet Furniture 1993
4 Teile; Gouache und Bleistift auf
Papier; je 28 x 35.6 cm
Courtesy die Künstlerin und Andrea
Rosen Gallery, New York

27
Study for A–Z Carpet Furniture 1993
2 Teile; Gouache und Bleistift auf
Papier; je 28 x 35.6 cm
Privatsammlung, Belgien

28 Abb. S. 39
Study for A–Z Carpet Furniture 1993
Gouache auf Papier; 28 x 38 cm
Courtesy die Künstlerin und Andrea
Rosen Gallery, New York

29
Study for A–Z Carpet Furniture 1993
Gouache und Bleistift auf Papier;
38 x 50.6 cm
Sammlung Goetz

30 Abb. S. 32
Study for A–Z Carpet Furniture 1993
Gouache und Bleistift auf Papier;
38 x 50.8 cm
Courtesy die Künstlerin und Andrea
Rosen Gallery, New York

31 Abb. S. 33
Study for A–Z Carpet Furniture 1993

Gouache und Bleistift auf Papier;
38 x 50.8 cm
Sammlung Martina Yamin

32 Abb. S. 38
Study for A–Z Carpet Furniture 1993
Gouache und Bleistift auf Papier;
38 x 50.8 cm
Sammlung Florence und Philippe
Segalot, Paris

33 Abb. S. 37
Study for A–Z Carpet Furniture 1993
Gouache und Bleistift auf Papier;
38 x 50.8 cm
Courtesy die Künstlerin und Andrea
Rosen Gallery, New York

34 Abb. S. 41
Study for A–Z Ottoman Furniture
1994
Gouache und Bleistift auf Papier;
23 x 30.5 cm
Sammlung Florence und Philippe
Segalot, Paris

35
Study for A–Z Ottoman Furniture
1994
Gouache und Bleistift auf Papier;
28 x 38 cm
Courtesy Tanya Bonakdar Gallery,
New York

36 Abb. S. 40u
Study for A–Z Ottoman Furniture
1994
Gouache und Bleistift auf Papier;
23 x 30.5 cm
The Museum of Modern Art,
New York, Geschenk von Patricia
und Morris Orden

37 Abb. S. 43
Study for A–Z Ottoman Furniture
1994
Gouache und Bleistift auf Papier;
28 x 38 cm
Courtesy die Künstlerin und Andrea
Rosen Gallery, New York

38 Abb. S. 44
Study for A–Z Ottoman Furniture
1994

Gouache und Bleistift auf Papier;
38 x 50.8 cm
Courtesy die Künstlerin und
Andrea Rosen Gallery, New York

39 Abb. S. 45
Study for A–Z Ottoman Furniture
1994
Gouache und Bleistift auf Papier;
38 x 50.8 cm
Courtesy die Künstlerin und
Andrea Rosen Gallery, New York

40 Abb. S. 40o
Study for A–Z Ottoman Furniture
1994
Gouache und Bleistift auf Papier;
38 x 50.6 cm
Sammlung Goetz

41 Abb. S. 46-47
My Linoleum Floor 1995-98
2 Teile; Gouache und Bleistift auf
Papier; je 28 x 38 cm
Courtesy die Künstlerin und Andrea
Rosen Gallery, New York

Raum 2

42 Abb. S. 49
Study for A–Z Personal Panels
1994
Gouache auf Papier; 38 x 50.8 cm
Sammlung Marjory Jacobson,
Boston, MA

43 Abb. S. 48u
Study for A–Z Personal Panels
1994
Gouache auf Papier; 30.5 x 23 cm
Monika Sprüth Philomene Magers
Köln München

44 Abb. S. 48o
Study for A–Z Personal Panels 1994
Gouache auf Papier; 30.5 x 23 cm
Monika Sprüth Philomene Magers
Köln München

45 Abb. S. 76
Me in A–Z Personal Panel in Front
of the A–Z 1998
Gouache auf Papier; 50.6 x 38 cm
Sammlung Goetz

paper; each 11 x 15"
Courtesy the artist and Andrea
Rosen Gallery, New York

Room 2

42 ill. p. 49
Study for A–Z Personal Panels
1994
gouache on paper; 15 x 20"
Collection of Marjory Jacobson,
Boston, MA

43 ill. p. 48b
Study for A–Z Personal Panels
1994
gouache on paper; 12 x 9"
Monika Sprüth Philomene Magers
Cologne Munich

44 ill. p. 48t
Study for A–Z Personal Panels
1994
gouache on paper; 12 x 9"
Monika Sprüth Philomene Magers
Cologne Munich

45 ill. p. 76
*Me in A–Z Personal Panel in Front
of the A–Z* 1998
gouache on paper; 20 x 15"
Goetz Collection

46 ill. p. 73t
*Pink A–Z Personal Panel on Table in
My Bedroom* 1998
gouache on paper; 10 x 15"
Goetz Collection

46a ill. p. 77r
*Me in Personal Panel Cleaning A–Z
Yard Yacht,* 1998
gouache on paper; 20 x 15"
Private Collection, Athens Greece

47 ill. p. 73b
*Grey A–Z Personal Panel on My
Bedroom Floor* 1998
gouache on paper; 10 x 15"
Monika Sprüth Philomene Magers
Cologne Munich

48 ill. p. 72
*Orange A–Z Personal Panel on Our
Kitchen Towel Rack* 1998

gouache on paper; 15 x 10"
Collection Mino and Barbara
Mazzocato

49 ill. p. 71
Drawstring Skirts 1998
gouache on paper; 15 x 10"
Martina Yamin Collection

50 ill. p. 53
My Fastest Most Complete Dress Plan
1998
gouache on paper; 20 x 15"
Private Collection, New York

51 ill. p. 50-51
Eight A–Z Personal Panels 1998
8 parts; gouache on paper; each
12 x 9"
Goetz Collection

52 ill. p. 78r
*Me in A–Z Personal Panel in our
Kitchen in Altadena* 1998
gouache on paper; 20 x 15"
Private Collection, Jersey

53 ill. p. 78l
*A–Z Personal Panel, Brooklyn, NY,
1994* 1999
gouache and pencil on paper; 30 x 22"
Courtesy Sadie Coles HQ, London

54
A–Z Cover in Use #1-11 1999
11 parts; pen and gouache on
vellum; each 11 x 14"
Private Collection

55
*A–Z Management and Maintenance
Unit: Model 003* 1992
steel, wood, carpet, plastic sink,
glass and mirror; 86 x 94 x 68"
Collection of Andrea Rosen, New York

56
A–Z Cover 1993
3 parts; wool, velvet and linen;
each 72 x 60"
Edition 30
Private Collection

57
A–Z Carpet: Bed 1995
wool and synthetic wool blend;

96 x 96"
Rennie Collection, Vancouver,
Canada

58
*A–Z Carpet Furniture: Drop-Leaf
Dining Room Table* 1997
nylon; 72 x 120"
Edition 5, 3AP
Collection of Andrea Rosen,
New York

59
A–Z Carpet Furniture: Living Room
2008
nylon; 120 x 180"
Edition 5, 2 AP, 1 exhibition copy
Courtesy the artist and Andrea
Rosen Gallery, New York

60
A–Z Carpet Furniture: Office 2008
nylon; 138 x 186"
Edition 5, 2 AP, 1 exhibition copy
Courtesy the artist and Andrea
Rosen Gallery, New York

**Uniforms nos. 61-74 and nos.
87-105 are owned by the
Emanuel Hoffmann Foundation,
on permanent loan to the
Öffentliche Kunstsammlung
Basel, and nos. 75-86 are owned
by the Goetz Collection.**

61
*A–Z Six-Month Personal Uniform:
Fall/Winter 1991-1992* 1991-1992
black woolen dress, sleeveless,
ankle-length and white cotton
man's shirt

62
*A–Z Six-Month Personal Uniform:
Spring/Summer 1991* 1991
black linen dress, sleeveless, 3/4-
length

63
*A–Z Six-Month Personal Uniform:
Spring/Summer 1992* 1992
black silk dress, sleeveless, ankle-

46 Abb. S. 73o
Pink A–Z Personal Panel on Table in
My Bedroom 1998
Gouache auf Papier; 25.3 x 38 cm
Sammlung Goetz

46a Abb. S. 77r
Me in Personal Panel Cleaning A–Z
Yard Yacht 1998
Gouache auf Papier; 50.8 x 38 cm
Privatsammlung, Athen Griechenland

47 Abb. S. 73u
Grey A–Z Personal Panel on My
Bedroom Floor 1998
Gouache auf Papier; 25.3 x 38 cm
Monika Sprüth Philomene Magers
Köln München

48 Abb. S. 72
Orange A–Z Personal Panel on Our
Kitchen Towel Rack 1998
Gouache auf Papier; 38 x 25.3 cm
Sammlung Mino und Barbara
Mazzocato

49 Abb. S. 71
Drawstring Skirts 1998
Gouache auf Papier; 38 x 25.3 cm
Sammlung Martina Yamin

50 Abb. S. 53
My Fastest Most Complete Dress
Plan 1998
Gouache auf Papier; 50.8 x 38 cm
Privatsammlung, New York

51 Abb. S. 50-51
Eight A–Z Personal Panels 1998
8 Teile; Gouache auf Papier;
je 30.4 x 22.7 cm
Sammlung Goetz

52 Abb. S. 78r
Me in A–Z Personal Panel in our
Kitchen in Altadena 1998
Gouache auf Papier; 50.8 x 38 cm
Privatsammlung, Jersey

53 Abb. S. 78l
A–Z Personal Panel, Brooklyn, NY,
1994 1999
Gouache und Bleistift auf Papier;
76.2 x 56 cm
Courtesy Sadie Coles HQ, London

54
A–Z Cover in Use #1-11 1999
11 Teile; Bleistift und Gouache auf
Velinpapier; je 28 x 35.6 cm
Privatsammlung

55
A–Z Management and Maintenance
Unit: Model 003 1992
Stahl, Holz, Teppich, Kunst-
stoffwaschbecken, Glas und
Spiegel; 218.4 x 238.8 x
172.7 cm
Sammlung Andrea Rosen,
New York

56
A–Z Cover 1993
3 Teile; Wolle, Samt und Leinen; je
182.8 x 152.4 cm
Edition 30
Privatsammlung

57
A–Z Carpet Furniture: Bed 1995
Wolle und Wollgemisch;
243.5 x 243.5 cm
Sammlung Rennie, Vancouver,
Kanada

58
A–Z Carpet Furniture: Drop-Leaf
Dining Room Table 1997
Nylon; 183 x 304.8 cm
Edition 5, 3AP
Sammlung Andrea Rosen,
New York

59
A–Z Carpet Furniture: Living Room
2008
Nylon; 305 x 457 cm
Edition 5, 2 AP, 1 Ausstellungskopie
Courtesy die Künstlerin und Andrea
Rosen Gallery, New York

60
A–Z Carpet Furniture: Office 2008
Nylon; 350 x 472 cm
Edition 5, 2 AP, 1 Ausstellungskopie
Courtesy die Künstlerin und Andrea
Rosen Gallery, New York

**Die „Uniforms" Nrn. 61-74
und Nrn. 87-105 sind im Besitz
der Emanuel Hoffmann-Stiftung,
Depositum in der Öffentlichen
Kunstsammlung Basel, Nrn. 75-
86 im Besitz der Sammlung
Goetz.**

61
A–Z Six-Month Personal Uniform:
Fall/Winter 1991-1992 1991-1992
schwarzes Kleid aus Wolle,
ärmellos, knöchellang und weisses
Herrenhemd aus Baumwolle

62
A–Z Six-Month Personal Uniform:
Spring/Summer 1991 1991
schwarzes Kleid aus Leinen,
ärmellos, dreiviertellang

63
A–Z Six-Month Personal Uniform:
Spring/Summer 1992 1992
schwarzes Kleid aus Seide,
ärmellos, knöchellang und schwarz-
weiss gestreiftes Oberteil aus
Baumwolle

64
A–Z Six-Month Personal Uniform:
Fall/Winter 1992-1993 1992-1993
schwarzer langer Rock aus Faille,
knöchellang, Unterrock, weisses
Herrenhemd aus Baumwolle und
Lederriemen

65
A–Z Six-Month Personal Uniform:
Spring/Summer 1993 1993
schwarzes Kleid aus Faille, mit
grauer Borte, kurzarm, dreiviertellang und Hosen aus Baumwolle

66
A–Z Six-Month Personal Uniform:
Fall/Winter 1993/1994 1993
schwarzes Wickelkleid aus Wolle
mit Satinfutter, Lederträger und
schwarzer Rollkragenpullover

67
A–Z Six-Month Personal Uniform:
Spring/Summer 1994 1994

length and black-and-white-striped
cotton T-shirt, long-sleeved

64

*A–Z Six-Month Personal Uniform:
Fall/Winter 1992-1993* 1992-1993
black faille skirt, ankle-length,
underskirt, white cotton man's shirt
and leather straps

65

*A–Z Six-Month Personal Uniform:
Spring/Summer 1993* 1993
black faille dress, grey border,
short-sleeved, 3/4-length and
cotton pants

66

*A–Z Six-Month Personal Uniform:
Fall/Winter 1993-1994*
1993
woolen wrap around panel, satin
lining, leather straps and black
turtleneck

67

*A–Z Six-Month Personal Uniform:
Spring/Summer 1994* 1994
black satin blend, leather straps,
snap fasteners and underskirt

68

*Green and White Curtain Fabric A–Z
Personal Panel Uniform and Spring
Green Under Panel* 1995-1998
Panel: green and white cotton
curtain fabric; 45 x 28"; Under
Panel: spring green fabric

69

*Grey Flannel A–Z Personal Panel
Uniform and Blue Shirt Material
Under Panel* 1995-1998
Panel: grey cotton flannel;
44 x 28 1/2"; Under Panel: white
and blue cotton

70

*Khaki Corduroy A–Z Personal Panel
Uniform and Navy Blue Striped
Under Panel* 1995-1998
Panel: cotton corduroy; 45 x 28 1/2";
Under Panel: navy blue striped
fabric

71

*Grey Wool with Black Embroidery
A–Z Personal Panel Uniform
and Dark Green Rayon Under Panel*
1995-1998
Panel: grey wool, embroidery and
elastic straps; 45 1/2 x 28"; Under
Panel: dark green rayon

72

*Grey Satin with Yellow Pattern A–Z
Personal Panel Uniform and Light
Yellow Silk Under Panel* 1998
Panel: grey satin with yellow pat-
tern; 46 x 28"; Under Panel: light
yellow silk

73

*RAUGH Brown Cotton A–Z Personal
Panel Uniform* 1998
cotton with straps and safety
pins

74

*RAUGH Blue Nylon A–Z Personal
Panel Uniform* 1998
nylon with straps and safety
pins

75

*Light Blue A–Z Personal Panel
Uniform* 1995-1998
cotton fabric; 45 x 28"

76

*Salmon and Red Silk A–Z Personal
Panel Uniform* 1995-1998
silk fabric; 44 1/2 x 28"

77

*Grey Taffeta with Black Velvet
Ribbon A–Z Personal Panel Uniform*
1995-1998
taffeta fabric with velvet ribbon;
46 x 28"

78

*Pale Silk Satin with Black Trim A–Z
Personal Panel Uniform* 1995-1998
silk and satin fabric with ribbon;
46 x 28"

79

*Red and Purple "Mondrian" A–Z
Personal Panel Uniform* 1998

wool, velvet, silk and satin fabric;
44 x 28 1/2"

80

*Brown Denim A–Z Personal Panel
Uniform* 1995-1998
cotton fabric (denim); 44 x 28"

81

*Navy Blue Nylon A–Z Personal
Panel Uniform* 1995-1998
nylon jacket material; 46 x 28"

82

*Olive, Red and Black "Window
Pane" A–Z Personal Panel Uniform*
1995-1998
velvet, wool and lining with black
elastic straps; 44 1/2 x 28"

83

Bright Orange A–Z Under Panel
1995-1998
cotton fabric; 34 1/2 x 51"

84

Tangerine Silk A–Z Under Panel
1995-1998
silk fabric; 35 1/2 x 42"

85

New Red A–Z Under Panel
1995-1998
cotton fabric; 35 x 42 1/2"

86

*Silver-Grey Metallic A–Z Under
Panel* 1995-1998
taffeta fabric; 35 1/2 x 43"

87

*A–Z Single-Strand Uniform: Fall
1998* 1998
green and black dress, wool and
mohair blend, sleeveless, knee-
length, black woolen shoulderbag
and black turtleneck

88

*A–Z Single-Strand Uniform: Winter
1998* 1998
grey, yellow and black dress, wool,
sleeveless, knee-length and
black turtleneck

schwarzes Satinmischgewebe, Lederriemen, Druckknöpfe und Unterrock

68
Green and White Curtain Fabric
A–Z Personal Panel Uniform and
Spring Green Under Panel 1995-98
Panel: grünes und weisses Baum-
wollvorhanggewebe; 117 x 71 cm;
Under Panel: hellgrüner Stoff

69
Grey Flannel A–Z Personal Panel
Uniform and Blue Shirt Material
Under Panel 1995-1998
Panel: grauer Baumwollflanell;
117 x 71 cm; Under Panel: weisser
und blauer Baumwollstoff

70
Khaki Corduroy A–Z Personal Panel
Uniform and Navy Blue Striped
Under Panel 1995-1998
Panel: Baumwollkord; 117 x 71 cm;
Under Panel: marineblau gestreifter
Stoff

71
Grey Wool with Black Embroidery
A–Z Personal Panel Uniform and
Dark Green Rayon Under Panel
1995-1998
Panel: grauer Wollstoff, Stickerei
und elastische Schulterriemen;
117 x 71 cm; Under Panel: dunkel-
grüner Rayon

72
Grey Satin with Yellow Pattern A–Z
Personal Panel Uniform and Light
Yellow Silk Under Panel 1998
Panel: grauer Satin mit gelbem
Muster; 117 x 71 cm; Under Panel:
hellgelbe Seide

73
RAUGH Brown Cotton A–Z Personal
Panel Uniform 1998
Baumwollstoff mit Schulterriemen
und Sicherheitsnadeln

74
RAUGH Blue Nylon A–Z Personal
Panel Uniform 1998

Nylon mit Schulterriemen und
Sicherheitsnadeln

75
Light Blue A–Z Personal Panel
Uniform 1995-1998
Baumwollgewebe; 117.2 x 71 cm

76
Salmon and Red Silk A–Z Personal
Panel Uniform 1995-1998
Seidengewebe; 113 x 70.5 cm

77
Grey Taffeta with Black Velvet
Ribbon A–Z Personal Panel Uniform
1995-1998
Taftgewebe mit Samtborte;
116.7 x 70.8 cm

78
Pale Silk Satin with Black Trim A–Z
Personal Panel Uniform 1995-1998
Seidensatingewebe mit Borte;
117 x 71 cm

79
Red and Purple „Mondrian" A–Z
Personal Panel Uniform 1998
Wolle, Samt, Seide und
Satingewebe; 112 x 71 cm

80
Brown Denim A–Z Personal Panel
Uniform 1995-1998
Baumwollgewebe (Denim);
111.5 x 71.7 cm

81
Navy Blue Nylon A–Z Personal
Panel Uniform 1995-98
Nylon-Jacket-Gewebe;
115 x 71.5 cm

82
Olive, Red and Black „Window
Pane" A–Z Personal Panel Uniform
1995-1998
Samt, Wolle und Futterstoff mit
elastischen Schulterriemen;
114 x 69.5 cm

83
Bright Orange A–Z Under Panel
1995-1998
Baumwollgewebe; 88.3 x 128.5 cm

84
Tangerine Silk A–Z Under Panel
1995-1998
Seidengewebe; 89.8 x 107.5 cm

85
New Red A–Z Under Panel
1995-1998
Baumwollgewebe; 89.9 x 106.3 cm

86
Silver-Grey Metallic A–Z Under
Panel 1995-1998
Taftgewebe; 89.8 x 106.3 cm

87
A–Z Single-Strand Uniform:
Fall 1998 1998
grünes und schwarzes Kleid aus
Wolle und Mohairmischung,
ärmellos, knielang, schwarze
Umhängetasche aus Wolle und
schwarzer Rollkragenpullover

88
A–Z Single-Strand Uniform: Winter
1998 1998
graues, gelbes und schwarzes Kleid
aus Wolle, ärmellos, knielang und
schwarzer Rollkragenpullover

89
A–Z Single-Strand Uniform: Spring
1999 1999
blaues, braunes und schwarzes
Kleid aus Rayon, ärmellos, knielang

90
A–Z Single-Strand Uniform:
Summer 1999 (L.A.) 1999
grün, gelb und lachsfarben
meliertes Kleid aus Rayon und
Baumwolle, ärmellos, knielang

91
A–Z Single-Strand Uniform:
Summer 1999 (Berlin) 1999
grünes, braunes und schwarzes
Kleid aus Wolle, ärmellos,
knielang, schwarzes Oberteil

92
A–Z Single-Strand Uniform: Fall
1999 1999
braunes und schwarzes Kleid aus

89

A–Z Single-Strand Uniform: Spring 1999 1999
blue, brown and black dress, rayon, sleeveless, knee-length

90

A–Z Single-Strand Uniform: Summer 1999 (L.A.) 1999
grey, yellow and salmon dress, rayon and cotton, sleeveless, knee-length

91

A–Z Single-Strand Uniform: Summer 1999 (Berlin) 1999
green, brown and black dress, wool, sleeveless, knee-length, black top

92

A–Z Single-Strand Uniform: Fall 1999 1999
brown and black dress, wool and mohair, sleeveless, knee length, black top

93

A–Z Single-Strand Uniform: Winter 1999 1999
brown and black dress, wool, long-sleeved, knee-length

94

A–Z Single-Strand Uniform: Spring 2000 2000
red and brown dress, rayon and mohair, sleeveless, knee-length

95

A–Z Single-Strand Uniform: Summer 2000 2000
light blue, red and black dress, cotton, sleeveless, knee-lenght

96

Special "Pocket Property" A–Z Single-Strand Uniform 2000 2000
blue, green, yellow and black hooded dress, wool, long-sleeved, floor-length

97

A–Z Single-Strand Uniform: Winter 2000 2000
brownish grey and black striped dress, mohair, long-sleeved, knee-length and black turtleneck

98

A–Z Single-Strand Uniform: Winter 2000 2001
green, grey and black striped dress, wool, long-sleeved, knee-length

99

A–Z Single-Strand Uniform: Spring 2001 2001
white, black and green striped dress, cotton, shortsleeve, knee-length

100

A–Z Single-Strand Uniform: Summer 2001 2001
yellow dress, cotton, sleeveless, knee-length

101

A–Z Handmade Single-Strand Uniform: Fall 2001 #1 (green and black top) 2001
green and black top, wool and mohair, long-sleeved, black skirt

102

A–Z Handmade Single-Strand Uniform: Fall 2001 #2 (grey and black top) 2001
grey and black top, wool, long-sleeved, black skirt

103

A–Z Handmade Single-Strand Uniform: Fall 2001 #3 (brownish-grey and black top) 2001
brownish-grey and black top, wool, long-sleeved, black skirt

104

A–Z Handmade Single-Strand Uniform: Fall 2001 #4 (grey and black dress) 2001
grey and black dress, wool and mohair, long-sleeved, knee-length, black turtleneck and skirt

105

A–Z Handmade Single-Strand Uniform: Winter 2001 (brown and black top) 2001
brown and black top, wool, long-sleeved, black skirt

Room 3 A

106 ill. p. 59

A–Z Escape Vehicle: "Exterior World Model" 1996
gouache on paper; 11 x 15"
Courtesy the artist and Andrea Rosen Gallery, New York

107 ill. p. 58

A–Z Escape Vehicle: "Interior World Model" 1996
gouache on paper; 11 x 15"
The Museum of Modern Art, New York. Gift of Patricia and Morris Orden

108 ill. p. 57

The A–Z Escape Vehicle... 1996
gouache on paper; 16 1/2 x 22"
Hort Family Collection

Room 3

109

Point of Interest in My Back Yard 1998
pencil on paper; 21 1/8 x 30 1/8"
Courtesy the artist and Andrea Rosen Gallery, New York

110

The Three of Us on Point of Interest 1998
pencil on paper; 21 1/8 x 30 1/8"
Courtesy the artist and Andrea Rosen Gallery, New York

111

Visit to Point of Interest 1998
pencil on paper; 21 1/8 x 40 3/8"
Courtesy the artist and Andrea Rosen Gallery, New York

112

My 1999 Winter Dress on a Model of Point of Interest 1999
pencil on paper; 22 x 30"
Private Collection

113

Two Public Sculptures 1999
pencil on paper; 22 x 30"
The Museum of Modern Art, New York. Gift of the Contemporary Arts

Wolle und Mohair, ärmellos,
knielang, schwarzes Oberteil

93
A–Z Single-Strand Uniform: Winter
1999 1999
braunes und schwarzes Kleid aus
Wolle, langarm, knielang

94
A–Z Single-Strand Uniform: Spring
2000 2000
rotes und braunes Kleid aus Rayon
und Mohair, ärmellos, knielang

95
A–Z Single-Strand Uniform:
Summer 2000 2000
hellblaues, rotes und schwarzes
Trägerkleid aus Baumwolle,
knielang

96
Special „Pocket Property" A–Z
Single-Strand Uniform 2000 2000
blaues, grünes, gelbes und
schwarzes Kleid mit Kapuze aus
Wolle, langarm, bodenlang

97
A–Z Single-Strand Uniform: Winter
2000 2000
blau-graues und schwarz gestreiftes
Kleid aus Mohair, langarm, knielang,
schwarzer Rollkragenpullover

98
A–Z Single-Strand Uniform: Winter
2000 2001
grün, grau und schwarz gestreiftes
Kleid aus Wolle, langarm, knielang,
schwarzer Rollkragenpullover

99
A–Z Single-Strand Uniform: Spring
2001 2001
weiss, schwarz und grün gestreiftes
Kleid aus Baumwolle, kurzarm,
knielang

100
A–Z Single-Strand Uniform:
Summer 2001 2001
gelbes Kleid aus Baumwolle, ärmellos, knielang

101
A–Z Handmade Single-Strand
Uniform: Fall 2001 #1 (green and
black top) 2001
grünes und schwarzes Oberteil aus
Wolle und Mohair, langarm,
schwarzer Rock

102
A–Z Handmade Single-Strand
Uniform: Fall 2001 #2 (grey and
black top) 2001
graues und schwarzes Oberteil aus
Wolle, langarm, schwarzer Rock

103
A–Z Handmade Single-Strand
Uniform: Fall 2001 #3 (brownish-
grey and black top) 2001
braungraues und schwarzes
Oberteil aus Wolle, langarm,
schwarzer Rock

104
A–Z Handmade Single-Strand
Uniform: Fall 2001 #4 (grey and
black dress) 2001
graues und schwarzes Kleid aus
Wolle und Mohair, langarm, knielang,
schwarzer Rollkragenpullover und
schwarzer Rock

105
A–Z Handmade Single-Strand
Uniform: Winter 2001 (brown and
black top) 2001
braunes und schwarzes Oberteil
aus Wolle, langarm, schwarzer Rock

Raum 3 A

106 Abb. S. 59
A–Z Escape Vehicle: „Exterior
World Model" 1996
Gouache auf Papier; 28 x 38 cm
Courtesy die Künstlerin und Andrea
Rosen Gallery, New York

107 Abb. S. 58
A–Z Escape Vehicle: „Interior World
Model" 1996
Gouache auf Papier; 28 x 38 cm
The Museum of Modern Art,

New York, Geschenk von Patricia
und Morris Orden

108 Abb. S. 57
The A–Z Escape Vehicle... 1996
Gouache auf Papier; 42 x 56 cm
Hort Family Collection

Raum 3

109
Point of Interest in My Back Yard
1998
Bleistift auf Papier; 53.7 x 76.5 cm
Courtesy die Künstlerin und Andrea
Rosen Gallery, New York

110
The Three of Us on Point of Interest
1998
Bleistift auf Papier; 53.7 x 76.5 cm
Courtesy die Künstlerin und Andrea
Rosen Gallery, New York

111
Visit to Point of Interest 1998
Bleistift auf Papier; 53.7 x 102.6 cm
Courtesy die Künstlerin und Andrea
Rosen Gallery, New York

112
My 1999 Winter Dress on a Model
of Point of Interest 1999
Bleistift auf Papier; 56 x 76.2 cm
Privatsammlung

113
Two Public Sculptures 1999
Bleistift auf Papier; 56 x 76.2 cm
The Museum of Modern Art, New
York, Geschenk des Contemporary
Arts Council, The Museum of
Modern Art in Erinnerung an
Patricia Orden

114
The Scientific Point of Interest
1999
Bleistift auf Papier; 38 x 50.8 cm
Martin und Rebecca Eisenberg

115
The Beatific Point of Interest 1999
Bleistift auf Papier; 38 x 50.8 cm
Martin und Rebecca Eisenberg

Council of The Museum of Modern
Art in Memory of Patricia Orden

114
The Scientific Point of Interest
1999
pencil on paper; 15 x 20"
Martin and Rebecca Eisenberg

115
The Beatific Point of Interest
1999
pencil on paper; 15 x 20"
Martin and Rebecca Eisenberg

116
The Recreational Point of Interest
1999
pencil on paper; 15 x 20"
Private Collection

117
Julien and Mike on Point of Interest
1999
pencil on paper; 17 x 14"
Courtesy the artist and Andrea
Rosen Gallery, New York

118
Maria's Friend on Point of Interest
1999
pencil on paper; 17 x 14"
Courtesy the artist and Andrea
Rosen Gallery, New York

119
Maria on Point of Interest 1999
pencil on paper; 17 x 14"
Courtesy the artist and Andrea
Rosen Gallery, New York

120
Mike on Point of Interest 1999
pencil on paper; 14 x 17"
Courtesy the artist and Andrea
Rosen Gallery, New York

121 ill. p. 62
*Point of Interest: An A–Z Land
Brand* 1999
gouache on paper; 13 x 20"
Courtesy the artist and Andrea
Rosen Gallery, New York

122 ill. p. 63
*Point of Interest: An A–Z Land
Brand* 1999
gouache and pencil on paper;
15 x 20"
The Museum of Modern Art,
New York. Gift of Patricia and
Morris Orden

123
Sprawl I 2002
color lithograph; 12 1/2 x 16"
Edition 9, 3 AP
Solo Impression Inc

124
Sprawl II 2003
color lithograph; 12 1/2 x 17"
Edition 9, 3 AP
Solo Impression Inc

125 ill. p. 105
A–Z Suburban Islands I 2001
1 unique gouache on paper and 19
inkjet prints; overall 38 1/8 x 39 1/8"
Courtesy Regen Projects, Los
Angeles, CA

126
A–Z Suburban Islands II 2001
1 unique gouache on paper and
15 inkjet prints; overall 31 x 31"
Courtesy Regen Projects,
Los Angeles, CA

127 ill. p. 106
A–Z Suburban Islands IV 2001
1 unique gouache on paper and
15 inkjet prints; overall 31 x 31"
Courtesy Regen Projects, Los
Angeles, CA

128 ill. p. 104
Sprawl #1 2001
1 unique gouache on paper and
15 inkjet prints; overall 40 x 28"
Courtesy the artist and Andrea
Rosen Gallery, New York

129 ill. p. 107
Sprawl #4 2001
1 unique gouache on paper and
15 inkjet prints; overall
35 4/5 x 32 3/5"

Emanuel Hoffmann Foundation, on
permanent loan to the Öffentliche
Kunstsammlung Basel

130
*A–Z Escape Vehicle Customized by
Andrea Zittel* 1996
shell: steel, insulation, wood, glass
interior: fiberglass, wood, papier-
mâché, colored lights, water, peb-
bles and paint; 60 x 40 x 84"
The Museum of Modern Art, New
York. The Norman and Rosita
Winston Foundation, Inc. Fund and
an anonymous fund, 1997

131
*A–Z Escape Vehicle Owned and
Customized by the Emanuel
Hoffmann Foundation* 1997
shell: steel, insulation, wood,
glass; interior: Deux Chevaux car
parts, plasma monitor, amplifier,
2 loudspeakers, 2 VHS players;
60 x 40 x 84"
Emanuel Hoffmann Foundation, on
permanent loan to the Öffentliche
Kunstsammlung Basel

132
*A–Z Escape Vehicle Owned and
Customized by Federica and Rolf
Fehlbaum for the Vitra* 1997
shell: steel, insulation, wood and
glass; 60 x 40 x 84"
Private Collection

133
A–Z Deserted Island VI 1997
fiberglass, wood, plastic, flotation
tank, vinyl seat and vinyl logo;
36 x 90 x 90"
Courtesy the artist and Andrea
Rosen Gallery, New York

134
A–Z Deserted Island VII 1997
fiberglass, wood, plastic, flotation
tank, vinyl seat and vinyl logo;
36 x 90 x 90"
Courtesy the artist and Andrea
Rosen Gallery, New York

116
The Recreational Point of
Interest 1999
Bleistift auf Papier; 38 x 50.8 cm
Privatsammlung

117
Julien and Mike on Point of Interest
1999
Bleistift auf Papier; 43.2 x 35.6 cm
Courtesy die Künstlerin und Andrea
Rosen Gallery, New York

118
Maria's Friend on Point of Interest
1999
Bleistift auf Papier; 43.2 x 35.6 cm
Courtesy die Künstlerin und Andrea
Rosen Gallery, New York

119
Maria on Point of Interest 1999
Bleistift auf Papier; 43.2 x 35.6 cm
Courtesy die Künstlerin und Andrea
Rosen Gallery, New York

120
Mike on Point of Interest 1999
Bleistift auf Papier; 35.6 x 43.2 cm
Courtesy die Künstlerin und Andrea
Rosen Gallery, New York

121 Abb. S. 62
Point of Interest: An A–Z Land
Brand 1999
Gouache auf Papier; 33 x 50.8 cm
Courtesy die Künstlerin und Andrea
Rosen Gallery, New York

122 Abb. S. 63
Point of Interest: An A–Z Land Brand
1999
Gouache und Bleistift auf Papier;
38 x 50.8 cm
The Museum of Modern Art,
New York, Geschenk von Patricia
und Morris Orden

123
Sprawl I 2002
Farblithographie; 31.7 x 40.6 cm
Edition 9, 3 AP
Solo Impression Inc

124
Sprawl II 2003
Farblithographie; 31.7 x 43.2 cm
Edition 9, 3 AP
Solo Impression Inc

125 Abb. S. 105
A–Z Suburban Islands I 2001
1 Gouache auf Papier und 19
Inkjetprints auf Papier; insgesamt
96.8 x 99.4 cm
Courtesy Regen Projects,
Los Angeles, CA

126
A–Z Suburban Islands II 2001
1 Gouache auf Papier und 15
Inkjetprints auf Papier; insgesamt
78.7 x 78.7 cm
Courtesy Regen Projects,
Los Angeles, CA

127 Abb. S. 106
A–Z Suburban Islands IV 2001
1 Gouache auf Papier und 15
Inkjetprints;
insgesamt 78.7 x 78.7 cm
Courtesy Regen Projects,
Los Angeles, CA

128 Abb. S. 104
Sprawl #1 2001
1 Gouache auf Papier und 15
Inkjetprints auf Papier; insgesamt
101.6 x 71 cm
Courtesy die Künstlerin und Andrea
Rosen Gallery, New York

129 Abb. S. 107
Sprawl #4 2001
1 Gouache auf Papier und 15
Inkjetprints auf Papier; insgesamt
91 x 83 cm; Emanuel Hoffmann-
Stiftung, Depositum in der
Öffentlichen Kunstsammlung Basel

130
A–Z Escape Vehicle Customized by
Andrea Zittel 1996
Gehäuse: Stahl, Isolationsmaterial,
Holz und Glas; Inneres: Glasfaser,
Holz, Papiermaché, farbige Lampen,
Wasser, Kieselsteine und Farbe;
157.5 x 101.6 x 213.4 cm

The Museum of Modern Art, New
York, The Norman and Rosita
Winston Foundation, Inc. Fund mit
einem Beitrag von anonymer Seite,
1997

131
A–Z Escape Vehicle Owned and
Customized by the Emanuel
Hoffmann Foundation 1996/1997
Gehäuse: Stahl, Isolationsmaterial,
Holz, Glas; Inneres: Deux-Chevaux-
Bestandteile, Plasma-Flachbild-
schirm, Verstärker, Lautsprecher,
2 VHS-Player; 152.5 x 213.5 x
101.5 cm
Emanuel Hoffmann-Stiftung,
Depositum in der Öffentlichen
Kunstsammlung Basel

132
A–Z Escape Vehicle Owned and
Customized by Federica and Rolf
Fehlbaum for the Vitra 1997
Gehäuse: Stahl, Isolationsmaterial,
Holz und Glas; 152.5 x 213.5 x
101.5 cm
Privatsammlung

133
A–Z Deserted Island VI 1997
Glasfaser, Holz, Kunststoff,
Schwebebehälter, Vinylsitz und
Vinylbeschriftung; 91.4 x 228.6 x
228.6 cm
Courtesy die Künstlerin und Andrea
Rosen Gallery, New York

134
A–Z Deserted Island VII 1997
Glasfaser, Holz, Kunststoff,
Schwebebehälter, Vinylsitz und
Vinylbeschriftung; 91.4 x 228.6 x
228.6 cm
Courtesy die Künstlerin und Andrea
Rosen Gallery, New York

Raum 4

135
Free Running Rhythms and
Patterns: Version II 2000

135

Free Running Rhythms and Patterns: Version II 2000
28 parts; walnut veneer, latex and oil-based paint, vinyl lettering and black-and-white photos; each 79 1/8 x 31 1/2 x 2"
Collection Olbricht

136

A–Z Time Tunnel: Time to Get Into Perfect Shape 2000
aluminum, walnut wood, steel, MDF, carpet, paint, vinyl adhesive, electrical lighting and sound machine; 39 x 48 1/4 x 80 1/4" closed without ladder; 46 3/4 x 48 1/4 x 94 1/4" open with ladder
Collection Olbricht

137

A–Z Time Tunnel: Time to Get to Know People Better 2000
aluminum, walnut wood, steel, MDF, carpet, paint, vinyl adhesive and electrical lighting;
39 x 48 1/4 x 80 1/4" closed without ladder; 46 3/4 x 48 1/4 x 94 1/4" open with ladder
Collection Olbricht

Room 5

138 ill. p. 60
A–Z Logo Study 1996
gouache and pencil on paper;
11 x 15"
The Museum of Modern Art, New York. Gift of Patricia and Morris Orden

139 ill. p. 87
My Neighbor Charles with His Carpet Furniture 1999
gouache on paper; 28 1/2 x 40"
Marta Moriarty Collection

140 ill. p. 86
Pit Bed vs. Platform Bed 1999
2 parts; gouache on paper;
each 24 x 34"
Hort Family Collection

141 ill. p. 82
The A–Z Chamber Pot 1999
gouache on paper; 24 x 34"
Zdenek Felix, Berlin

142 ill. p. 61
A–Z Emblem 1999
gouache on paper; 15 x 11"
Courtesy the artist and Andrea Rosen Gallery, New York

143 ill. p. 91l
A–Z Food Group: The Compounds of Life 2001
gouache on paper; 30 x 22"
Goetz Collection

144 ill. p. 85
Find New Ways to Position Yourself in the World 2001
gouache on paper; 30 x 22"
Courtesy the artist and Andrea Rosen Gallery, New York

145

A–Z Cellular Compartment Units #1 2001
10 parts; stainless steel, birch plywood, glass and mixed media each 48 x 48 x 96"; overall 96 x 144 x 192"
Courtesy the artist and Andrea Rosen Gallery, New York

146

A–Z Cellular Compartment Communities #2 2002
4 parts; latex paint, tape and pen on birch plywood; each 49 5/16 x 97 3/8"; overall 98 5/8 x 266 7/8"
Emanuel Hoffmann Foundation, on permanent loan to the Öffentliche Kunstsammlung Basel

147

A–Z Cellular Compartment Communities #5 2002
5 parts; latex paint, tape, and pen on birch plywood; each 49 5/16 x 97 3/8"; overall 147 15/16 x 194 3/4"
Courtesy the artist and Andrea Rosen Gallery, New York

148 ill. p. 161
Prototype for Billboard at A–Z West: These Things I Know for Sure #1 2005
Flashe, vinyl lettering and polyurethane on birch plywood;
41 x 71 1/4"
Hort Family Collection

149 ill. p. 157
Prototype for Billboard at A–Z West: Things I Know for Sure #3 2005
Flashe, vinyl lettering and polyurethane on birch plywood;
41 x 71 1/4"
Private Collection, Madrid

150 ill. p. 155
Prototype for Billboard at A–Z West: These Things I Know for Sure #4 2005
Flashe, vinyl lettering and polyurethane on birch plywood;
41 x 71 1/4"
Courtesy Martha Macks-Kahn and Goya Contemporary

151 ill. p. 147
Prototype for Billboard at A–Z West: These Things I Know for Sure #10 2005
Flashe, vinyl lettering and polyurethane on birch plywood;
41 x 71 1/4"
Emanuel Hoffmann Foundation, on permanent loan to the Öffentliche Kunstsammlung Basel

152 ill. p. 141
Prototype for Billboard at A–Z West: These Things I Know for Sure #14 2005
Flashe, vinyl lettering and polyurethane on birch plywood;
41 x 71 1/4"
Private Collection New York

153 ill. p. 151
Prototype for Billboard at A–Z West: These Things I Know for Sure #4 2006
Flashe, vinyl lettering and poly-

28 Teile; Walnussfurnier, auf Latex
und Öl basierte Farbe,
Vinylbeschriftung und schwarz-
weiss Fotografien; je 201 x 80 x 5 cm
Sammlung Olbricht

136
A–Z Time Tunnel: Time to Get Into
Perfect Shape 2000
Aluminium, Walnussholz, Stahl,
MDF, Teppichboden, Farbe, Vinyl,
Elektroinstallation, Soundmaschine
99 x 122 x 201 cm geschlossen
ohne Leiter; 118.8 x 122 x 239.4 cm
offen mit Leiter
Sammlung Olbricht

137
A–Z Time Tunnel: Time to Get to
Know People Better 2000
Aluminium, Walnussholz, Stahl,
MDF, Teppichboden, Farbe, Vinyl,
Elektroinstallation; 99 x 122 x 201
cm geschlossen ohne Leiter; 118.8 x
122 x 239.4 cm offen mit Leiter
Sammlung Olbricht

Raum 5

138 Abb. S. 60
A–Z Logo Study 1996
Gouache und Bleistift auf Papier;
28 x 38 cm
The Museum of Modern Art, New
York, Geschenk von Patricia und
Morris Orden

139 Abb. S. 87
My Neighbor Charles with His
Carpet Furniture 1999
Gouache auf Papier; 72.40 x
101.5 cm
Sammlung Marta Moriarty

140 Abb. S. 86
Pit Bed vs. Platform Bed 1999
2 Teile; Gouache auf Papier:
je 62 x 87.4 cm
Hort Family Collection

141 Abb. S. 82
The A–Z Chamber Pot 1999
Gouache auf Papier; 62 x 87.4 cm
Zdenek Felix, Berlin

142 Abb. S. 61
A–Z Emblem 1999
Gouache auf Papier; 38 x 28 cm

143 Abb. S. 91l
A–Z Food Group: The Compounds
of Life 2001
Gouache auf Papier; 76.2 x 56 cm
Sammlung Goetz

144 Abb. S. 85
Find New Ways to Position Yourself
in the World 2001
Gouache auf Papier; 76.2 x 56 cm
Courtesy die Künstlerin und Andrea
Rosen Gallery, New York

145
A–Z Cellular Compartment Units
#1 2001
10 Teile; Edelstahl, Birkensperrholz,
Glas und Einrichtungsgegenstände
je 122 x 122 x 244 cm; insgesamt
244 x 366 x 488 cm
Courtesy die Künstlerin und Andrea
Rosen Gallery, New York

146
A–Z Cellular Compartment
Communities #2 2002
4 Teile; Latex Farbe, Klebeband
und Filzstift auf Birkensperrholz;
je 125 x 247 cm; insgesamt
250.5 x 678 cm
Emanuel Hoffmann-Stiftung,
Depositum in der Öffentlichen
Kunstsammlung Basel

147
A–Z Cellular Compartment
Communities #5 2002
5 Teile; Latex Farbe, Klebeband und
Filzstift auf Birkensperrholz;
je 125 x 247 cm; insgesamt
250.5 x 678 cm
Courtesy die Künstlerin und Andrea
Rosen Gallery, New York

Raum 6

148 Abb. S. 161
Prototype for Billboard at A–Z
West: These Things I Know for
Sure #1 2005

Flashe-Vinylfarbe, Vinylbeschriftung
und Polyurethanlack auf
Birkensperrholz; 104 x 181 cm
Hort Family Collection

149 Abb. S. 157
Prototype for Billboard at A–Z
West: Things I Know for Sure #3
2005
Flashe-Vinylfarbe, Vinylbeschriftung
und Polyurethanlack auf
Birkensperrholz; 104 x 181 cm
Privatsammlung

150 Abb. S. 155
Prototype for Billboard at A–Z
West: These Things I Know for
Sure #4 2005
Flashe-Vinylfarbe, Vinylbeschriftung
und Polyurethanlack auf
Birkensperrholz; 104 x 181 cm
Courtesy Martha Macks-Kahn und
Goya Contemporary

151 Abb. S. 147
Prototype for Billboard at A–Z
West: These Things I Know for
Sure #10 2005
Flashe-Vinylfarbe, Vinylbeschriftung
und Polyurethanlack auf
Birkensperrholz; 104 x 181 cm
Emanuel Hoffmann-Stiftung,
Depositum in der Öffentlichen
Kunstsammlung Basel

152 Abb. S. 141
Prototype for Billboard at A–Z
West: These Things I Know for
Sure #14 2005
Flashe-Vinylfarbe, Vinylbeschriftung
und Polyurethanlack auf
Birkensperrholz; 104 x 181 cm
Privatsammlung, New York

153 Abb. S. 151
Prototype for Billboard at A–Z
West: These Things I Know for
Sure #4 2006
Flashe-Vinylfarbe, Vinylbeschriftung
und Polyurethanlack auf
Fichtensperrholz; 120 x 186 cm
Courtesy Sadie Coles HQ,
London

urethane on fir plywood;
47 1/4 x 73 1/4"
Courtesy Sadie Coles HQ, London

154 ill. p. 159
*Prototype for Billboard at A–Z West:
These Things I Know for Sure #1
(AZ in fiber form holding scarf)* 2006
Flashe, vinyl lettering and
polyurethane on fir plywood;
47 1/4 x 73 1/4"
Courtesy Sadie Coles HQ, London

155 ill. p. 149
*Prototype for Billboard at A–Z West:
These Things I Know for Sure #8*
2006
Flashe, vinyl lettering and poly-
urethane on fir plywood;
47 1/4 x 73 1/4"
Collection Maja Hoffmann

156 ill. p. 145
*Prototype for Billboard at A–Z West:
These Things I Know for Sure #11*
2006
Flashe, vinyl lettering and poly-
urethane on fir plywood;
47 1/4 x 73 1/4"
Courtesy Sadie Coles HQ, London

157 ill. p. 167
*Prototype for Billboard at A–Z West:
Radiating Arenas of Enhancement
#1* 2006
Flashe, vinyl lettering and poly-
urethane on birch plywood;
47 1/4 x 73 1/4"
Courtesy Sadie Coles HQ, London

158 ill. p. 143
*Prototype for Billboard at A–Z West:
These Things I Know for Sure #13*
2006
Flashe, vinyl lettering and poly-
urethane on fir plywood;
47 1/4 x 73 1/4"
Gemma De Angelis Testa Collection

159 ill. p. 165
*Prototype for Billboard at A–Z West:
Voids and Avoids* 2007
Flashe, vinyl lettering and poly-
urethane on fir plywood;

47 1/4 x 73 1/4"
Collection Freeman, Los Angeles

Room 7

160
A–Z Homestead Units #1 2001
acrylic, gouache and pen on paper;
18 x 23"
Courtesy Sadie Coles HQ, London

161 ill. p. 111
A–Z Homestead Units #2 2001
acrylic, gouache and pen on paper;
18 x 23"
Collection Deutsche Bank

162
A–Z Homestead Units #3 2001
acrylic, gouache and pen on paper;
18 x 23"
Addison Gallery of American Art,
Philipps Academy, Andover, MA

163 ill. p. 112
A–Z Homestead Units #6 2001
acrylic, gouache and pen on paper;
18 x 23"
Collection Deutsche Bank

164
*sfnwvlei (Something for Nothing
with Very Little Effort Involved) Note
#1* 2002
gouache and pen on birch plywood;
24 x 36"
Diez-Cascón Collection

165
*sfnwvlei (Something for Nothing
with Very Little Effort Involved) Note
#2* 2002
gouache and pen on birch plywood;
24 x 36"
Diez-Cascón Collection

166
*sfnwvlei (Something for Nothing
with Very Little Effort Involved) Note
#3* 2002
gouache and pen on birch plywood;
24 x 36"
Diez-Cascón Collection

167
*sfnwvlei (Something for Nothing
with Very Little Effort Involved) Note
#4* 2002
gouache and pen on birch plywood;
24 x 36"
Diez-Cascón Collection

168 ill. p. 163
*Prototype for Billboard at A–Z West:
Single Strand* 2006
flashe and polyurethane on fir
plywood; 47 1/4 x 73 1/4"
Collection J. Rubner, Italy

169 ill. p. 169
*Prototype for Billboard at A–Z West:
Ribbon* 2007
flashe and polyurethane on fir ply-
wood; 47 1/4 x 73 1/4"
Courtesy the artist and Andrea
Rosen Gallery, New York

170
A–Z Paper Pulp Panels #4 2008
3 parts; powder coated steel frame,
adhesive and paper pulp panel
(paperwaste and cement);
96 x 72"; 84 x 72"; 72 x 72"
Courtesy the artist and Andrea
Rosen Gallery, New York

171
*A–Z Homestead Unit from A–Z
West with RAUGH Furniture*
2001-2005
powder-coated steel, birch paneling
with paint and polyurethane,
corrugated metal roof, sculpted
foam furniture, fleece blanket, pillows with pillowcases, A–Z Fiber
Form Containers (felted wool),
campstove with tea; 308 x 183"
Los Angeles County Museum of
Art, Modern and Contemporary Art
Council and the Contemporary Art
Deaccession Fund

172
*A–Z Fiber Form Uniform: White
Felted Dress #2* 2002
felted wool; 57" length
Angelika Taschen, Berlin

154 Abb. S. 159
Prototype for Billboard at A–Z
West: These Things I Know for
Sure #1 (AZ in Fiber Form holding
scarf) 2006
Flashe-Vinylfarbe, Vinylbeschriftung
und Polyurethanlack auf
Fichtensperrholz; 120 x 186 cm
Courtesy Sadie Coles HQ, London

155 Abb. S. 149
Prototype for Billboard at A–Z
West: These Things I Know for
Sure #8 2006
Flashe-Vinylfarbe, Vinylbeschriftung
und Polyurethanlack auf
Fichtensperrholz; 120 x 186 cm
Sammlung Maja Hoffmann

156 Abb. S. 145
Prototype for Billboard at A–Z West:
These Things I Know for Sure #11
2006
Flashe-Vinylfarbe, Vinylbeschriftung
und Polyurethanlack auf
Fichtensperrholz; 120 x 186 cm
Courtesy Sadie Coles HQ, London

157 Abb. S. 167
Prototype for Billboard at A–Z West:
Radiating Arenas of Enhancement
#1 2006
Flashe-Vinylfarbe, Vinylbeschriftung
und Polyurethanlack auf
Birkensperrholz; 120 x 186 cm
Courtesy Sadie Coles HQ, London

158 Abb. S. 143
Prototype for Billboard at A–Z West:
These Things I Know for Sure #13
2006
Flashe-Vinylfarbe, Vinylbeschriftung
und Polyurethanlack auf
Fichtensperrholz; 120 x 186 cm
Sammlung Gemma De Angelis Testa

159 Abb. S. 165
Prototype for Billboard at A–Z
West: Voids and Avoids 2007
Flashe-Vinylfarbe, Vinylbeschriftung
und Polyurethanlack auf
Fichtensperrholz; 120 x 186 cm
Sammlung Freeman, Los Angeles

Raum 7

160
A–Z Homestead Units #1 2001
Acryl, Gouache und Filzstift auf
Papier; 46 x 58.6 cm
Courtesy Sadie Coles HQ, London

161 Abb. S. 111
A–Z Homestead Units #2 2001
Acryl, Gouache und Filzstift auf
Papier; 46 x 58.6 cm
Sammlung Deutsche Bank

162
A–Z Homestead Units #3 2001
Acryl, Gouache und Filzstift auf
Papier; 46 x 58.6 cm
Addison Gallery of American Art,
Philipps Academy, Andover, MA

163 Abb. S. 112
A–Z Homestead Units #6 2001
Acryl, Gouache und Filzstift auf
Papier; 46 x 58.6 cm
Sammlung Deutsche Bank

164
sfnwvlei (Something for Nothing
with Very Little Effort Involved)
Note #1 2002
Gouache und Filzstift auf
Birkensperrholz; 61 x 91.5 cm
Sammlung Diez-Cascón

165
sfnwvlei (Something for Nothing
with Very Little Effort Involved)
Note #2 2002
Gouache und Filzstift auf
Birkensperrholz; 61 x 91.5 cm
Sammlung Diez-Cascón

166
sfnwvlei (Something for Nothing
with Very Little Effort Involved)
Note #3 2002
Gouache und Filzstift auf
Birkensperrholz; 61 x 91.5 cm
Sammlung Diez-Cascón

167
sfnwvlei (Something for Nothing
with Very Little Effort Involved)

Note #4 2002
Gouache und Filzstift auf
Birkensperrholz; 61 x 91.5 cm
Sammlung Diez-Cascón

168 Abb. S. 163
Prototype for Billboard at A–Z
West: Single Strand 2006
Flashe-Vinylfarbe und
Polyurethanlack auf
Fichtensperrholz; 120 x 186 cm
Sammlung J. Rubner, Italien

169 Abb. S. 169
Prototype for Billboard at A–Z
West: Ribbon 2007
Flashe-Vinylfarbe und Polyurethanlack
auf Fichtensperrholz; 120 x 186 cm
Courtesy die Künstlerin und Andrea
Rosen Gallery, New York

170
A–Z Paper Pulp Panels #4 2008
3 Teile; pulverbeschichteter
Stahlrahmen, Klebstoff und Panel
aus Papierabfall und Zement;
243.8 x 183 cm; 213.4 x 183 cm;
183 x 183 cm
Courtesy die Künstlerin und Andrea
Rosen Gallery, New York

171
A–Z Homestead Unit from A–Z
West with RAUGH Furniture
2001-2005
pulverbeschichtetes Stahl, Birken-
sperrholz mit Farbe und Poly-
urethanlack, Wellblechdach,
Schaumstoff, Vliesdecke, Kissen
mit Kissenbezug, A–Z Fiber Form
Behälter (gefilzte Wolle), Camping-
kocher mit Tee; 782 x 465 cm
Los Angeles County Museum of
Art, Modern and Contemporary Art
Council und Contemporary Art
Deaccession Fund

172
A–Z Fiber Form: White Felted
Dress #2 2002
gefilzte Wolle; 144.8 cm lang
Angelika Taschen, Berlin

173
*A–Z Fiber Form Uniform: White
Felted Dress #5* 2002
felted wool; 57" length
Courtesy Paula Cooper Gallery

174
*A–Z Fiber Form Uniform: White
Felted Dress #7* 2002
felted wool; 57" length
Collection of Eileen Harris Norton,
Santa Monica

175
*A–Z Fiber Form Uniform: White
Felted Dress #8* 2002
felted wool; 57" length
Iann Stolz Collection

Room 8

176 ill. p. 69
Me in a RAUGH Dress on a Field Trip
1998
gouache on paper; 20 x 15"
Private Collection, Jersey

177
Martha with A–Z Food Group 2001
gouache on paper; 30 x 22"
Courtesy the artist and Andrea
Rosen Gallery, New York

178 ill. p. 89
A–Z Food Group for You 2001
gouache on paper; 30 x 22"
Courtesy the artist and Andrea
Rosen Gallery, New York

179
Eat Your Food Group RAUGH 2001
gouache on paper; 22 x 30"
Tullio Leggeri Collection

180
*A–Z Advanced Technologies: Me
Wearing a Black Fiber Form Sitting
on the Sofa at A–Z West #1* 2002
gouache and pen on paper;
9 x 12"
Emanuel Hoffmann Foundation, on
permanent loan to the Öffentliche
Kunstsammlung Basel

181 ill. p. 119
*A–Z Advanced Technologies: Me in
a Green Fiber Form in Front of A–Z
West* 2002
gouache and pen on paper; 9 x 12"
Emanuel Hoffmann Foundation, on
permanent loan to the Öffentliche
Kunstsammlung Basel

182 ill. p. 120b
*A–Z Advanced Technologies: Me
Wearing a Brown Fiber Form While
Working at RAUGH Desk* 2002
gouache and pen on paper; 9 x 12"
Emanuel Hoffmann Foundation, on
permanent loan to the Öffentliche
Kunstsammlung Basel

183 ill. p. 120t
*A–Z Advanced Technologies: Me
Wearing a Flame Fiber Form in Front
of A–Z West #1* 2002
gouache and pen on paper; 9 x 12"
Emanuel Hoffmann Foundation, on
permanent loan to the Öffentliche
Kunstsammlung Basel

184 ill. p. 121t
*A–Z Advanced Technologies:
Me Wearing a Green Fiber Form and
Cooking at "Food Prep Station" #1*
2002
gouache and pen on paper; 9 x 12"
Emanuel Hoffmann Foundation, on
permanent loan to the Öffentliche
Kunstsammlung Basel

185
*A–Z Advanced Technologies: Me
Wearing a Grey Fiber Form in Front
of Mountains at A–Z West* 2002
gouache and pen on paper;
9 x 12"
Courtesy the artist and Andrea
Rosen Gallery, New York

186 ill. p. 134
*Filing System, Joshua Tree, March
2004* 2004
gouache and pencil on paper;
9 x 12"
Private Collection

187 ill. p. 133m
*Carving New RAUGH Furniture, A–Z
West, October 2004* 2004
gouache and pencil on paper;
9 x 12"
Courtesy the artist and Andrea
Rosen Gallery, New York

188 ill. p. 129
Rock in Wash Behind A–Z West
2004
gouache and pencil on paper;
9 x 12"
Courtesy the artist and Andrea
Rosen Gallery, New York

189 ill. p. 133t
*Working on Nightstand at Secret
L.A. House, December 2004* 2004
gouache and pencil on paper;
9 x 12"

190 ill. p. 135
*Favorite Felted Bowl (that I want to
keep)* 2004
gouache and pencil on paper;
9 x 12"
Courtesy the artist and Andrea
Rosen Gallery, New York

191 ill. p. 128
*Snow on Regenerating Field, A–Z
West, November 2004* 2004
gouache and pencil on paper;
9 x 12"
Private Collection, Los Angeles

192 ill. p. 133b
*First Flaw in New RAUGH Furniture
at A–Z West, January 2005* 2005
gouache and pencil on paper;
9 x 12"
Courtesy the artist and Andrea
Rosen Gallery, New York

193
Prototype for RAUGH Desk #2 2001
MDF, paint, polyurethane, fabric
and foam cushion, with miscella-
neous accessories; 28 x 126 x 126"
Emanuel Hoffmann Foundation, on
permanent loan to the Öffentliche
Kunstsammlung Basel

173
A–Z Fiber Form: White Felted
Dress #5 2002
gefilzte Wolle; 144.8 cm lang
Courtesy Paula Cooper Gallery

174
A–Z Fiber Form: White Felted Dress
#7 2002
gefilzte Wollc; 144.8 cm lang
Sammlung Eileen Harris Norton,
Santa Monica

175
A–Z Fiber Form: White Felted Dress
#8 2002
gefilzte Wolle; 144.8 cm lang
Sammlung Iann Stolz

Raum 8

176 Abb. S. 69
Me in a RAUGH Dress on a Field
Trip 1998
Gouache auf Papier; 50.8 x 38 cm
Privatsammlung, Jersey

177
Martha with A–Z Food Group 2001
Gouache auf Papier; 76.2 x 56 cm
Courtesy die Künstlerin und Andrea
Rosen Gallery, New York

178 Abb. S. 89
A–Z Food Group for You 2001
Gouache auf Papier; 76.2 x 56 cm
Courtesy die Künstlerin und Andrea
Rosen Gallery, New York

179
Eat Your Food Group RAUGH 2001
Gouache auf Papier; 56 x 76.2 cm
Sammlung Tullio Leggeri

180
A–Z Advanced Technologies: Me
Wearing a Black Fiber Form Sitting
on the Sofa at A–Z West #1 2002
Gouache und Filzstift auf Papier;
23 x 30.5 cm
Emanuel Hoffmann-Stiftung,
Depositum in der Öffentlichen
Kunstsammlung Basel

181 Abb. S. 119
A–Z Advanced Technologies: Me in
a Green Fiber Form in Front of A–Z
West 2002
Gouache und Filzstift auf Papier;
23 x 30.5 cm
Emanuel Hoffmann-Stiftung,
Depositum in der Öffentlichen
Kunstsammlung Basel

182 Abb. S. 120u
A–Z Advanced Iechnologies: Me
Wearing a Brown Fiber Form While
Working at RAUGH Desk 2002
Gouache und Filzstift auf Papier;
23 x 30.5 cm
Emanuel Hoffmann-Stiftung,
Depositum in der Öffentlichen
Kunstsammlung Basel

183 Abb. S. 120o
A–Z Advanced Technologies: Me
Wearing a Flame Fiber Form in
Front of A–Z West #1 2002
Gouache und Filzstift auf Papier;
23 x 30.5 cm
Emanuel Hoffmann-Stiftung,
Depositum in der Öffentlichen
Kunstsammlung Basel

184 Abb. S. 121o
A–Z Advanced Technologies: Me
Wearing a Green Fiber Form and
Cooking at „Food Prep Station" #1
2002
Gouache und Filzstift auf Papier;
23 x 30.5 cm
Emanuel Hoffmann-Stiftung,
Depositum in der Öffentlichen
Kunstsammlung Basel

185
A–Z Advanced Technologies: Me
Wearing a Grey Fiber Form in Front
of Mountains at A–Z West 2002
Gouache und Filzstift auf Papier;
23 x 30.5 cm

186 Abb. S. 134
Filing System, Joshua Tree, March
2004 2004
Gouache und Bleistift auf Papier;

23 x 30.5 cm
Privatsammlung

187 Abb. S. 133m
Carving New RAUGH Furniture,
A–Z West, October 2004 2004
Gouache und Bleistift auf Papier;
23 x 30.5 cm
Courtesy die Künstlerin und Andrea
Rosen Gallery, New York

188 Abb. S. 129
Rock in Wash Behind A–Z West
2004
Gouache und Bleistift auf Papier;
23 x 30.5 cm
Courtesy die Künstlerin und Andrea
Rosen Gallery, New York

189 Abb. S. 133o
Working on Nightstand at Secret
L.A. House, December 2004 2004
Gouache und Bleistift auf Papier;
23 x 30.5 cm
Courtesy die Künstlerin und Andrea
Rosen Gallery, New York

190 Abb. S. 135
Favorite Felted Bowl (that I want to
keep) 2004
Gouache und Bleistift auf Papier;
23 x 30.5 cm
Courtesy die Künstlerin und Andrea
Rosen Gallery, New York

191 Abb. S. 128
Snow on Regenerating Field, A–Z
West, November 2004 2004
Gouache und Bleistift auf Papier;
23 x 30.5 cm
Privatsammlung, Los Angeles

192 Abb. S. 133u
First Flaw in New RAUGH Furniture
at A–Z West, January 2005 2005
Gouache und Bleistift auf Papier;
23 x 30.5 cm
Courtesy die Künstlerin und Andrea
Rosen Gallery, New York

193
Prototype for RAUGH Desk #2
2001
MDF, Farbe, Polyurethan, Schaum-

194

Sufficient Self 2004
Power Point projection; 17min 29s
Emanuel Hoffmann Foundation, on
permanent loan to the Öffentliche
Kunstsammlung Basel

Uniforms **nos. 195-206 are
collection Emanuel Hoffmann
Foundation, on permanent loan to
the Öffentliche Kunstsammlung
Basel, and nos. 207-219 are
Courtesy the artist and Andrea
Rosen Gallery, New York.**

195

*A–Z Fiber Form Uniform: Spring
2002 #2 (green and black top)* 2002
green and black top, felted merino
wool, sleeveless, black turtleneck
and skirt

196

*A–Z Fiber Form Uniform: Spring
2002 #1 (brown with black top)*
2002
brown and black top, felted merino
wool, sleeveless, black turtleneck
and skirt

197

*A–Z Fiber Form Uniform: Summer
2002 #1 (maroon and white top)*
2002
maroon and white top, felted merino wool, sleeveless, black skirt

198

*A–Z Fiber Form Uniform: Summer
2002 #2 (sunset colored top)* 2002
sunset colored top, felted merino
wool, sleeveless, black skirt

199

*A–Z Fiber Form Uniform: Summer
2002 #3 (green and white top)*
2002
green and white top, felted merino
wool, sleeveless, black skirt

200

*A–Z Fiber Form Uniform: Fall 2002
(maroon dress)* 2002
maroon dress, felted merino wool,
sleeveless, black top

201

*A–Z Fiber Form Uniform: Winter
2002 (beige dress)* 2002
beige dress, felted merino wool,
sleeveless, black top

202

*A–Z Fiber Form Uniform: Spring
2003 #1* 2003
brown tunic, felted Icelandic wool,
sleeveless, black top

203

*A–Z Fiber Form Uniform: Spring
2003 #2* 2003
light brown tunic, felted Icelandic
wool, sleeveless, black top

204

*A–Z Personal Uniform: Summer
2003 #1* 2003
cotton broadcloth dress with
embroidery thread, sleeveless

205

*A–Z Personal Uniform:
Spring/Summer 2003 #2* 2003
cotton broadcloth dress with
embroidery thread, sleeveless

206

*A–Z Personal Uniform:
Spring/Summer 2003 #3* 2003
cotton broadcloth dress with
embroidery thread, sleeveless

207

*A–Z Fiber Form Uniform: Fall/Winter
2003 #1* 2003
olive green tunic, felted merino
wool, sleeveless, short brown skirt,
black top and blue and olive green
silk scarf

208

*A–Z Fiber Form Uniform: Fall/Winter
2003 #2* 2003
dark and light green tunic, felted
merino wool, sleeveless, short
black skirt, black turtleneck and
green plaid scarf

209

*A–Z Fiber Form Uniform: Fall/Winter
2003 #3* 2003
black, red and gold tunic, felted
merino wool, sleeveless, black
miniskirt and green turtle neck

210

*A–Z Fiber Form Uniform: Spring-
Summer 2004 (maternity)* 2004
salmon and beige tunic, felted
Icelandic wool, sleeveless and short
black skirt

211

*A–Z Fiber Form Uniform: Fall 2004
(breastfeeding)* 2004
green, blue and grey poncho,
crocheted wool, grey plaid skirt and
blue man's shirt

212

*A–Z Fiber Form Uniform: Winter
2004* 2004
brown and white dress, felted
Icelandic wool, black skirt and
maroon top

213

*A–Z Fiber from Uniform, Fall/Winter
2005 #1* 2005
red dress, felted merino wool,
brown skirt and white man's shirt

214

*A–Z Fiber Form Uniform, Fall/
Winter 2005 #2* 2005
black and white dress, felted
merino wool, sleeveless, hounds-
tooth plaid skirt and white man's
shirt

215

*A–Z Fiber Form Uniform: Fall 2005
(green with horizontal stripes)* 2005
green, black and beige dress, felted
merino wool, black skirt and black
top

216

*A–Z Fiber Form Uniform: Winter
2005 (brown with black cross)*
2005
brown and black dress, felted

stoffkissen mit Stoffüberzug,
verschiedene Gegenstände;
71 x 320 x 320 cm
Emanuel Hoffmann-Stiftung,
Depositum in der Öffentlichen
Kunstsammlung Basel

194

Sufficient Self 2004
Power Point-Projektion; 17min 29s
Emanuel Hoffmann-Stiftung,
Depositum in der Öffentlichen
Kunstsammlung Basel

**Die „Uniforms" Nrn. 195-206 sind
im Besitz der Emanuel Hoffmann-
Stiftung, Depositum in der
Öffentlichen Kunstsammlung
Basel, Nrn. 207-219 sind Courtesy
die Künstlerin und Andrea Rosen
Gallery, New York.**

195

A–Z Fiber Form Uniform: Spring
2002 #2 (green and black top) 2002
grünes und schwarzes Oberteil aus
gefilzter Merinowolle, ärmellos,
schwarzer Rollkragenpullover und
Rock

196

A–Z Fiber Form Uniform: Spring
2002 #1 (brown and black top)
2002
braunes und schwarzes Oberteil
aus gefilzter Merinowolle, ärmellos,
schwarzer Rollkragenpullover und
Rock

197

A–Z Fiber Form Uniform: Summer
2002 #1 (maroon and white top)
2002
rötlichbraunes und weisses Oberteil
aus gefilzter Merinowolle, ärmellos,
schwarzer Rock

198

A–Z Fiber Form Uniform: Summer
2002 #2 (sunset colored top) 2002
orangegelbes Oberteil aus gefilzter
Merinowolle, ärmellos, schwarzer
Rock

199

A–Z Fiber Form Uniform: Summer
2002 #3 (green and white top)
2002
grünes und weisses Oberteil aus
gefilzter Merinowolle, ärmellos,
schwarzer Rock

200

A–Z Fiber Form Uniform: Fall 2002
(maroon dress) 2002
rötlichbraunes Kleid aus gefilzter
Merinowolle, ärmellos, schwarzes
Oberteil

201

A–Z Fiber Form Uniform: Winter
2002 (beige dress) 2002
beiges Kleid aus gefilzter
Merinowolle, ärmellos, schwarzes
Oberteil

202

A–Z Fiber Form Uniform: Spring
2003 #1 2003
braune Tunica aus gefilzter
Islandwolle, ärmellos, schwarzes
Oberteil

203

A–Z Fiber Form Uniform: Spring
2003 #2 2003
hellbraune Tunica aus gefilzter
Islandwolle, ärmellos, schwarzes
Oberteil

204

A–Z Personal Uniform: Summer
2003 #1 2003
Kleid aus Baumwolle mit Stickerei,
ärmellos

205

A–Z Personal Uniform:
Spring/Summer 2003 #2 2003
Kleid aus Baumwolle mit Stickerei,
ärmellos

206

A–Z Personal Uniform:
Spring/Summer 2003 #3 2003
Kleid aus Baumwolle mit Stickerei,
ärmellos

207

A–Z Fiber Form Uniform:
Fall/Winter 2003 #1 2003
olivgrüne Tunica aus gefilzter
Merinowolle, ärmellos, kurzer brauner
Rock, schwarzes Oberteil und blauer
und olivgrüner Seidenschal

208

A–Z Fiber Form Uniform:
Fall/Winter 2003 #2 2003
dunkel- und hellgrüne Tunica aus
gefilzter Merinowolle, ärmellos, kurzer
schwarzer Rock, schwarzer
Rollkragenpullover und grünkarierter
Schal

209

A–Z Fiber Form Uniform:
Fall/Winter 2003 #3 2003
schwarze, rote und goldene Tunica
aus gefilzter Merinowolle, ärmellos,
kurzer schwarzer Rock und grüner
Rollkragenpullover

210

A–Z Fiber Form Uniform: Spring-
Summer 2004 (maternity) 2004
rosa-beige Tunica aus gefilzter
Islandwolle und kurzer schwarzer
Rock

211

A–Z Fiber Form Uniform: Fall 2004
(breastfeeding) 2004
grüner, blauer und grauer Poncho,
aus Wolle gehäkelt, graukarierter
Rock und blaues Herrenhemd

212

A–Z Fiber Form Uniform: Winter
2004 2004
braunes und weisses Kleid aus
gefilzter Islandwolle, schwarzer
Rock und bordeaux Oberteil

213

A–Z Fiber From Uniform,
Fall/Winter 2005 #1 2005
rotes Kleid aus gefilzter
Merinowolle, brauner Rock und
weisses Herrenhemd

merino wool, black skirt and white
man's shirt

217

*A–Z Fiber Form Uniform: Special
2005: Hiking Uniform #1 (dark
brown and white)* 2005
brown and white dress, felted
merino wool, orange crocheted
skirt, black shirt and light brown
crocheted neck piece with safety pin

218

*A–Z Fiber Form Uniform: Special
2005: Hiking Uniform #2 (grey)*
2005
grey dress, felted merino wool,
black, green and orange crocheted
skirt and black top

219

*A–Z Fiber Form Uniform: Special
2005: Hiking Uniform #3 (light
brown)* 2005
light brown dress, felted merino
wool, green crocheted skirt, black
top and orange neck piece

Room 9

220

Rules of RAUGH 2005
portfolio in wooden crate, consisting of 2 front pages, 9 plates and 1
editorial page; etching and aquatint
on chine collé; each 13 1/2 x 15"
Edition 20
Emanuel Hoffmann Foundation, on
permanent loan to the Öffentliche
Kunstsammlung Basel

221

*Single-Strand Shapes: Forward
Motion Landscape* 2004
black cotton, crocheted; 21 x 86"
Emanuel Hoffmann Foundation, on
permanent loan to the Öffentliche
Kunstsammlung Basel

222

*Single-Strand Shapes: Forward
Motion #4 (brown and black)* 2005

sheep wool, crocheted; 63 x 63"
Courtesy the artist and Andrea
Rosen Gallery, New York

223

*Single-Strand Shapes: Forward
Motion #2 (white)* 2005
sheep and llama wool, crocheted
and Flashe on birch plywood;
76 x 46"
Goetz Collection

224

*Single-Strand Shapes: Forward
Motion #3 (red)* 2005
sheep and llama wool, crocheted
and Flashe on birch plywood;
49 x 49"
Private Collection

225

*Single-Strand Shapes: Forward
Motion #5* 2006
wool, crocheted; 60 1/4 x 39"
Courtesy Sadie Coles HQ, London

226

*Single-Strand Shapes: Forward
Motion (geometric black and white)*
2007
black and white wool, crocheted
65.2 x 42.3"
Collection J. Rubner, Italy

227

*Single-Strand Shapes: Forward and
Backward Motion (black cross with
tapered ends)* 2007
wool, crocheted; 86.6 x 94.5"
Collection J. Rubner, Italy

228

RAUGH Mantle 2006
laminated fir plywood, carpet, collection of rocks with horizontal
stripes, a stone clock, stone vase,
felt container, 2 white ceramic
cups, mounted plaster boxes;
overall 68 1/2 x 77 x 27";
RAUGH element 63 x 47 x 7 1/2";
carpet 95 x 77"
Collection Maja Hoffmann

229

RAUGH Furniture: Woody 2007
laminated fir plywood, plaster
boxes, carpet, three felted bowls,
wooden objects and driftwood;
RAUGH element approx. 84 x 30 x 7"
Collection J. Rubner, Italy

214

A–Z Fiber Form Uniform, Fall/
Winter 2005 #2 2005
schwarzes und weisses Kleid aus
gefilzter Merinowolle, Rock mit Karo-
muster und weisses Herrenhemd

215

A–Z Fiber Form Uniform: Fall 2005
(green with horizontal stripes) 2005
grünes, schwarzes und beiges Kleid
aus gefilzter Merinowolle, schwar
zer Rock und schwarzes Oberteil

216

A–Z Fiber Form Uniform: Winter
2005 (brown with black cross) 2005
braunes und schwarzes Kleid aus
gefilzter Merinowolle, schwarzer
Rock und weisses Herrenhemd

217

A–Z Fiber Form Uniform: Special
2005: Hiking Uniform #1 (dark
brown and white) 2005
braunes und weisses Kleid aus
gefilzter Merinowolle, orangener
gehäkelter Rock, schwarzes Hemd
und hellbrauner, gehäkelter Kragen
mit Sicherheitsnadel

218

A–Z Fiber Form Uniform: Special
2005: Hiking Uniform #2 (grey) 2005
graues Kleid aus gefilzter
Merinowolle, schwarzer, grüner und
orangener, gehäkelter Rock und
schwarzer Rollkragenpullover

219

A–Z Fiber Form Uniform: Special
2005: Hiking Uniform #3 (light
brown) 2005
hellbraunes Kleid aus gefilzter
Merinowolle, grüner gehäkelter
Rock, schwarzes Oberteil und rot-
orangener Schal

Raum 9

220

Rules of RAUGH 2005
Portfolio in Holzkiste bestehend

aus zwei Titelseiten, neun Tafeln
und einer Textseite; Radierung
und Aquatinta auf Chine collé
je 34.3 x 38.1 cm
Edition 20
Emanuel Hoffmann-Stiftung,
Depositum in der Öffentlichen
Kunstsammlung Basel

221

Single-Strand Shapes: Forward
Motion Landscape 2004
schwarze Baumwolle, gehäkelt;
53.3 x 219.7 cm
Emanuel Hoffmann-Stiftung,
Depositum in der Öffentlichen
Kunstsammlung Basel

222

Single-Strand Shapes: Forward
Motion #4 (brown and black) 2005
Schafwolle, gehäkelt; 161.29 x
161.29 cm
Courtesy die Künstlerin und Andrea
Rosen Gallery, New York

223

Single-Strand Shapes: Forward
Motion #2 (white) 2005
Schaf- und Lamawolle, gehäkelt
und Flashe-Farbe auf Birkensperr-
holz; 190.6 x 114.3 cm
Sammlung Goetz

224

Single-Strand Shapes: Forward
Motion #3 (red) 2005
Schaf- und Lamawolle, gehäkelt
und Flashe-Farbe auf Birkensperr-
holz; 124.5 x 124.5 cm
Privatsammlung

225

Single-Strand Shapes: Forward
Motion #5 2006
Wolle, gehäkelt; 153 x 99.1 cm
Courtesy Sadie Coles HQ, London

226

Single-Strand Shapes: Forward
Motion (geometric black and white)
2007

schwarze und weisse Wolle, gehäkelt;
165.5 x 107.5 cm
Sammlung J. Rubner, Italien

227

Single Strand Shapes: Forward and
Backward Motion (black cross with
tapered ends) 2007
Wolle, gehäkelt; 220 x 240 cm
Sammlung J. Rubner, Italien

228

RAUGH Mantle 2006
laminiertes Fichtensperrholz,
Teppich, Sammlung von Steinen
mit horizontalen Streifen, Steinuhr,
Steinvase, Filzbehälter, 2 weisse
Keramiktassen, befestigte
Gipsboxen; insgesamt 164 x 195.6
x 68.6 cm; RAUGH Element 160 x
120 x 19 cm; Teppich 241.3 x
195.5 cm
Sammlung Maja Hoffmann

229

RAUGH Furniture: Woody 2007
laminiertes Fichtensperrholz,
Gipskisten, Teppich, 3 Filzbehälter,
Holzobjekte, Treibholz ; RAUGH
Element ca. 213 x 76 x 18 cm
Sammlung J. Rubner, Italien

Ausstellung   Exhibition Credit

Konzept/Concept – Theodora Vischer, Andrea Zittel; **Kuratorin/Curator** – Theodora Vischer; **Planung und Organisation/Planning and Organisation** – Heidi Naef; **Registrar** – Charlotte Gutzwiller; **Öffentlichkeitsarbeit/Public Relations** – Stephan Graus; **Sekretariat/Administration** – Gabriella Brancher, Michèle Meyer; **Technischer Dienst/Technical Management** – Christoph Kym; **Aufbau Ausstellung/Exhibition Team** – Aufbau Architektur/Installation exhibition walls: Marius Hatt, Ralph Hauswirth, Bruno Steiner, Bruno Trembley, Tobias Voss; Aufbau Werke/Installation exhibition: Yvo Hartmann mit/with Urs Cavelti, Jo Dunkel, Pia Gisler, Kaspar Müller, Bruno Steiner, Manuel Strässle, Muriel Utinger, und/and Jim Kanter, Los Angeles; **Konservatorische Betreuung/Conservation** – Markus Broecker; **Führungsprogramm/Guided Tours** – Beate Florenz

Andrea Zittel wurde 1965 in Escondido in Kalifornien geboren. Nach der Schule besuchte sie die San Diego State University, und schloss 1988 mit einem BA in Painting and Sculpture ab. Im Anschluss daran zog Zittel an die Ostküste, an die Rhode Island School of Design in Providence, und erlangte dort 1990 den MA of Sculpture. Die nächste und erste selbständige Station war New York, wo sie sich in Brooklyn niederliess. In New York begründete Zittel 1991 ihr künstlerisches Unternehmen A–Z, ein Projekt, in dessen Rahmen sie seither alle ihre Recherchen durchführt und ihre Werke entwirft, produziert und testet. Mit A–Z schafft sich Zittel den experimentellen Raum für eine Parallelwirklichkeit, in der die Unterscheidung von Kunst und Realität obsolet geworden ist. In dieser Zeit setzt auch die Ausstellungstätigkeit ein, die seither Teil ihrer Arbeit geworden ist. In der zweiten Hälfte der 1990er Jahre verlässt Zittel für längere Perioden New York, während denen sie sich in Europa aufhält oder auf längeren Reisen das Land Amerika erkundet. Immer wieder führt in diesen „Wanderjahren" die Reise in den Westen. 2000 schliesslich beginnt Zittel ein neues Kapitel in und um Los Angeles. Sie erwirbt südöstlich von Los Angeles in der Wüste von Kalifornien (Joshua Tree) eine verlassene Unterkunft (ein ehemaliges sog. *homestead cabin*) und das dazugehörige Stück Land, das Zittel nun A–Z West nennt und zu ihrem neuen Versuchsfeld macht. Dort und in Los Angeles lebt sie seither.

Literaturhinweis: *Andrea Zittel: Critical Space*, hrsg. von Paola Morsiani und Trevor Smith, Houston: Contemporary Arts Museum Houston, New York: New Museum of Contemporary Art, München/Berlin/London/New York: Prestel, 2005.

Andrea Zittel was born in Escondido, California. After completing secondary school, she attended San Diego State University, receiving her Bachelor of Arts in Painting and Sculpture in 1988. Zittel then moved to the East Coast to attend the Rhode Island School of Design in Providence, where she received her Master of Arts in Sculpture in 1990. Her next stop—the first one on her own—was New York, where she settled in Brooklyn. In New York in 1991, Zittel founded her A–Z art enterprise, a project that has provided the framework within which she has conducted her research and designed, produced, and tested her works ever since. With A–Z, Zittel creates an experimental space for a parallel reality in which the difference between art and reality has become obsolete. During this period, too, her exhibition activity began, and it has since become part of her works. In the second half of the 1990s, Zittel left New York repeatedly for extended periods, during which she stayed in Europe and explored nonurban America on long trips. Her travels during these "years of wandering" took her repeatedly to the West. Finally, in 2000, Zittel began a new chapter in and around Los Angeles. She purchased an abandoned home—a former so-called homestead cabin—and the associated property in Joshua Tree, in the desert east of Los Angeles. Zittel called it A–Z West and has made it her new site for experiment. Since then she has been living there and in Los Angeles.

Further Reading: *Andrea Zittel: Critical Space*, ed. by Paola Morsiani und Trevor Smith, Houston: Contemporary Arts Museum Houston, New York: New Museum of Contemporary Art, München/ Berlin/London/New York: Prestel, 2005.

Dank

Der herzliche Dank des Schaulagers und der Künstlerin geht als erstes an alle privaten und öffentlichen Leihgeber, die durch ihr grosszügiges Entgegenkommen die Ausstellung ermöglicht haben. Danken möchten wir auch allen Personen, die mit Rat und Tat, Geschick und Engagement die Realisierung der Ausstellung und der Publikation unterstützt haben, insbesondere den Galerien von Andrea Zittel, Andrea Rosen Gallery, New York, namentlich Teneille Haggard und Laura Mackall, Regen Projects, Los Angeles, Sadie Coles HQ Ltd., London, Galleria Massimo De Carlo, Mailand.

Acknowledgments

Schaulager's and the artist's profound thanks are due to all public and private lenders whose generous cooperation made this exhibition possible. We would also like to thank all those who supported the making of the publication and the exhibition for their invaluable help and advice, skill, and labor, in particular the galleries of Andrea Zittel, including Andrea Rosen Gallery, New York, especially Teneille Haggard and Laura Mackall; Regen Projects, Los Angeles; Sadie Coles HQ Ltd., London; Galleria Massimo De Carlo, Milan.

Erste Auflage 2008

© 2008 für die Werke: Andrea Zittel
© 2008 für die Texte bei den Autoren
© 2008 für diese Ausgabe: Laurenz-Stiftung, Schaulager Basel, Schweiz (www.schaulager.org) / Steidl Verlag Göttingen

Herausgegeben von Theodora Vischer
Redaktion: Annamira Jochim und Theodora Vischer mit Bettina Friedli und Stephan Hauser
Übersetzung Deutsch-Englisch und Redaktion der englischen Texte: Steven Lindberg, Berlin; Übersetzung Englisch-Deutsch: Niklaus G. Schneider, Berlin

Buchgestaltung: Steidl Design / Sarah Winter
Scans: Steidl's digital darkroom
Gesamtherstellung und Druck: Steidl, Göttingen

Steidl
Düstere Str. 4, D-37073 Göttingen
T +49 551 49 60 60 / F +49 551 49 60 649
E-mail: mail@steidl.de
www.steidlville.com/www.steidl.de

ISBN 978-3-86521-722-6 (Steidl)
ISBN 978-3-9522967-7-6 (Schaulager)

Printed in Germany

First edition 2008

© 2008 for the artwork: Andrea Zittel
© 2008 for the texts by the authors
© 2008 for this edition: Laurenz Foundation, Schaulager Basel, Switzerland (www.schaulager.org) / Steidl Publishers, Göttingen

Edited by Theodora Vischer
with the assistance of Annamira Jochim, with Bettina Friedli and Stephan Hauser
German-English Translations and Copyediting of English Texts: Steven Lindberg, Berlin; English-German Translations: Niklaus G. Schneider, Berlin

Book Design: Steidl Design / Sarah Winter
Scans: Steidl's digital darkroom
Production and Printing: Steidl, Göttingen

Steidl
Düstere Str. 4 / D-37073 Göttingen
Phone +49 551-49 60 60 / Fax +49 551-49 60 649
E-mail: mail@steidl.de
www.steidlville.com / www.steidl.de

ISBN 978-3-86521-722-6 (Steidl)
ISBN 978-3-9522967-7-6 (Schaulager)

Printed in Germany

Umschlag / Cover: My Linoleum Floor 1995-1998 (Detail), S. / p. 47
Vorsatzblatt / Endpaper: Study for A–Z Cellular Compartment Unit #1 2002 (Detail), S. / p. 101

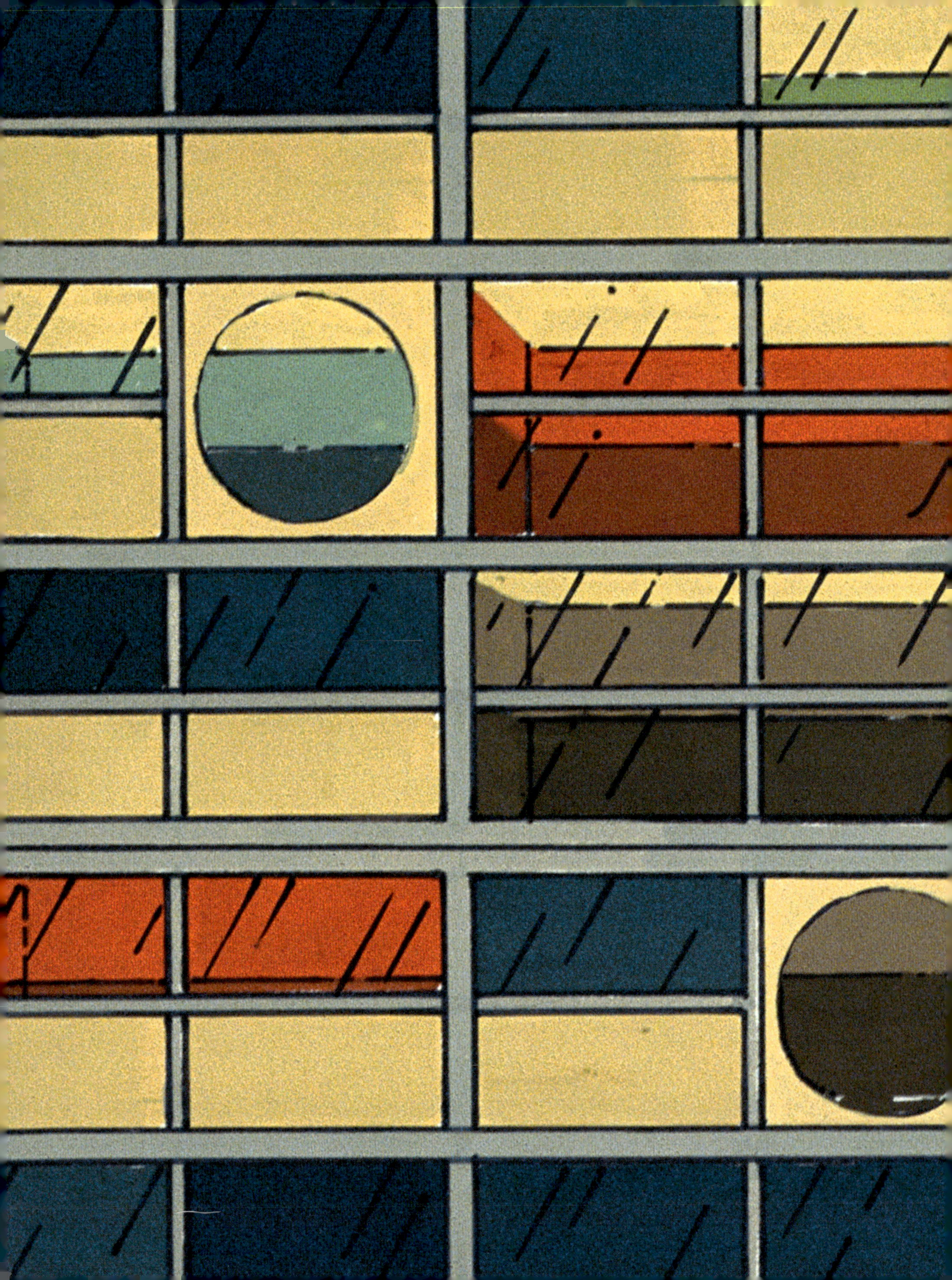